THE RED ARMY YEARS

Also by Richard Kurt

United We Stood
Despatches From Old Trafford
As The Reds Go Marching On
Cantona

THE
RED ARMY
YEARS

Manchester United in the 1970s

Richard Kurt and Chris Nickeas

HEADLINE

First published in 1997
by HEADLINE BOOK PUBLISHING

10 9 8 7 6 5 4 3 2 1

British Library Cataloguing in Publication Data

Kurt, Richard
    The Red Army years :
        Manchester United in the 1970s
    1.Manchester United Football Club - History
    I.Title II.Nickeas, Chris
    796.3'34'0942733'09047

ISBN 0 7472 1919 2

Typeset by
Letterpart Limited, Reigate, Surrey

Printed and bound in Great Britain by
Mackays of Chatham PLC, Chatham, Kent

HEADLINE BOOK PUBLISHING
A division of Hodder Headline PLC
338 Euston Road
London NW1 3BH

To the memory
of Jim Holton

Contents

Acknowledgements

'You're Supposed To Be At Home!' is the title of the regular nostalgia column which is a highlight of the fanzine *United We Stand*. The authors would like to thank especially the column's writer and compiler, the Huddersfield Red Andrew Pollard, for all his help with archives and research as well as his comments and pointers – not to mention the original inspiration his column provided. Nice one, Andy.

Thanks are due also to Tony for prolonged access to his literary collection; and to everyone else who sent in contributions whether they were used or not; to all United personalities who spared some time for us; and to those Red Army soldiers who spoke at last and whose anonymity we guaranteed.

The authors are particularly indebted to Michael Crick's scholarship as definitively exhibited in *Betrayal of a Legend*.

A Note About Transfer Fees

The wheeling and dealing of Docherty and Sexton in the transfer market is clearly an important part of following the way United's teams and players developed through the seventies. However, such has been the rate of inflation over the years – and in particular football industry inflation – that quoting seventies prices is pretty meaningless. To give an idea of what players were really worth, we have calculated a formula that allows us to approximate any seventies player's value at 1996 rates. Our formula compares average ticket prices for the Stretford End/E Stand/Paddock throughout the seventies, with mid-nineties rates; so each player's value in the text is given both at seventies fees and, in brackets, what he'd have cost us to day taking into account 'football inflation'. The true seventies transfer fees, net of VAT and League levy as tabulated by Michael Crick, are used throughout. The base for all calculations is that a £100,000 player purchased in each of the following seasons would now be worth the fee quoted below:

1972–73: £2.5m *1973–74:* £2.4m *1974–75:* £2.2m *1975–76:* £1.7m *1976–77:* £1.5m *1977–78:* £1.3m *1978–79:* £1m *1979–80:* £850,000

So Jim Holton, bought in 1972–73 for £91,000, would have cost £2.2m at today's prices.

Introduction

This is a book about United in the seventies. If history divided itself up in neat little decennial packages to suit our categorical fetishes, then we'd have kicked off at 1 January 1970. (Or New Year's Day 1971, if you're the kind of hopeless pedant who'll be celebrating the millennium alone in 2001.) History doesn't behave like that. Example: the sixties truly began in 1963, alongside Philip Larkin's sexual intercourse and the Beatles first LP. Perhaps, at a push, late '63: JFK's splattered brains cross-fertilized with 'I Want To Hold Your Hand'. So too at Old Trafford: the white-out winter of 1962–63 gave way to a bright new dawn of Law, Crerand and then Best, the final instruments in Busby's sixties hit beat-combo. Swinging London didn't have all the best tunes, as Swingin' Salford could tell you.

So where did United's seventies really begin? In pop music's literature, once mined most richly in the seams of *Rolling Stone* magazine, the decade doesn't start until 1972 when Bowie, Bolan, Ferry and the monoliths of Metal wrested the initiative away from the post-Altamont sixties survivors. The Stones made their last great album in '72, whilst John Lennon teetered on the brink, the one remaining relevant Beatle about to fall from godhead to agitprop joke with his *New York City* album-abortion. The pop literati will also tell you that, contrary to popular belief, the seventies were not an empty musical decade; instead, they were stuffed with the crashes, wails and bad reunion LPs of slowly decaying sixties dinosaurs. The less charitable say the same of some of the Old Trafford personnel in the new decade's early years. Whichever side one took in the political debate at early seventies United, no one could

1

deny the dominance of the underlying theme, as repetitive and inescapable as a *Led Zep 4* riff – the struggle to modernize and move forward without losing what Sir Matt and his boys of '68 still had to offer.

So to pick a date that marks the true beginning of the seventies at Old Trafford is to mark a seismic moment, a day after which the enduring drama of the Theatre of Dreams became less of an epilogue to a classic sixties episode but instead took on fresh actors and a new glammed-up, bolshie, in-yer-face seventies character. Less *Z-Cars*, more *The Sweeney* – in other words, goodbye Frank O'Farrell: hello Tommy Docherty. Surely 19 December 1972 is the only place to begin. If you're enough of a Dr Masoch fan to enjoy compiling lists of worst United defeats, then the 5-0 slaughter suffered by the Reds at Crystal Palace three days earlier must make your Top Ten. The presence of the canny Don Rogers on the Palace team-sheet should not fool you. Our opponents were undoubtedly one of the crappiest sides ever to play in the seventies First Division and were rightly relegated at the end of the season. Yet their chairman felt able to say afterwards that United were the worst team he'd seen at Selhurst Park for a long time. That it should have come to this: for United to be pitied by a man in such a position, barely three and a half years after being robbed of a second European Cup Final appearance. As shatteringly rapid declines go, only the New Kids On The Block can compete. Saddest sight of the night? One of the oldest kids on our block, Denis Law, sporting the worst hairstyle seen outside a monastery. He looked overweight and out of sorts after a series of wrecking injuries but it was the bewildered glaze of horror in his eyes that spoke loudest: 'We are fucked', echoed on terraces and in boardroom.

As it happened, the board had long been busy signing death warrants. George Best's was already public knowledge, O'Farrell's ready for proclamation but its existence still secret, though half of Manchester appeared to know it was coming. David Meek wasn't one of them; his 'Be Fair To Frank' article, as so often supplying the pro-boss line right until the end, had upset the board sufficiently for them to have him prevented from going on the team bus for a while. (You and I may think that 'being David Meek' would be offence enough to get thrown off any bus. In fact, the board were miffed because they thought Meek knew Frank was for the chop and was simply 'making trouble'. David Meek making trouble for United's board? The absurdity of the very concept reminds you just how long ago this all was . . .)

Poor Frank wouldn't have long to wait. Did he know Tommy Docherty had been offered the United job during half-time at Selhurst Park? Apparently not: however, he had no illusions as to his fate when summoned by the board on the morning of the 19th. First looking up to the blue sky and then forward into his own dark and clouded future, he uttered the one quotable quip of his footballing life: 'Nice day for an execution.' Given the state of the team and its morale, and glancing at United's bottom-of-the-table position with attendant tabloid piss-taking merriment, perhaps it was more a case of putting a suffering animal out of its misery.

O'Farrell never saw it like that, of course. By all accounts, he never forgave Sir Matt for what he saw as unwarranted interference, nor the 'Busbyite' players who supposedly undermined him. This is not the place to delve into the mire and murk that surrounds the O'Farrell period – as we've said, that's a strictly sixties bag, man. Eamon Dunphy gives a fairly pro-Frank account in his book, *A Strange Kind Of Glory*, whilst Sir Matt fires one or two succinct and targeted bullets back in his own *Soccer At The Top*. Was Frank a victim of an aged Busbyite mafia which is solely to blame for United's decline and relegation? Or was he incapable of handling this size of club and its personalities, a poor buyer with only Martin Buchan to his credit and too diffident a character who, in Law's words, 'came and left a stranger'?

Fittingly for a man who remains such a historical enigma, O'Farrell's own book co-written with James Lawton never appeared, shelved amidst legal wrangling and second thoughts; he resurfaced in calmer Persian fields, via Cardiff, before retiring to Torquay. Lawton himself tells me he liked and admired Frank, 'a true football intellect', but significantly demurs from backing the Dunphy school's view on O'Farrell versus Busby: 'Eamon's book was very good and well researched but I'm not convinced his

conclusions were wholly justified.' Quite: any manager can
only blame so much of a disaster such as the condition of
United in December 1972 on others. Harry S. Truman
talked a lot of bollocks at times but 'the buck stops here'
was one of his less testicular epithets. So the morality at
Old Trafford post-Busby was not ideal; but, as Somerset
Maugham put it, 'a morality is only accepted by the weak –
the strong form their own'. If O'Farrell was indeed in
constant battle with conservative forces, then his failure
was not only a function of the power of his enemies but
also, surely, of the weakness in the self.

Enough already: this is about the seventies, not the
unfinished business of the sixties. When the Doc was
called to tend to the sickness at United, a seventies archetype replaced the last of the sixties gents. Poor Frank – can
O'Farrell ever be mentioned without a sympathetic and
pathetic prefix? – always appeared to belong to a former
era. Those awful pictures showing Frank with stern expression, plastered-down hair and ramrod tie seem to come
from the same time-frozen stock as those iconic snaps of
Ian Brady and Lord Lucan. His manner placed him alongside Stan Cullis, Bill Nicholson and Alf Ramsey in a world
of clenched buttocks, stiff lips and correct behaviour. Frank
did everything above board and by the book whereas
Docherty didn't know where the book was and virtually
lived under the table. A seventies Old Trafford was surely
no place for an O'Farrell – but it was made for the Doc,
Seventies Man incarnate. Put him in a kipper tie, in *Man
About The House*, next to a Party Seven or behind the
wheel of a Capri – does he not fit perfectly within your
mental image? Now try the same with poor Frank . . . see
what I mean? Faced with the svelte Paula Wilcox, Frank
would surely have told her to put some less indecent
clothes on, while you could imagine the Doc hiding Cup
Final tickets down her bra and asking if she fancied some
horizontal training. To take on the shambles at United in
December 1972 required some sly, brash, courageous,
savvy, charming and brutal flair. Whatever your opinion of
the Doc as a person, manager or courtroom witness, he was
the ideal man for the moment. If the footballing sixties
were dead, then so too were the concomitant integrity,
gentlemanly codes, correct reserve and modest rewards: for

4

the cynical, flash, hardbitten and loudly moneyed seventies, United had a man who understood his era to take the helm.

Naturally, this has its risks, as United were to discover: like the live TV shows which invited the Sex Pistols on, anticipating a viewing figures bonanza, you can't complain when they shout 'Dirty Fucker!' at the screen. It goes with the territory. United were to be so scarred by their own Johnny Rotten that they were to appoint his absolute opposite as successor. And just as the smooth blandishments of disco rushed in to engulf spiky punk, so United discovered the price of suburban Sextonite cosiness: 4-3-3, tedium and 'Cold Trafford'.

That's all a few years away from a starting point whose selection we've explained in football terms. But this book is also about the fans; indeed, our title is a direct homage to them. We're not going to pretend that December 1972 marks any great significant development in the growth of the Red Army, a process which Chris will outline and illustrate throughout this book. You could probably plump for any 'incident' between West Ham away in 1967 and the pitch invasion against City in 1974 and claim that it heralded the birth of the Red Army phenomenon as a mass experience or generalized psychosis. But the 1972–73 season marks at least a psychological development in that those who were there in the thick of it recognized that something tangible had developed; this was more than mere isolated outbreaks of trouble. That's not to say disorder had become organized *per se* – indeed, there is an argument that organization never happened until the eighties casual era. But it did mean you could chant 'Red Army' and you would understand that this meant more than simply 'we are United fans'. By 1972–73 the phrase had, subconsciously at least, a meaning that was more sinister of delectable, depending on your viewpoint.

Undoubtedly, the cult of supporting United in a particular fashion which was to produce both mass disorder and unforgettable terrace celebrations throughout the seventies was well established by 1972 and about to grow exponentially. The paradox, of course, is that the Red Army grew to gigantic strength and power almost in inverse proportion to the status of the first team. Thus there are plenty of forty-something blokes who, basing their judgements on football as an all-round emotional experience, will happily cite 1974–75 as their favourite season ever, a year when United's status as a club was at a half-century low.

The fascination is not purely about the violence in itself. The endlessly repeated question sociologists asked back then as to why football fans fight was always easily answered: they like it. The lure is surely about the overwhelming sense of self-confidence and intoxicating power of the mass which will sometimes produce violence but in other circumstances will satisfy itself in outrageous celebration of team, hometown and self. Sure, a lot of lads will get off on footage of downright dirty terrace aggro but they are also likely to be equally enthralled by, say, the famous film of the Stretford End in full jubilatory mode at the end of the 1974–75 season. There is more to Red Army cultism than mere aggro and domination: it's also about a sheer joy in being Red, United and, more often than not, Mancunian. Add the magic of mass intoxication, both literal and spiritual, and it is no wonder the seventies Stretford End and its travelling divisions still inspire modern Reds twenty years later.

One suspects that another element must be added to explain the fervour of Reds in the seventies: class. This book begins at a period of historic ascendancy for the British working class – the middle of the Heath government. Ted had just been forced into his infamous U-turn, abandoning hard-right Selsdonomics for a softer corporatist approach. The three-day week and miners' strike were a few months around the corner, culminating in the removal of the government by the organized working class. For the Thatcher generation, it is hard to grasp; but that decade was one in which to be a member of the industrial proletariat was to be blessed, doubly so if you had a good union. Unemployment of one million or less, rising wages, the TUC at Downing Street, ever-pleading management on its knees ... The worship of the bourgeoisie with which we're so familiar now had no place in a Britain dominated politically and economically by organized labour. One could read the February 1974 Labour manifesto and honestly believe a socialist country was there to be had.

More than that, the sixties cultural revolution had freed

the working class from eternal deference, or so it seemed. Popular culture was thoroughly proletarianized, whether it be in the music of the day (glam rock, northern soul, pub rock, new wave) or the fashion of the street: gone were the suit-and-dress styles evolved from the 1950s and 1900s which dominated modwear and dandyish psychedelic foppery, to be replaced by oceans of denim and leather in rugged, dressed-down stylings. Cinema and TV had long since jettisoned Whitehouse-friendly cosiness and clean-cut 'naice' boys 'n' girls as heroes; realism was dominant, full of rough lads, earthy dialogue and revolutionary sentiment. Dirk Bogarde and *School For Scoundrels* seemed nineteenth century in comparison to Michael Caine or *Frenzy*. The 'class war' was becoming a walk-over.

Despite decades of meandering and gentle decline, Manchester remained industrial and working-class in character, United fans overwhelmingly so. To be a Red then was to have the world at your feet: in work, on top and full of power. No wonder the Establishment took such fright at the sight of stuffed, vibrant and uncontrollable terraces. Down the ages this was their worst nightmare – Britain's *hoi polloi* collectivized, confident and courageous. To be a Red, politically or not, a Mancunian and a working lad amidst thousands of comrades at such a time must have been a delirious pinnacle. No wonder those guys now tell us that was the time to be alive. Mind you, the Cantona Double Double is some consolation, isn't it?

Managers, like any other professionals, need references: that Tommy Docherty's came courtesy of Denis Law and Willie Morgan must be a cause of wry reflection for all concerned. Within a couple of years, the Doc was to buy both men one-way tickets on the slow train to the Old Bailey, via the Palookavilles of Moss Side and Turf Moor. But when Sir Matt called in his two Scottish stalwarts for the lowdown on Docherty, he was looking for confirmation that Tommy had indeed now become the character the *Daily Mail* had prescribed for Old Trafford: 'He has restored his reputation as a man for big-time football – United need a soccer evangelist like Bill Shankly and Docherty could be such a man.'

Conventional wisdom, which the two Scots shared, was that the Doc's Scottish managerial assignment had been the making of him. Back in the mid-sixties this Seventies Man archetype had actually tried the authoritarian, strait-laced and hands-off approach that sat happily alongside the stylisms of football's O'Farrells; a mad night out in Blackpool by Venables and his Chelsea cohorts marked the beginning of the end of that bizarre chapter. Picking up a burgeoning reputation for, um, 'eccentricity' as the decade turned, the subsequent Scottish job gave him gravitas, a true 'name' and an insatiable taste for buying anyone who'd ever been near tartan underwear. The meandering drift through the wastelands of Rotherham, Villa, Hull, QPR and Oporto were forgiven: that so few laughed out loud when the Doc was linked to United demonstrated how far he'd been rehabilitated. So Willie and Denis spoke up for him in all good faith: they could later spend the rest of the decade ruminating on the pernicious nature of 'conventional wisdom'.

It never ceases to amaze me how, if repeated sufficiently, one image in a newspaper can con all manner of observers into believing its message. The ubiquitous shot of Sir Matt, opening his office outer door to find the step covered in discarded rosettes and scarves, seemed to speak of fans' disgust of the 'betrayal' of O'Farrell. For a few days the press played the violins for Frank with Wagnerian overkill, assuming most Red sympathy was with him. It transpired that the detritus on the doorstep in the closely cropped shot had all been left by one girl; Red response to the execution had been impassive, like 1790s Parisians now inured to the daily sight of rolling heads. Whilst Ladbrokes were offering 2 to 1 against United's relegation, there were pub odds to be had on the Doc surviving 1973 – even money.

These were not, after all, times to be clinging on to hopes of permanence and security. Governments rewrote manifestos weekly, rock stars broke worldwide then immediately 'retired' or died in plane smashes, Arabs yo-yoed oil prices like tarts' knickers . . . so who could tell when the next 0-5 hammering, disappearing drunk superstar or managerial *coup d'état* might occur? Anyway, football fans are notoriously adept as coping with regime revolutions. In *Nineteen Eighty-Four*, crowds at a rally instantly convert when Big Brother announces his military allies are now enemies. It's a chilling moment in the book but one that football fans understand, Cantona's 1992 equivalent being a perfect example. When Docherty received a trademark Red roar from the Strettie at his first match in charge, you can bet there were many hoarse voices which only a week before had been shouting support for Frank. Those who wonder how some football fans get so psychically warped should consider the effect of these emotional blood-changes season after season.

Everybody – fans, players, officials – feels the electric baton up the arse of a new manager's arrival. You can always bet that the first performance will be the best of the season so far, causing every fan to spit blood in the belief that 'the bastards haven't been trying'. Forty-six thousand were there for the visit of treble-chasing Leeds (a permanent and, I suppose, redundant adjective in the seventies for Leeds, like 'laughing-stock City' or 'thrice-convicted Scouser' these days). That attendance figure was 10,000 up on the miserable showing against the Saints in November, although admittedly the fact that it was pissing icicles that day hadn't exactly encouraged flocking crowds. Allan Clarke sniffed a last-minute equalizer to rob us of our deserved Christmas present – how typical of seventies Leeds. (Imagine a Leeds-supporting Santa: he'd shit in your selection box, make an aeroplane shape with the tinsel and fuck the family Fido.) But we'd fought well and showed some belief – and Ted MacDougall had scored again to make it four in seven. As a 'Let's impress the boss' exercise, it had been a complete success, MacDougall in particular apparently overcoming criticism that his early-ball-to-near-post demands were out of order at Old Trafford.

How wrong they all were. New bosses at OT are expected to trot out the usual clichés: 'This is the finest club in the land', 'These fans are the greatest', 'I am here for the honour not the money (though thanks for the fifty per cent hike and flash car)'. The Doc duly conformed, but demurred from the fourth: 'Every player here will get a good chance to show me what he can do.' He had, it seemed, made his mind up long since. Later he would talk of approaching the job with scalpel in hand – they had called the Doc so he was ready for surgery. Docherty talked of the 'cancer' and 'canker' within, mixing metaphors to add 'dead wood'; lumberjack or butcher, the Doc was about to start culling. And the influence of his managerial year spent watching Scots throughout Britain was about to become apparent – there would soon be more hairy Scots knocking about than at any time since Bonnie Prince Charlie's boys stopped off in town for a 1745 piss-up.

Boxing Day at Derby: the champions win 3-1 and Ian Storey-Moore scores his last goal of the season. The first wave of casualties are O'Neill, Dunne and Davies who play for United only twice more between them; Wyn will be a-leaping no more, thankfully. At Arsenal on 6 January, another 3-1 stuffing marks the end for David Sadler and virtually Denis Law's last game up front. Ian Moore's main run comes to an end too though no one, least of all the Doc, wished to lose him – he was about to become the seventies' second most lamented injury victim after Big Jim. In between those dank holiday defeats which fixed us to the foot of the table, the Tartan Terror had begun. George Graham and Alex Forsyth arrived within forty-eight hours of the Baseball Ground match – £220,000 spent in a day, which amounted to a third of O'Farrell's entire outlay. Imagine the impact: the exact equivalent of Alex Ferguson if he'd spent over £5 million within a week of arriving.

Amidst the general swooning, few took issue with the Doc as he gushed to the media about George's 'Netzer-like skill and arrogance' that would lift all around him. 'The Stroller' would captain us out of the danger zone and his innate class place him among the fans' Pantheon of Heroes. Graham was an old teacher's pet of Docherty's – one might almost say of Fergie/Choccy proportions, except that the Doc did at least eventually sell his own particular has-been. This was the third time he'd bought Graham and perhaps he should have checked the sell-by date: his boots surely had 'Use Before April '73' stamped on the sole.

So we got 'the Stroller' a touch too late in his career, on the verge of becoming 'the Staggerer'. At least Forsyth was coming to his peak, such as it was. The hairiest and roughest-looking Scottish invader of them all, he would have fitted in perfectly hanging from a Wembley crossbar in '77. Any picture of Alex invariably shows him high-kicking like a Rockette, ball already at 80 mph in the clouds, roaring 'get on the end o' that' to hapless chasing forwards. Like every modern full-back nowadays, he had his winger fantasy sessions bombing down the line which back then was both pretty funny and quite exciting; his free-kicks proved he could boot a ball in the goalie's face as hard as he could clear it at the back. By the time he really established himself in the spring of '74, his ability to get stuck in was all that mattered for the relegation rottweiler-fight; when more sophisticated times arrived, his lack of pace did for him. But for now, it was his arrival that did for Tony Dunne, who departed to Preston without a murmur of discontent, a loyal gentleman to the end.

Tommy Cavanagh came as coach on New Year's Eve to

make it a hat-trick of new boys. A Scouser within the walls: always a disturbing prospect. Phrases like 'tactical game-plan' and 'Method football' (what's that? Marlon Brando at sweeper?) began to surface in United's publications, a shock to those used to the Busbyesque 'just go out and play'. However, Cavanagh was a modern coach for a different era. By the end of '73, he stood accused in the great debate over United's 'defensive' new breed but as his career shows, he was to be a man who could transform playing styles completely – all he required was the managerial order. You can say one thing for modernity: it's functional and adaptable.

Those who thus far remained distinctly underwhelmed got what they wanted in the fortnight after the Arsenal game: two seismic purchases and genuine heroes, with an ugly new midfielder and FA Cup defeat sandwiched in between. To go out of the Cup at Wolves was a blessing – United had quite enough blood-curdling competition on their hands as it was. Mick Martin's arrival may have scared the kids but at least introduced an element of trundling reliability to help stabilize a mercurial team. He had 'stop-gap' written all over him but the niceties of long-term planning had to wait – when you're 22nd, you're just looking for plugs to fill leaking holes. (And Martin was 'Plug' himself, moonlighting from the *Beano*.)

Jim Holton and Lou Macari were the main event, of course, heralded everywhere as the smartest of buys. At nearly 300 grand (£6.7m), that brought Docherty's spending to the equivalent of almost £12 million in three weeks. If O'Farrell had dallied too long for the critics, then, according to some, the Doc risked over-compensation: was this premature ejaculation on a virginal scale? Macari, unbelievably given the circumstances, knocked back Shankly to join us, thus missing three trophies and getting relegated as a reward. Stuck up front for the rest of the season in the out-and-out role he loathed, he received the Stretford End bird too. We were soon to forgive each other.

Holton was the rough, granite-hewn terminator both we and the silky Martin Buchan had been praying for. It was no surprise that, as all five of Forsyth, Graham, Holton, Martin and Macari made February home debuts against West Ham and Everton, gates soared up to 59,000. At last,

12

with reinforcements from the clans, we were ready to fight. But would this be Bannockburn or Culloden?

Actually, if the Doc had had any more cash to spend, he could easily have added Eddie Colquhoun and John Brownlie too. The '74 World Cup could conceivably have seen United's entire first team turning up under the name of Scotland. But Brownlie broke a leg and the board's piggy bank rattled only with spare ha'penny bits. On the eve of the Hammers game, Docherty announced he was 'happy with the squad', thanking the directors for their largesse: 'I have never known anything like this support in my life.' It had indeed been an extraordinary plunge; one wonders whether the modern plc could have moved so swiftly and accommodatingly as the old OT cabal. Speculation now centred on who might be sold in offset. Ted MacDougall found himself the butt of a whispering campaign – now I wonder who could have started that? – but was in the team for West Ham. He was to play only four more games.

It's 3.28 p.m. Saturday 22 January. Best has scored at Old Trafford; but it's the genial black Hammer Clyde, not our seista'd George. United are 2-0 down and Big Jim's been made to look a fool on his debut, no thanks to the atrocious '92-style pitch. But the 51,000 have not given up hope and nor has Lou Macari. 'He combines the non-stop aggression of Hughie Gallagher and the strength of Bobby Collins,' raves the *Mail*'s Ron Crowther as Lou gives an exasperated Billy Bonds the run-around. Charlton, the only old Busby Boy still in favour, slams home the dodgiest of penalties but it is Lou who pops up for the late equalizer to spark rampant celebrations. A lucky home point should not have been an excuse for raving but it felt to everyone like a turning point; Docherty appeared close to tears as he spoke of the crowd's fervour.

For the Wednesday night game against Everton 59,000 thronged to OT; a goalless point got us off the foot of the table. The team had hardened up, playing tight 4-4-2 and kicking chunks out of every Scouser who came near the box. Big Jim, on the steepest learning curve of his life, bashed about manfully, getting away with an obvious penalty-shove. The fates were with us once more after months of desertion. But not perhaps with MacDougall: he missed a late one, came off for Kidd and must have known that the Strettie chants for him as he departed wouldn't delay the Doc's scalpel for long.

A point at Highfield Road too, thanks to Holton's goal; after Jim blotted out the smooth John Richards on Wolves' visit to OT, he was on his way to cult status. As one hero arrives, another is on the point of departure. Bobby Charlton scored his last competitive Old Trafford goals that Saturday, the second a drive as vintagely Bobby as his performance. A last gasp of grace in a grim, hard season – he didn't look like a man out of his time merely because of the tonsorial contrast with the hirsute battlers around him. Macari's fistfight with Shaw simply added counterpoint.

Amidst much media ballyhoo, Scotland picked five Reds only to receive 5-0 drubbing by the Sassenachs. Martin Buchan must never have had a worse week as the retreating Scots then partook in United's 1-4 humiliation at Ipswich. Docherty took advantage of the shell-shock to cash in on MacDougall; the £170,000 virtually paid for Macari. Some will tell you MacD never had a chance. One seventies veteran colleague of mine, agreeing with the Doc for the first time in years, dismisses this with 'he was never a United player'. Unlike Tony Dunne, Mac would not go quietly. His subsequent career, never truly at the top flight, seemed to bear out the Doc's judgement; at least it gave Collyhurst hero Kidd a last sustained run of success.

That final switch seemed to settle the team for the final, highest slopes of the mountain. The change from the outfit that opened the season with nine winless games can be seen thus; from this:

Stepney; O'Neill, Sadler, Buchan, Dunne, Morgan, Charlton, Best, Davies, MacDougall, Moore

to this basic line-up:

Stepney; Young, Holton, Buchan, Forsyth, Morgan, Charlton, Graham, Kidd, Macari, Martin.

United amazed their fans by entering the much-ridiculed Anglo-Italian Cup, which proved to be beneficial for the team's gelling process, though not for poor Ian Storey-Moore. He scored on his comeback game against Bari on 4 April, only to break down once more; however much United strapped him up and kept him training wherever possible, he was to appear just twice more in a Red shirt.

United played five crunch relegation battles during the run-in; only Birmingham beat us, at a vicious St Andrews with a late killer. Lou Macari's second crucial intervention of the season had seen off West Brom and by the time he scored at Stoke in a 2-2 draw, United were favourites to beat the drop. Charlton had already scored his last Red goal at The Dell, whilst King Denis pulled on the Number 10 shirt for the final time against Norwich – fittingly, both games had been won.

The dénouement was as beautiful as 1974's would be hideous. A kid called Trevor Anderson (only the tenth player to be hailed as the new George Best and already an Irish cap) scored the winner at Elland Road, helping Leeds lose the title fight in the process. 'Looked like Peter Wyngarde as *Jason King*,' notes Andy Pollard, 'unfortunately played football like him too.' Still, the zapata'd one's great contribution was much appreciated by those Reds in the 45,000 crowd brave enough to acknowledge it. A point in the derby would suffice; a season's record gate of near 62,000 rejoiced in a nil-nil as much as they had back in darker days against Everton. It turned out that the largely good-humoured pitch invasion was to be merely a staging post towards a far more searing incursion, twelve months down the rockiest of roads . . .

It may be a literally inaccurate description but the summer of 1973 had a truly *fin-de-siècle* atmosphere about it; the sun setting on the Busby Empire, the Young Turks emerging to man the ramparts. United had closed the season, and an era, at Stamford Bridge. The calm eye inside a turbulent Old Trafford storm, Bobby Charlton had characteristically wrought some personal dignity in which to wrap himself on his way to retirement. A 754th United appearance for the very last true Busby Babe, going out on his terms and at his timing; relegation itself would not sully him. Just as after the day Ramsey substituted him in Mexico, a team would plunge to previously unplumbed depths in the wake of his departure. They gave him the full guard of honour rigmarole at Chelsea and the tears duly flowed but dull United's grim defeat, surrounded by the sensational battle for the Shed, said more about post-imperial realities than any ceremonials could.

Charlton had woken up one mid-season morn to realize he wasn't enjoying the game any more: that much had become apparent to many who spoke of his wordless, depressive presence at OT in the final months. Relations between the Holy Trinity of Best, Law and Charlton had never been lower than late '72, fatally destabilizing O'Farrell's efforts to build team morale. Charlton's last major contribution to United was to be a player in Frank's disposal. So, in a twisted fashion, the Doc owed Bobby; he certainly admitted a debt of gratitude in that he'd been spared the awful prospect of telling yet another legend he had to go. After all, he'd already used up all his legend-crushing capital in the Denis Law Affair.

Old Trafford was to be granted a sentimental curtain call days later when two Bobby Dazzlers helped beat Verona. At Number 11 for the Reds that day was another symbol of the changing times – Gerry Daly. A scorer for Bohemians when United played them in February, his shop-window dreams came true within weeks as United quietly snapped him up. Daly had other young fellow combatants who would soon be emerging to create the new seventies United. There was Sammy McIlroy, recovering from his car crash and still only on the verge of 19, who'd impressed the Doc enough in comeback friendlies to secure the promise of a Red future; Brian Greenhoff, a Barnsley boy getting rave reviews from Bill Foulkes in the youth team; and Arthur Albiston, touted as the best 15-year-old full-back in Britain. Three Busby favourites had left: Bobby, Denis and the wretchedly unlucky John Fitzpatrick, finally conceding defeat to his injuries at the age of 26. But at the very moment when Busbyism appeared to be in retreat, at least in terms of his physical legacy, the essence of Sir Matt's vision was reborn. Once again the future would belong to young, hungry lads, trained up in United's ways before other big clubs warped them with their alien philosophies. Jimmy Greenhoff apart, United would buy no more ready-made,

16

pre-packaged stars until long after Docherty's departure. For these new emerging Babes, metaphorical baptism, death and resurrection were to tumble upon them with unholy haste.

❀ ❀ ❀

Fin de siècle perhaps; *fin de régime* certainly. Docherty deposed Old Trafford's King Denis with a Cromwellian ruthlessness. Actually, he was harsher than the old Lord Protector. At least Charles I was allowed to show a dignity and bravery on the block, dying with proud words and a certain regal flourish. Law's execution was just as public, I suppose, live on lunchtime TV rather than a Westminster scaffold. But its manner meant few could claim 'nothing befitted the man so much as his passing' in this instance. He deserved a glorious and graceful finale, replete with deep bows and curtain-calls; what he got was a shitty, two-faced farrago which spoke more of the executioner than the honour of the victim. So not at all 1640s England – but sadly very much 1970s United.

When Docherty arrived, talking of 'dead wood' and 'cancers', he had Law in mind more than most. He sneered that Denis had 'stopped trying', that he spent 'four days a week on the treatment table', that 'all he cared about was how long he could continue playing'. The first of those suggestions was simply pure calumny, the third a bizarre *non sequitur* – what else should a man who loved playing for United have as his first priority? The second revealed that Docherty had no understanding of Law's career. Here was a player who only became truly heated in public when discussing two subjects: persecution by disciplinary authorities and being forced to play when not fully fit. The latter had been a curse all his life. For much of the late sixties he had battled to gain recognition that his knee was severely damaged; in echoes of the Kanchelskis affair, his anger increased as he was left to suffer and coralled into playing when he couldn't produce the goods. Remember, this man had missed a European Cup medal because of injury – no wonder, as his career drew to a close, that he was more concerned than ever to protect his own pride and

17

potential. At least he was still desperately trying to keep his hand in, rather than chuck in the towel; at least he was reaching Saturdays able to present himself for selection and bearing his omissions with stoicism. But none of that cut much ice with the Doc. The scalpel was ready for a final surgery, without anaesthetic.

In early 1973, as the Doc began to negotiate his way around Old Trafford's political minefields, he took to dining with the Crerands and Laws – a Fifth Columnist operating in the midst of a Busbyite mafia (*sic*) perhaps. Whatever information Docherty gained from people he later characterized as the enemy, he foolishly gave up a hostage to fortune – in front of witnesses he offered Denis a 'job for life' on more than one occasion. No surprise in that: half-a-dozen Busby Boys had ended up on the payroll post-retirement. Denis, who didn't want to leave the club or become a fully fledged manager, was delighted. Here was the reassurance every loyal thirty-something player wants to hear, the promise of a kind of footballing private pensionhood.

Later, Docherty would deny ever having given such assurances: 'How could I promise a job for life when I only had a contract for three years myself?' he claimed with some sophistry. When full of bonhomie, such grandiose back-slapping is precisely the kind of guff you'd expect from 'characters' such as Docherty. Pointing out, in day's sober light, the true limitations of one's own largesse is scarcely proof that one couldn't have said such a thing. There's little mileage in denial when perfect witnesses such as the Crerands are on hand.

April 27 1973. Bobby's about to get the full-colours career burial next day at Chelsea and Denis knows he'll enjoy a similar tear-jerking ceremony sometime in the next year or so. He gambols through training in wide-eyed innocence, completely unaware that Docherty has been to the board to secure a free transfer for him; only Busby himself objected. As Law heads for home, Tommy calls him into the office to hand over what Denis himself termed 'a sentence of death'. To paraphrase Macbeth, another tragic Scot: is this a dagger I feel behind me, waggling between my shoulder-blades, you fat two-faced twat?

18

Somehow, despite the shock of seeing promises smashed before his eyes, Denis found the presence of mind to cobble together a compromise on the spot. If he couldn't have the future he'd been assured, or even just another season as a player, then at least he could stagger on towards his testimonial, keeping his public dignity and reputation. Docherty agreed: Law could remain a player and announce his retirement from football on the day of his testimonial, which was only four months away after all. The two old warriors had saved face, as important to Scots as to Japanese samurai. If Law had been unwillingly shafted – which he undoubtedly had – then at least it had been in the dark, with lubrication and a condom. The world outside would only see a royal abdication in August, with the full pomp and circumstance. No one would know of Docherty's duplicity or Law's disappointment.

Saturday lunchtime. Denis is in an Aberdeen pub, surrounded by friends and well-wishers as ever. *Football Focus*, babbling from a telly above the bar, announces curtly that Law and Tony Dunne have been dumped by Docherty on freebies. Denis tries hard in his book to explain how this fist smashing into his emotional solar plexus hurt: adjectives fail him. The last vestiges which Docherty had left him to cover his nakedness were ripped away in seconds. 'Look mam, the King's got no clothes.' This was treachery of an unforgivable sort.

Law hared back to Manchester in frantic search of an explanation and a culprit, which was the only consolation on offer. The damage couldn't be repaired, of course. If this hadn't been Docherty's doing, to suspend disbelief for a moment, then a prompt denial from Tommy within the hour might've done the trick. By the time Denis reached Manchester, no such statement had materialized. Docherty later suggested that the news could've been leaked by Law's dining partners, or even indirectly by Sir Matt himself. To what end would that have been? As a defence, it was about as credible as OJ's. Docherty's own silence in the wake of the report was rather more convincing to this jury. When he himself admitted he 'might have let it slip to David Meek or someone like that', the ring of truth sounded. This was more like the Docherty of legend, shooting from the hip around town to any who'd listen and not caring overmuch whom his stray bullets struck.

Denis was told at Old Trafford that 'pressure from the media' had forced the release of the news. 'That explanation wasn't worth two bob – according to my agreement reached with Tommy, there should have been no news to release,' judged Denis correctly. Docherty's own 1981 version leaves a gaping hole at this point – he simply doesn't address it. Perhaps he's learned one thing from his legal tribulations after all: sometimes, rather than incriminate yourself through verbal contortion and evasion, it's better to keep schtum completely. Suddenly, the image of a New York *consigliere* growling 'I'm taking the Fifth' comes to mind.

Denis took his free, went to City and proved a couple of points to Docherty in a painfully forceful way. Typically, he took no pleasure in this, nor did he reveal the truth about his ignominious experience until the Morgan court case years later. Even then, he didn't look forward to blowing Docherty out of the water from the witness box and was hugely relieved to be reprieved by Tommy's surrender. 'I don't bear a grudge,' says Denis, 'but what he did to me was unforgivable.' And if Law was the first notable victim of the Docherty Treatment, he wouldn't be the last.

Disciples and Enemies is a dangerous game to play. For most of his period in charge, Tommy thought he had enough of the former to counteract the activities of the latter. Surprisingly for a man so adept at wheeler-dealing and reckoning up the readies, it appears he couldn't keep count. The events of 1977 and their aftermath illustrated his miscalculation. It's a pity for him that he didn't share his successor's interest in Oriental maxims: he might then have recalled: 'Be careful lest you make too many enemies on the way up – they'll all be there to help you on your way down.'

⚽ ⚽ ⚽

The greatest lost artists of all-time? In my opinion, a toss-up between Nick Drake, whose suicide after three LPs robbed the seventies of its soul, and Gerry Daly. It seems fitting that one of Gerry's good mates was Alex Higgins, another Irish genie who never quite delivered as much as he should have – but the stellar moments provided by both will never leave the memory.

Nineteen years old when he arrived from Dublin, he rarely tipped ten stone on the scales. He always looked pale, slightly ill and 'interesting': a natural indiepop frontman but surely not one for the hurly-burly of English midfieldery. Such was his elegance, grace and touch, however, that on his day he could overcome any collection of ferocious hatchetmen and muscle-heads. Until Hill's arrival, he was indisputably the team's one true artist, the nearest thing we had to Bobby Charlton.

So Docherty would later call him 'a Fancy Dan type with not a lot of grey matter' as if this was supposed to put any adoring Stretford Enders off: his intelligence on the pitch was all that counted. Off the pitch, it did admittedly appear that he hadn't given much thought to his lifestyle. The man lived on chips: chips and Tizer, chips and beer, chips and scampi . . . add several fags plus the frequent late nights and his pallid demeanour is thus explained. But he looked as though he'd be completely at home on the Stretford End, which only added to his appeal.

Best of all, he had the full-on Red Attitude – a bubbling, buzzing self-confidence which made him believe he could succeed at anything, be it football, darts, pool or chip-scoffing competitions. The marriage of sharp skill and cool confidence made him a penalty-taking natural, much as it has done for our modern equivalent, Eric. But he was so much more than that: his energy, passing, vision and shot were all top-rank. His only weakness, supposedly, was consistency – and his good friend Sammy's alleged superiority in that department proved to be his undoing.

Others suggest his troublesome relationship with Docherty was a far more telling factor. What an Odd Couple they proved to be: Tommy bought him, sold him, refused to sell him when he ended up in Derby, then farmed him out. At various times they've slagged each other, supported each other and damaged each other – but, above all, they shared a sadly similar fate. Mid-seventies Manchester would be as good as it got, for Gerry and the Doc. And nothing else in the future would quite bring out the best in them again.

❀ ❀ ❀

Red Army Despatches

An Introduction to Aggro
Pinpointing the birth of the Red Army is not a difficult task. There'd been sporadic outbreaks of trouble involving United fans in the sixties, most notably at Blackpool in 1965, where a knife was pulled from a police helmet. In 1965 Everton had been the first (and to date only) side ever to have taken the Stretford End; but the true birth of the Red Army can be traced to Upton Park on 6 May 1967.

'We had to go to West Ham and win to win the League, much as we would twenty-five years later. We all got the Friday night coach down to London, so that we were in East Ham for six o'clock in the morning. Already there were thousands of Reds roaming the streets. As we walked down the high road that morning I can recall hearing a massive rumbling sound from behind, and turning to see five United fans riding one of those big old-fashioned washing machines as three of their mates pushed it down the road. They were careering into parked cars with a guy chasing them in hot pursuit. They'd obviously nicked it from outside a shop somewhere: it was that sort of a day.

'We got to the ground hours before any West Ham fans or officials were even there, and kicked in the gates to their end. By 12.30 there must have been 200 of us playing football on the pitch. The police asked us to get off it so that they could open the gates to paying customers. An hour later, their end was full of United fans – there must have been 10,000-plus. In those days you used to be able to buy bottles of brown ale inside the ground and by 2.45, empties were flying over between ourselves and the small knot of West Ham fans to one side of their end. I got hit on the back of the head by one and decided I was going to do something about it. I

22

barged my way through the United fans and headed in the direction of where the bottle had come from, intent on getting a West Ham fan – any West Ham fan.

'As I came to where they were stood, I stopped dead in my tracks. I couldn't believe the clothes the West Ham fans were wearing! At the time I was dressing myself at the army surplus store on Chester Road. But they were all wearing faded denims, Dr Marten Boots, pink Ben Sherman shirts, braces and jackets with the sleeve cuffs turned up and brandishing chains, bottles and iron bars. I was frozen to the spot. One of them looked at me and said, "What's your number, sweetpea?" I just ducked down and disappeared back into the United crowd. They were proper blokes: we were just teenagers.

'As the bottles continued going back and forth, some bright spark threw one into the rafters so it shattered all over the West Ham heads. That was it then; bottles just seemed to be clattering into the roof and shattering down for the rest of the game. One old bloke was almost choking on his brown ale, such was his hurry to empty the bottle and throw it. At the end of the game, we all went on to the pitch to celebrate the win. As we came out of the ground, I saw one Red walking down the road wearing an outrageous hat with feathers in it, the sort you'd expect to find some la-di-dah woman wearing at Ascot. Then another Red went past wearing a similar hat, then another. Bobby Moore's wife owned a milliner's near the ground, and it had been broken into. You've never seen anything like it – Reds, scruffy as fuck, sporting the most expensive headwear imaginable!

'But that day really was the birth of the Red Army. Up to that point, we'd all been a bit too young. After West Ham, however, we began to reckon we could hold our own with anybody.' – *Rick, Stretford*

With the winning of the European Cup, attendances rocketed away from home as well as at Old Trafford. At the start of the 1969–70 season, the centre section of the Stretford End was closed after missiles had been thrown at the AC Milan keeper. The following term, more missile throwing incidents led to United's opening fixtures of the 1971–72 season being switched to the Victoria Ground for the match against West Brom and to Anfield for the Arsenal game. At Anfield, Reds had invaded the pitch from the Kop end as the players were warming up, in protest at the closure of Old Trafford. Outside afterwards, 'gangs of youths wearing the red and white colours of United hurled stones at cars streaming away from the ground and police control rooms were swamped with calls from householders who'd had their windows smashed by beer bottles.'

Two years previously on an away trip to Arsenal, United supporters had turned their thoughts to community service, though not of the kind handed out by lenient magistrates. In September 1969 a group of hippies had invaded and squatted in the Piccadilly Mansion at 144 Park Lane overlooking Hyde Park; United fans on their way to Highbury stopped off en route and told waiting policemen outside, 'We can get them out'. Reds always preferred to have a 'mission' to prevent aimlessness:

'It would be easy to make out that it was all trouble in those days, but to be honest we seemed to spend a lot of our time bobbing up and down the road running to where we thought there was trouble. Often as not, with a mob of fifteen hundred to two thousand United fans in a small town centre, if there was any trouble it was always the ones at the front who copped it. The rest of us would be bobbing up and down to see what was going on rather than joining in. United were really no worse than the others; Everton in particular used to give us a torrid time when we went over there. With United it was just the sheer numbers that made us more of a handful than anyone else.

'One of the big things amongst United fans was the wearing of scarves, and it was always the task to try and get one of the scarves of the opposition to show how hard you were; as with a Red Indian scalp, the wearing of an opponent's scarf marked you down as a hard nut. Truth is, it was easy to get their scarves most of the time. They'd come to Old Trafford and be so outnumbered that we'd just walk up to them and tell them to give us their scarves. In most instances they were so scared they just handed them over though we still wore them as trophies all the same. On one occasion, however, I went up to this big Arsenal fan at Old Trafford and told him to give me his colours – he just told me to fuck off. I ended up rucking with him with all my mates stood watching, laughing at me.'

By the end of Docherty's first season, 'activity' at away games had died down somewhat from the period of 1967–71; no doubt the poverty of our football had some part to play in this. What point was there to travelling the length and breadth of the country to see a side for whom Denis Law made only all-too-rare appearances, from which George Best had retired and in which Bobby Charlton was playing out his final few games? What incentive was there in a trip to Southampton at the end of March to watch George Graham, Martin, James and Anderson? The biggest United turnout of that season would be at Stamford Bridge, where every Red present was in the ground by twelve thirty, ostensibly to see Bobby get his silver cigarette case and nothing else. (Although, as it happened, they got more than they bargained for . . .) There'd been a few kick-offs at Newcastle, Liverpool and Sheffield United but nothing on the scale of what had been before nor indeed would come later. Nevertheless, there was still a certain 'atmosphere' about away travel and an ever-present potential for trouble, as these Reds recall in the following Despatches, beginning with a trip to Newcastle in 1972.

'I had to make my way to Victoria as the ManU special left there for the trip north. Once on board I soon made friends with some Chorley Reds who exchanged some good repartee with the travelling Greater Manchester constabulary. In those days the special trains had a carriage for parcels converted into a cage where misbehavers were kept. The nearest me and the Chorley lads got to that was a slap round the ear from a sergeant's gloves. The atmosphere was good and everybody was trying to make up new songs to wind up the Geordies.

'At York the train came to a brief halt at signals; streams of abuse and missiles were hurled at a Leeds special heading in the opposite direction. As we edged closer to Tyneside, a plan was put together on how best to get to the ground and the leader of the Chorley Reds made up our minds for us that it would be best to go through the town centre. It was a brilliant feeling as we marched through singing "There's only one United!" and "B for B and Georgie Best". We eventually closed in on the ground and came to a massive pub where an unfortunate Red had taken a beating but he was all for having another go once the army had arrived.

'The match itself ended 2-2 with Bestie getting one of his specials. So it was time to face up to getting back to the station in one piece. When I got back to Newcastle Central, I could not see a single Red – where were they all? Once inside the station it was like being on an iceberg with a colony of penguins. I could not understand a word they were saying and I hoped no one would ask me a question – or the time. I was hoping to catch a porter on his own, out of earshot, to ask where the Manchester special was going from. Just as I was about to give up hope I saw someone doing the fastest unrecorded 200 yards in history, with a red scarf hanging out of his pocket. Call it instant intuition but I burst through the gate at the end of the platform and chased after him. There was a small three-carriage train about to leave the platform and he jumped on quickly followed by me. Once on board we were totally surrounded by more penguins so I quietly asked him where he was going, hoping that he was not a Geordie Red. After a quick chat it appeared that they had failed to tell us that the special did not depart from Newcastle Central, but a small station called Manors. As we got off the train the Manchester special was on the adjacent platform; not until we got on board did the penguins stop hurling missiles and abuse at us, having realized that we'd been Red infiltrators. The great escape was successfully completed, for another year at least.'

Red Robbie recalls Anfield 1971:

'I remember not being able to get in the Anfield Road End occupied by United. With bells ringing at each turnstile, a cavalry charge was made to join the queues for the Kop. We pushed and shoved our way through

the turnstiles, down to the front of the Kop and stood
in the bottom left-hand corner. It soon became apparent who we were and the police escorted us along the
pitch to join the Anfield Road end.

'The walk back from Anfield to Lime Street was as
eventful as ever. There was a lot of demolition work
taking place and bricks were not in short supply; the
police escort had their work cut out preventing us from
stealing half house bricks but they did little to stop the
Scousers who managed to obtain quite an arsenal. It
was a relief to get to the station by other means than an
ambulance.

'The following season we got ambushed at the station
itself. My mate Micky made the mistake of answering
back when he was asked the time and before he knew it
he was on the floor minus his jacket, ticket and money.
We thought that once aboard the train to Crewe, that
would be it, but the train was one of those single com-
partment types, not a walk-through. So at every stop on
the way, you had this tragi-comic scene: United and
Liverpool supporters would dash out of the doors on to
the platform, have an almighty scrap on the spot and
then hurriedly pile back into their compartments as the
train pulled out, leaving the injured at the station. After
two searches of the train en route – they were looking for
some mad Scouser with a shovel! – we got to Runcorn
where most of the remaining Mickeys were chased
across the rails and away up the embankment. It was two
in the morning before we got to Crewe.' – *Robbie*

Clearly, football was not an entirely safe family experience
in the early seventies – but equally, as *Foul* magazine's
Chris Lightbown explained in December '73, the late sixties
surge of 'Boot Power' did not seem to have survived the
turn of the decade:

Whatever the press may say, football hooliganism is all
but over. Back in 1968, any young person could start a
fight upon the flimsiest of excuses. This was the period
of weapons crazes, bordering on the use of guns in
some London areas. Train-wrecking was far more frequent; hardly a Football Special ended its Saturday

without wrecked lights, seating and windows. Skin-headism and social violence were a spent force by 1971. Just as violence came into football because the youth movement was going through a violent phase, and not because of any inherent defect in the game itself, so it ended because violence stopped being *the* criterion for young people.

'In the last couple of years, the age group that caused havoc five years ago have hung up their boots. There was an 18-month gap before younger kids started to fill the vacuum. Indeed, there was literally a changing of the guard at three London clubs, where End leaders in their early twenties gave way to new teenage leaders. Shortly after that the new but still very over-rated round of violence that we are beginning to hear about started up.

'But the big uncertainty is the younger generation who, so far, hardly stand boot-high to their predecessors. As long as the fans who are involved in violence – and there are a lot more than the ridiculous 2 per cent estimates – have at least tacit support from the rest of their generation, then there is no way that the football violence movement can be completely stamped out. The ordinary lad of 15 who goes to football and who would never dream of getting involved in a "normal" fight, is interested in the Ends fighting and in which gang has done what to whom recently. And if the new generation becomes involved in football violence, then it will be because they find themselves expected to carry on the tradition of their elders.' – *Chris Lightbown*, Foul

Within the year, *Foul*'s prediction came to pass. A new Red Army joined the willing remnants of 1967's veterans: 'youth fashion' had changed again and made aggro 'in'. This time, the authorities wouldn't wait for fashion to take on a more pacifistic hue – eventually, in United's case, they took 'stamping out' action. But again, *Foul* was right: 'You can't stamp out any such subversive movement.' By the end of the seventies, aggro at United and elsewhere mutated into another form, one which could evade the new restrictions – casualism. That, however, is another story and another book . . .

1973–74

In the autumn and winter of 1973, whistling in the dark wasn't the sole preserve of cowering householders during the endless power cuts; it was *de rigueur* at Old Trafford too. Before August's kick-off, Martin Buchan had bravely declared in the *Supporters' Yearbook*: 'We look forward to the opportunity of showing our true capabilities, now that the pressure is off.' (Arf!) That summer light-headedness didn't last long; soon all Reds were back in the now familiar crouching position with the pressure of an entire League table bearing down on our shoulders. The Doc, to his credit, kept on a-whistling all season, drawing tributes that ooze retrospective irony from Morgan and Stepney for his morale-building efforts. But by April, he was merely 'whistling Dixie'.

Yet that darkest of winters for both United and country seemed a long way off on the Saturday night of 1 September. Sure, we'd had an opening day tonking at Arsenal, despite Gerry Daly's decent debut, but that was normal. Four thrashings in a row at Highbury had established it as a seventies graveyard for all Red teams from which we didn't escape alive until '78. But victories over Stoke and QPR, both better sides than us, lifted the spirits of eternal optimists. Trevor Anderson received rave reviews – Oh, such surreal days – McIlroy was temporarily back both making and scoring goals and the Rumour Machine was rampant, linking United with Archie Gemmill, Tony Currie, Asa Hartford and, strongest of all, Celtic's David Hay. For months we tracked the cultured Celt, offering the unsettled Forsyth (whom Tony Young had replaced) in part-ex; when George Graham's decline became increasingly obvious to

29

fans, our failure to pick up any of these smart operators stung all the more.

The pessimists, as ever, had a better grip on reality. We'd beaten Stoke partly by kicking them off the park, one seventies prerequisite skill we did have in abundance; QPR were simply robbed after Bowles and Venables had taken the piss for an hour and forced Stepney into six class saves. (How the balance of power had shifted since their last visit: United 8, Rangers 1 . . .) The comparison between the two Strollers, Bowles and Graham, was painful to note; the Strettie chanted Storey-Moore's name at the end, knowing full well that the absentee winger was a better bet than George for inspiration. Three defeats followed to cheer up the G-Stand Grumblers. All by the odd goal, mind – the United relegation team only ever got truly stuffed twice. The newly formed United Travel Club had merely a rare Trev Anderson header as reward for its expedition to the wilds of Suffolk though later they could appreciate having witnessed the debut of Brian Greenhoff. For the 41,000 at OT for Leicester's visit, seeing Stepney beat a stunned Peter Shilton from the spot had to suffice as the afternoon's inspiration; the symbolic value of a penalty-taking keeper was to be seen as immense. When Alex was still joint top scorer at Christmas, the novelty lost its joke appeal, although his miss against Wolves did result in an amusingly cartoonish Schmikes-scramble back to his area.

Before United plunged into a five-month decline to the foot of the table which saw us win just twice, Old Trafford enjoyed its last, almost carefree afternoon of innocent pleasure before crappy angst took over. Brian Kidd, back for his final and ultimately tragic run in the side, hammered the Irons with two sensational strikes, and Ian Storey-Moore got the other in what was his farewell appearance. When one notes that Georgie Buchan, who my mate Eamonn claims was created with all the non-footballing chromosomes left over from Martin, made a goal and played a blinder, you can appreciate how ethereal a game this had been. Docherty gushed with relief about Kiddo's comeback, hoping he'd found the self-belief and consistency which had been deemed to be missing from his game. He spoke too soon.

Whatever criticisms there were of United's lack of style

and forward power – and there were plenty, as we shall see – they could never be accused of lacking the stomach and enthusiasm for a scrap. This team almost always gave 100 per cent; it's just that 100 per cent of a three-cylinder engine isn't usually enough and it certainly wasn't expected to be sufficient to get anything from the sleek V12 machines we faced in late September, Leeds and Liverpool.

Fortunately for us, the Elland Roaders had just embarked on a PR campaign, promising to clean up their game and drop their characteristic cynicism. Now that they had a team brilliant enough to win without their customary evil-doing – and we caught them on the way to twenty-nine games unbeaten and the championship – they were attempting to take on some of the credo of old Busby United, ironically just at the moment we were resembling Leeds-lite. (Or, in view of the results, Leeds-shite.) As it happened, our respective futures demonstrated how karma punishes you for working against your nature. We got relegated for pretending to be sheepshagging assassins whilst their efforts to become Yorkshire's Red Devils prompted a rapid post-'74 decline. Poor Leeds: they'll always be the club of Hunter and Carlton Palmer at heart.

Ten thousand Reds infiltrated Elland Road to watch this amusing role-reversal – a dreadful game, enlivened by Greenhoff booting Bremner all over the pitch and Big Jim predating Vinnie Jones by getting booked three minutes after kick-off. Leeds, straining at the leash, kept their cool but lost a point. Their fans tried to gain 'compensation' from Reds afterwards and were amazed to discover how many had mobbed up – bedlam ensued from ground to station and beyond. 'The most violent I've seen Elland Road,' notes Andy Pollard; indeed, none would be more relieved at United's eventual relegation than the West Yorkshire Police.

Another dull 0-0 against Liverpool followed, the Scousers so miffed when robbed of a blatantly good early goal that they appeared to sulk for the rest of the game, taking the ball back into their half so that the other nasty kids couldn't play with it. So we'd proved we could mix it with the hardest and defend against the best; what became increasingly apparent was that we couldn't create enough – and couldn't score in any event. In the next twenty-five

League games, we scored more than once on just five occasions – and won only one of those – which essentially meant that once the opposition scored, we couldn't win. Dull draws, but mainly defeats, were the inevitable and doomladen results. The apparent paradox of defenders Holton and Buchan emerging as nationally renowned greats in a relegation season is easily explained: United lost their top-table seat up front, not at the back.

No surprise then that the comeback of George Best should have been greeted with Cantonesque fervour. So what if he was still bulging, boozed and fully birded-up; we had to take whatever attacking chances we were offered. With Moore out, Anderson exposed, Kidd inconsistent, McIlroy unfit and Macari unhappy out of position, the Doc needed this gamble to come off. Seven thousand turned up to watch his reserves comeback whilst the first team were at Molineux; given the rival attraction, arguably a pulling power on the Cantona vs Leeds reserves scale. Later, as United slumped at home to Derby after Forsyth fucked up his return, the Stretford End chanted the absent Best's name. Of course it was a leap of faith, not reason – what did doubters think we were, thick? – but Best had a talismanic status not unlike Eric's. Watching the Reds thrice hit woodwork, seeing Kidd struggle for the break his work deserved and coming away with nothing for a third match in a row could convince even the most existential that the Fates had abandoned us. George had always been lucky; he'd carried us for three seasons at least and saved us on innumerable occasions. So, just as they saluted grinning Formby in 1940: 'Let George Do It!' No ukulele on show here, though; unfortunately, George was largely unable to hit a cow's arse with his metaphorical banjo either.

They turned out in force for him – third-best crowd of the season in fact – only to see a slow shadow of former glory get hacked about by a Brummie centre-half. Or should that be centre-back? Welcome to the seventies on both counts, George. It rained and the goalie scored a penalty: a normal day at Old Trafford.

Ten thousand-plus Reds at Turf Moor rose to Buchan's majesty as we scabbed another point – George did all right, Kidd was as unlucky as ever. But time was running out for

all our yesterday's men. These two had ten games left
between them, substitute David Sadler none. Four nights
before, Old Trafford had said a final farewell to Tony
Dunne; Denis the King had had his formal abdication
against Ajax three weeks further back. By season's end,
only three Busby Boys remained and only one would see
out the decade with us.

It's embarrassing to talk about 'bad luck' and 'fate'
because objectively there's no such thing; statistically it all
evens out in the long run and to talk in such terms makes
you sound like Mystic Meg or – worse, this – one of her
readers. But for United to come out of November without a
win was ballot-riggingly scandalous. How entirely understandable that Jim Holton should engage in a mighty
punch-up with Mike England at White Hart Lane; this
ill-wind business is hard to take. Another massive Red
Army invasion in London saw a tremendous game (a shock
to the system in 1973–74) and thrilled to Best's best.
Laughter at what was in fact a Knowles own goal prompted
some Red wag to sing "Nice one Cyril, let's have another
one'; the sod duly obliged by popping one in at the other
end.

Leading 2-1 at St James' Park, those Reds who'd braved
the ends and slipped in everywhere must have thought our
luck had turned. George Graham's smashing goal into the
roof of the net stunned them, his supplier Best and, to
judge from his slack-jawed head-scratching reaction, the
scorer himself. We still lost. Naturally. The memory of our
fightback against Chelsea two weeks earlier, when Tony
Young thumped home from 25 yards and Greenhoff opened
his account bang on time, suddenly seemed like a long
time ago.

So too did Christmas 1971, when United had been five
points clear at the top. Xmas '73: Slade's seasonal greetings
at Number One rang hollow in Manchester. We were in
depressing disarray – five games, four at home, without a
win, the Scousers taking advantage in particular. Gates
crashed to a hard core of 28,500 who saw George Best's
last-ever United goal in the defeat by Coventry. The Doc
had begun to lose patience. Trevor Anderson's Red run was
finished whilst Graham lost his place, and the captaincy to
Morgan. Only the return of a fit McIlroy brought any timely

33

good cheer. Kidd's mini-revival was over as Everton hovered ready to bid for the unhappy hero; Moore had officially retired, destroying the Doc's ambitions to run a 4-2-4 system. When Sheffield United scored a last-minute winner at a Boxing Day Old Trafford, we had reached a nadir; fans trooped glumly home to their cold turkey, three-day week and candle-lit toilets. Merry Fucking Christmas everybody.

For some reason, Stewart Houston was mad enough to want to step into this miserable morass, signing from Brentford within days for £45,000 (£1m). We didn't know it at the time but his intervention saved us from what would have been the biggest blow of all – the loss of Martin Buchan. Unhappy at having to play right-back because we had no other decent cover, he had discussed transferring with the Doc. Houston slotted in immediately; with Young then Forsyth coming back at Number 2, Buchan returned to his triumphant generalissimo role. All these manoeuvres and the late winners that beat Ipswich to keep our heads above water in 19th spot were soon lost amidst the last lamentable Georgie Best scandal which engulfed the New Year – just as QPR drowned us in goals on 1 January itself. Best was poor that day; he never played for us again. God's most blessed creations deserve better codas than that.

That January day on which Best last approached the Reds' dressing room in anger (or in-ebriation? Or in-the-arms-of-a-dollybird?), United faced little Plymouth in the Cup. We struggled as much without Best as we had with, Macari heading the only goal. Graham produced his worst game of the season, an award granted amidst stiff competition, ending his run in the team at West Ham a week later. He'd only play twice more for United and finished the season on offer. From the new Gunther Netzer to club captain and thence to expensive reject in eighteen months: no wonder there didn't seem to be any boardroom cash available to Docherty.

Losing to yet another late winner at Upton Park reignited transfer talk; Chelsea's Osgood, over whom Docherty had drooled lasciviously after the 2-2, and team-mate Alan Hudson were available but United stayed silent. As regards the latter, perhaps it was a case of having just dumped one pisshead . . . A local Red called Anthony Blair made a splash in the press by offering to set up a supporters' fund to buy players; fans mostly understood and believed the board when they said the bank account was bare. (In a way, this was the first call for flotation, except no one had conceived of football plcs back then.) Yet by March, United had found £60,000 (£1.4m) for Jim McCalliog and two months later, a mammoth £200,000 (£4.8m) for Stuart Pearson. Curious. Admittedly, the sales of Fletcher, O'Brien and Rimmer raised half the Pearson fee, but even so . . .

So United embarked on the run-in with a limited squad, having to scrape the bottom of the barrel. Actually, they went through the barrel-bottom into the rotten earth below, digging up beetling creatures who should never have seen the light of an Old Trafford day. (Take a bow, Messrs Bielby, Fletcher and Griffiths.) Rock-bottom had been touched already; on 9 February a season's-best 60,000 saw Leeds win 2-0 and send us to the basement. A joyous nation – never believe ABUs (Anyone But United) are a purely modern phenomenon – intoned our last rites. Joe Jordan and Mick Jones had scored, symbolizing the seemingly effortless transition from old to new generations at Elland Road. How the savages would enjoy their title and our simultaneous relegation. April '77 and February '78 couldn't come soon enough for us. Tony Young was the Doc's scapegoat this time – he'd only play twice more, in April. The manager admitted he'd buggered the lad about in five different positions and his confidence and form were shot. A decent Urmston lad, was Tony: nonetheless, he was never going to captain England, if you get my drift.

Nemesis approached for the incarnation of United that had dominated the Docherty era thus far; the hard, dour, defensive side which had struggled to find flair and crea-tion was into its last half-dozen games. When relegation appeared inevitable, it would transform itself into an almost complete opposite. So some say in retrospect, any-way. In the month between 23 February and 23 March, United played five League games: they scored only one goal, Lou's winner at Bramall Lane in front of possibly 12,000 Reds. A sign of the desperate state of our attack – Brian Greenhoff drafted in as emergency striker on the strength of a goal in a 'friendly' against Glasgow Rangers. (It was a miracle that they found time to score five in between the pitch-invasion battles.)

Tempers were as fraught on the pitch as on the terraces; Macari and ultimate Bluenose Mike Doyle were sent off for a set-to in the goalless derby, unwittingly at one with the marauding hordes roaring down Claremont and Princess roads. The final axe fell on Graham and Kidd as they made their last Red starts in the defeats against Brum and Spurs; Jim McCalliog arrived as a rearguard battling reinforcement (the Doc seeing him as long-term, the Stretford Enders as stop-gap); Gerry Daly was given his first chances in mid-field . . . but all this frenzied shuffling and dealing didn't alter the way the cards were eventually stacked. Losing the crunchiest of crunch relegation battles at St Andrews – to yetafuckinother last-gasp goal – was crippling; slumping to the old baldie Ralph Coates's goal against Spurs was virtually death itself. United were now, quite rightly, odds-on for the drop with only nine games left, having shown little of the goalscoring qualities they would need to survive.

Sometime in that last week of March, the clouds lifted and an Indian Summer arrived. Legend has it that Sir Matt said to Docherty: 'If we're going to go down, let's do so in style.' The critics who had carped about United's style for the best part of two seasons were blown away as United scored twelve goals in five games, even winning three in a row for the first time in twelve months. The criticism had always been a sore point; as Martin Buchan had pointed out, when the only functioning part of your team is the defence and you're fighting for survival, what can you expect but hardened spirits and barely controlled aggression? If we'd played the purists' way, we'd never have left the bottom spot we occupied in December 1972.

What also stuck in the craw was the provenance of the complainants, places like Derby, Leeds and London where negativity, cynicism and percentage play had long ruled the roost. There is a myth that seventies football was a golden age on the park, a myth the nineties nostalgia industry has shamelessly exploited. Watching the execrable *There's Only One Brian Moore* the other night, I listened in amazement as some has-been wittered on about the feast of attacking footie that characterized the decade. What utter bollocks. The seventies were dominated by endless hand-wringing about the dreadful state of the game as England missed two World Cups and the goals-per-game ratio slipped to an all-time low. It was a commonplace not worth repeating that a tedious defensive mentality had overrun the game; observers decried the mechanical nature of virtually every champion side, from Arsenal to Liverpool, Derby to Leeds. Even Leeds at their most 'beautiful' in '74 were no match for the delights offered by a 1994 United or even a 1988 Liverpool. Most sides that United played in '73 and '74 were as tight-arsed as we were – the difference was that such was expected of them. Britain looked to us to uphold older values; it was the childish disappointment that we wouldn't so sacrifice ourselves which caused the grumbling. All those god-awful trundling Midlands sides, stuffed full of anonymous beards and butlers at Castle Dracula – that made for a golden age? Of course not. What made the seventies golden was the experience of the fans revelling in true traditional fandom. What inspires nostalgia is the memory of being in the Stretford End when 63,000 are celebrating a winner. Most seventies footie was shite: the very reason why United's '75–'77 team was so lionized then and now is that its flair and style stood so dramatically apart from the calculated mediocrity around it. Bob Mills, you should know better.

Now that United were the underdogs, condemned men with nothing expected of them, they got 'gate-happy' with merciful release in sight. The youngsters McIlroy, Greenhoff and Daly flourished once the burden was lifted – and McCalliog may not have been the greatest player but he was undoubtedly just the ticket at that juncture. Driven on by an inspired Captain Morgan, April became a rum old month.

We won all three vital crunch games: at Chelsea, despite Steve James's near-decapitation making his grin toothier than ever; at Norwich, where Stepney outwitted the vengeful MacDougall and Holton out-savaged Howard; and when Cup Finalists Newcastle tried a half-strength team on us, receiving rightful punishment as the second Supermac of the week finished second best. And after months of Old Trafford sterility, what fabulous refreshment to be reminded of the good old days: a bonkers six-goal thriller against Burnley, complete with mad penalties, last-minute equalizer and atrocious goalkeeping, then a 3-0 obliteration of high-flying Everton that was as overwhelming as any sixties demolition. Docherty had found something here he could use for the future. If not yet quite the youthful, purring 4-2-4 that was to come, at least it was on the way. From the wreckage of his initial plan which had counted on Moore, Kidd and Graham, he had retrieved an Easter resurrection substitute that might yet prove superior.

A point at The Dell sent us to Goodison for an infamous Wednesday night, still fighting the odds yet still with hope. We had to win and hope Birmingham didn't beat a good QPR side; having murdered Everton at home only days before, United went in at half-time goalless but confident they could finish the job. As they left the field, a mischievous tannoy announcer chose to broadcast just one of the night's other half-times: Brum 2, QPR 0. And in case the team missed it, he helpfully piped a repeated announcement directly into the dressing room. United came out, heads down and lost to a Mick Lyons goal whilst the Brummies sealed victory. Sly Scouse sharp practice had triumphed again. But it was fellow Mancs who awaited on Saturday to help complete the job.

Saturday, 27 April 1974 – the day that United's fate is surely to be decided. 'What a bloody moment for a bloody derby,' mutters my bloody uncle. To have a hope of staying up, we must beat City at home, something that even Best, Law and Charlton hadn't managed in the League since September 1966. But the true incarnation of Fate that day are the other Blues, of Birmingham. Should they beat doomed Norwich at St Andrews, no amount of Old Trafford heroics can save us. Our ground hadn't seen so many transistors clapped to earholes since 11 May 1968 – on reflection, not a good omen. These two dates must feature in every Bertie wet dream.

The midday atmosphere in town can only be described as surreal. After two years of scrabbling to escape a yawning trapdoor, the actual sensation of finally slipping through to the hell below is too savagely original to be fully appreciated. You have to be well into middle age to recognize what is happening from previous experience; the vast majority in the Strettie have no such compass. Some

Blues dare to make the trip into the Scoreboard End, salivating at the prospect of capping five years of supremacy with a final humiliation but equally fearing the inevitable result at 90 minutes – win, lose or draw, the Stretford would be coming for them. The day is certain to end in tears – but for whom?

Two minutes gone – with two practice pitch invasions chalked up already – and Norwich score at Birmingham. It takes an eternity for this to be announced but United's players already know: they're going for it, rattling Corrigan, hacking at Lee, teasing Doyle. The midfield is ours but the goal won't come and Tueart, as ever, is a threatening pain in the arse wherever he marauds. The real daggers up the rectum are wielded in Brum, however: Bob Hatton and Kenny Burns score just before the break. The Beast that is Division Two licks its lips in anticipation.

This is Old Trafford, not Goodison. Second-half heads don't drop: proud hearts drive tired bodies on. McIlroy and Daly never stop running. But however much you strain to hear the warbling medium wave, there's nothing good coming out of Birmingham – as usual. City, who've played it cool, move in for the kill with ten to go. Summerbee hits the bar, Stepney brilliantly denies Tueart. We've almost nothing left to offer. The good old days are over: there's no George Best for a match-turning hat-trick, no Bill Foulkes for a galloping late header, no Denis Law for a winner-out-of-nothing. But there is a Denis Law for City. Seven minutes from time, instinct takes over; Bell and Lee feed him in the box and his smart back-heel bamboozles Stepney on its way into the Scoreboard goal. Never has a man enjoyed his revenge less. For five seconds or so, Old Trafford is completely stunned, scarcely able to believe the cruelty of the moment. Bell slaps Law around the face, trying to rouse him from his stupor to share his team-mates' enjoyment. But Denis knows who his eternal, true comrades are – the frozen, horrified hordes on the terraces.

Thankfully, it wasn't the King who'd killed his subjects. As every schoolboy knows – though apparently not many football writers – we were down anyway as Birmingham held on to their 2-1 lead. But of course everyone then and since found the symbolism and poetic cruelty of the image irresistible. No relegation and no fall from grace will ever be so 'celebrated', so full of ironies and so utterly desperate as United's that day. Typical United: even in disaster, there's always a strange kind of glory, however perverted. As a distraught Denis came off, the Stretford came on; City fans exited stage right. The invaders secured the abandonment they wanted but, like United's final Easter charge, it had come too late: with only four minutes left on the clock, the result was allowed to stand. Docherty and several players wept in the dressing room as the Red Army ran riot. For the Stretford Enders, there'd be plenty of time to cry into their beers later that deathly night. The rest of football rejoiced, of course. The national delight of 29 May 1968 was another world: the modern United would henceforth always shed their tears of triumph or despair alone. 'No one likes us . . .' and, at such a moment, 'we don't care.'

An oft-repeated declaration at the time was that United should never have allowed themselves to get relegated. To some, that smacked of the kind of arrogance that had put us on the ruinous road to start with, complacently fannying about in the early seventies when surgery and proper planning were required. But it was the truth: clubs of this size and pedigree can only go down when an almost inconceivable set of calamities occur simultaneously. All the greats have had such moments – even Arsenal, who bribed their way out of it in 1915. (The 'Bank Of England Club' my arse: more like 'The BCCI Club'.) We've touched on most of the immediate causes that combined to doom us: unexpected injuries and loss of form in players we relied on like Kidd, Moore and Graham; kids coming in under pressure who didn't get time enough to learn what they needed; lack of finances to add the two extra players we could've done with; playing Macari and Buchan out of position for too long; sheer ill-luck and bad timing. David Meek then claimed we shouldn't have sold Davies and MacDougall, although hindsight hasn't flattered that Meekian judgement; but since he was the keenest to argue that we couldn't afford to spend during 1973–74, how could he have expected us simply to keep hold of the players we had if the Doc hadn't handsomely cashed in on the duo?

In one respect, Meek was right though: in remarking that

'all management changes are expensive', he pinpointed the underlying cause of which all other reasons are mere functions. The board as a whole had mismanaged the succession to Busby, and those managers in turn had to some degree mismanaged the teams. There was no long-term planning: no strategy, just tactics. Arrogance and complacency festered where urgency and bravery were needed. This all may seem obvious but is worth restating. No trophies are won or relegations suffered on the strength or weakness of one season alone; they are summations of an era. And perhaps, as George Best has always argued, this particular era had really begun the night United won the European Cup.

⚽ ⚽ ⚽

Writers in the seventies looking for metaphors of perennial occurrences had three choices: 'as frequent as . . .' sterling crises, Sinatra farewell tours or George Best comebacks. Actually, the last mentioned were probably the most numerous of all, if you count every single transatlantic or lower division debut as a fresh attempt. But in truth, the last serious resuscitation of a generation's greatest talent began in August 1973; he was barely 27. Instead of approaching the climax of a career, he was five months from virtual retirement. For a player such as Best, matches at outposts like Craven Cottage and LA could only ever be seen as Sunday-style kick-abouts.

This is not the place to dissect Best's downfall, how a combination of drink, gambling and women so weakened an already precariously balanced character that he was unable to carry the twin burdens of permanent public scrutiny and an ailing United team. Michael Parkinson's seventies book documents this wretched process best and is the dolly-birds-and-doubles romp *non pareil*. By August '73, Best's footballing obituaries had already been twice written. Sacked by United in December '72, George had provided the tabloids with a steady stream of stories throughout the early years of the decade, including at least two AWOL crises and an infamous weekend shacked up with the scrumptious Sinead Cusack. In a world without Di and Fergie, Best was surely Fleet Street's Royal *manqué*.

41

The bubbling excitement surrounding his possible return that autumn genuinely reflected Reds' sense of anticipation – but also that of the hacks, sniffing those padded expense accounts and two-page splashes to come.

Best had spent most of the preceding eight months in Spain. If it hadn't been for the fact that he was the world's greatest player wasting half a season of potentially historic achievement, who could resist admiring his luck? Eight months of sun, cheap booze, beach footie and a succession of bikini'd blondes: what more can a lad want? Yet, like Eric Cantona eighteen years later, he missed proper football. He missed the heroism; he missed the buzz. But it took a serious thrombosis to drive him back to England and into the embracing arms of United: he would never have gone crawling back voluntarily. When he awoke from his Manchester operation, there by his bed sat Matt Busby, bearing grapes and a wry smile. 'Isn't it time you were back playing again?' Matt remarked in a parting aside. That, and a ground-rules meeting at Paddy McGrath's house with the Doc, was all it took: George could go back into Old Trafford, head held high.

There were some who thought it 'off', the same kind of people who would later decry Cantona's second resurrection: he'd had his chances and should've stayed sacked in order to preserve the club's integrity and honour. However, United, ever the good Catholic club, spoke of forgiveness and absolution. Sure, he'd been forgiven before and had still let us down again. But he'd done eight months' penance, said his metaphorical Hail Marys and received Sir Matt's blessing – the old training shirt numbered 33 awaited the prodigal son.

So he was as hairy as Jim Morrison, ten pounds overweight and with muscles as soft as his drinks should have been. Yet after two months of the Cav regime, he was deemed ready to start. One insider quipped that United were training him labour-camp hard so as to ensure he'd be shagged-out long before he could get his hands on any jugs, of either kind. He trained with the pros in the morning and the apprentices after a non-liquid lunch; the world marvelled at his application. Again as Eric would discover, the media loves the apparent penitent – you had to be a right Woolnough not to applaud.

And for most of his twelve-match run, the media and fans alike were prepared to overlook his deficiencies on the pitch in the hope of a brighter tomorrow. For if his pace had not yet returned, the skill had clearly never left him. He was beating players but not quite getting away from them; at times he would disappear from the game completely but then display visionary spells of which his team-mates were so clearly incapable. To be thrown into the maelstrom of a relegation dogfight was hardly ideal but he was battling as manfully as he could. And there were moments, such as at White Hart Lane, when the football world could believe the best of Best was not entirely behind him. Three days of pigheadedness wrecked that faith.

George Best had memorized what he claims Docherty said to him when he rejoined and he'll repeat it verbatim whenever asked: 'If you have a night out and miss training, you'll have to come back and do it in the afternoon. But no one will ever know about it. It will remain between you and me – *I promise you.*' The test, eventually, came in the week of United's January Cup tie with Plymouth. George, for the first time since September, missed training on the Wednesday morning. Anxious to keep his word, he did the extra stint that afternoon; no one said a word about it to him for the next two days and, for George, the matter was forgotten. A mistake made but immediately repaired – hadn't that been the deal? Clearly, the lessons of the Law Affair hadn't been fully learned by this particular player . . .

Saturday match-day. The Doc has told the players to report to the Grill Room at 11.30. And on this much, it is agreed: Georgie didn't roll up at the ground until 2.30. But then, that had always been the Best way. If Sir Matt had accepted it, why not lesser men? Docherty now says he took Best aside into the ref's room and told him he was being dropped for his lateness – and for not being in a fit state to play, accusing Best of having had a lunchtime drop or two. (Better a Best with a double inside him than a completely sober Mick Martin, you might suggest.) No one else who saw Best before kick-off has suggested he was even vaguely pissed, however. Docherty also claims now that Best simply wasn't up to it anymore, that his comeback had failed on football terms. Yet he picked Best throughout the period and had him down to play that Cup tie; clearly at this point he was deemed good enough for a Doc team.

You may, therefore, find Best's version rather more persuasive. Especially in the light of the mysterious leak to Thursday's press that Best had missed training. For by Saturday, the tabloid blood-sport zealots had hyped up a triviality into a trial of strength between Docherty and Best. Once again, the Cantona comparison comes to mind: how a minor foul becomes evidence of near psychotic outbreak when translated by the *Sun*. The jackals wanted to see Best slapped down, humiliated; no secret pact between the Doc and George could survive such pressure. Best remembers his version of the 2.30 confrontation: 'Docherty said he wasn't playing me. I asked why. "Because you didn't turn up for training." "But I came in on the afternoon as we agreed." Docherty said it didn't matter. "I can't let it be seen that you are bigger than me." Tommy Docherty had lied to me.'

This, then, was the Best variation of the Docherty Treatment, as patented elsewhere via Denis Law and Willie Morgan. But then, in a moment of stubbornness which echoes with poignancy, Best refused a lifeline. Paddy Crerand jumped in to offer a fresh start on the Monday morning; the Doc didn't demur either. Best refused, perhaps in the heat of the moment but also on principle. As far as he was concerned, 'Docherty was a liar' – and he wouldn't work for a man who didn't have integrity, in whom he couldn't place his own trust. Perhaps George had been spoiled by having had Sir Matt to believe in and to rely upon, leaving him unsuited for the grim machinations of most other managerial regimes; perhaps this is just his *post facto* rationalization for an overly hasty decision which finished his career. In leaving United for good on such a precise note, he displayed both nobility and wretchedness, a combination that typified his early-seventies life. Sadly, as his slow descent continued over the years, the latter would tend to overshadow the former.

George is a familiar face around OT nowadays but only returned publicly a couple of times during the rest of the seventies; as he was still of playing age then, these occasions carried an emotional charge lacking today. You couldn't help asking yourself, 'What if . . .?' From time to time bizarre rumours would surface from Manchester's drinkeries that Best was planning a comeback at United, usually when the team was struggling to live up to our illustrious past; few ever believed them, but the stomach would still tingle despite the absurdity. I only ever saw him once at Old Trafford, in Paddy Crerand's testimonial; the reception he received that night told me more than anything I'd ever read about the faithful's reverence for his genius. I know that Law was King Denis and that Charlton was 'Our Bobby' – but George was The Best, wasn't he?

And for all the regrets for what might have been, never let such idiocies pass as 'he blew it' or 'left promise unfulfilled', as once was fashionable. Thirty years on he's still being voted the world's greatest-ever sportsman, having left a legacy of performances, goals and personal style that will never be matched. Would that we could all 'wreck our careers' to such eternal effect. *Ne regrette rien*, as Eric says . . .

⚽ ⚽ ⚽

Red Army Despatches

Hooliganism's obituaries had been a touch premature: this season built like a pressure cooker, as all the right ingredients began to combust together before providing the mammoth explosion that was 1974–75. Early season trips to Leeds and Sheffield had made press headlines once again; over forty had been arrested as United halted Leeds' eight-game winning start to the season at Elland Road. At Bramall Lane a contingent of United took their Kop with over fifty arrested. If you were looking for signs of things to come, they were there – younger kids replacing those who'd 'retired' from aggro's first wave, a realization that the authorities' recent complacency could be freshly exploited and, in the light of United's grim football, some fans desiring a replacement form of matchday entertainment. Three fixtures in particular were to provide ample illustration of the new mood during the last months of the season.

'As we became aware that there really was little hope we would stay up, a "fuck it" attitude seemed to take over many of the Reds I knew. We had a reputation but nothing much had been happening on the grand scale of things. Sure, there'd been a few skirmishes at the usual places like Leeds and Newcastle, but nothing to compare to the late sixties days. Then Rangers came to Old Trafford and it seemed to spark everyone off again.' – *Kevin H, Salford*

On 9 March 1974, with United long since knocked out of the FA Cup, the club took the decision to invite Glasgow Rangers to Old Trafford for a so-called 'friendly' game. Rangers too had been knocked out of the Scottish Cup and both clubs were facing blank Saturdays on what was sixth-round day. The visit of Rangers was not as well publicized as might have been expected. A crowd of less than 25,000 were to witness the worst scenes ever seen inside Old Trafford.

'We found out about it watching *On The Ball* during Saturday lunchtime. Before the match, word went round Manchester that Rangers were going about the town taking fucking liberties. At that time, no one was allowed to run around our town so everyone just headed down to Old Trafford to take them on.' – *Mick, Collyhurst*

'They were in the Scoreboard end and K Stand before the game – it was the biggest away following I'd ever seen at Old Trafford. In the mid-seventies it was unusual to see anyone bring more than a few hundred to Old Trafford; they just didn't do it 'cos they were too scared. About a quarter of an hour before the game kicked off, Rangers all ran on to the pitch and just stood in front of the Stretford End, daring us to come on. We all got on to the pitch – this was before the fences went up – and it kicked off something rotten. The police brought the horses and dogs out to try and stop it; in the end, Docherty and Jock Wallace came over the loudspeaker and made an appeal to everyone to stop. My abiding memory is of their women fans pissing in the seats.' – *John, Harpurhey*

In Manchester before the game, running battles had taken place, with fans of both sides using building material from the under-construction Arndale Centre as missiles. It was, in the words of the *Manchester Evening News*, 'the worst outbreak of hooliganism the city has ever seen'. Seventy-seven fans were arrested at the ground, thirty injured and twenty locked up in custody for the weekend, before appearing in court the following Monday on charges that in one instance included the use of an axe to attack a police officer. Alderman Kenneth Collis, then Mayor of Manchester, was in no doubt that Rangers fans should be banned from any future friendlies in Manchester, and called for a total ban on their travelling to England.

Only four days after the visit of Rangers to Old Trafford, United went to Maine Road for a rearranged derby match. One Red remembers: 'We used to go to Maine Road where the Kippax was split into two with just a line of ticker tape between us – United were simply steaming through the tape and the coppers to get at the City fans.'

The match itself was one of the most bad-tempered in derby history with Doyle and Macari getting their marching orders from Clive Thomas, who took the teams off the field to calm them down for seven minutes. Outside, the two mobs of United and City fought almost continuously for an hour before kick off; running battles saw every window in the houses down one side of Kippax Street put through. Cars were turned over everywhere, with the fire brigade having to hose them down for fear of fire breaking out. Inside the ground scuffles broke out, with both sets of supporters trying to take the others' section of the Kippax at various stages. So many fans were ejected that police stopped counting although there were no really serious injuries amongst the 45 taken to hospital.

Everyone was aware of the requirements of the United side as they took to the field to play Manchester City at Old Trafford on 27 April. Even before the teams had left the dressing rooms, there had been two pitch invasions with hundreds ejected; as the two teams came out, there were still fans on the pitch, one Red bowing down in mock prayer to Willie Morgan.

'There were less than 2,000 City at that game. They were occupying a section of the terracing at the front of the Scoreboard Paddock – there was no proper segregation.

I was stood at the back on the old wooden boards which used to bounce when things really got rocking. Suddenly, with about ten minutes to go – and that was before Denis scored – I heard this rumble and a mob of United burst up the stairs which were in the centre of the terracing and piled into the City fans at the front with total ferocity. That was truly the worst aggro I saw that day – the stuff on the pitch was really just an attempt to get the game abandoned.' – *Rick, Stretford*

With seven minutes to go, Denis scored. United fans invaded the pitch and the players were taken from the field, temporarily at first. But when a second invasion occurred before the final three minutes could be played out, the game was abandoned. The sight of thousands of scarf-bedecked flare-sporting youngsters careering across the Old Trafford pitch is one of the images of the decade.

Louis Edwards was quick to defend those who invaded. 'This was not a riot,' he told David Meek. 'There was a 57,000 crowd and a lot of noise with everyone whistling for the end of the game. The kids had been waiting to come on, as they do at the end of our last game of the season. They were over-eager of course. It was a matter of excitable youngsters rather than malicious thugs.'

Others were not so generous: 'Fence in the louts!' and 'Clear the terraces!' screamed the tabloid headlines. There was little doubt amongst commentators that United would have to pay the price for the FA's inaction over the St James' Park fiasco seven weeks previously when Geordie invaders were allowed to secure an abandonment and a replay. The press and FA assumed that the pitch invasion had been sparked by a desire to have the match replayed but everyone in the ground was fully aware of the Birmingham score and the fact that a United win would make no difference to their relegation. The fans just wanted a simple abandonment, however futile, to make a nihilistic point of sorts. For the start of the following season, Manchester United fans would be the first ever supporters to have to watch their football from behind bars.

Reds were left with one First Division swansong before the delights of Division Two – at Stoke on the following Monday night. Outside, United and Stoke fought more running battles through their city centre before pelting each other with bricks next to the ground. Inside, supporters burnt their scarves in an act that, for many, spoke of the depths to which a team they had seen lift the European Cup only six years previously had plummeted.

'I swore that night I'd never go to watch United again I was that gutted, but three months is a long time in football and like everyone else I was back in August.'
– *Mark, Chorlton*

And indeed, from the ashes of those burned scarves would rise a phoenix – and a pretty scary bird at that, waving broken bottles and half-bricks at any who fancied a pop. The resurrected Red Army would do rather more than merely emulate its predecessors; the Second Division would end 1974–75 hoping they never caught sight of us again. The feeling would be mutual. But that didn't stop a lot of Likely Lads having a ball in the meantime . . .

Following the pitch invasion against City, one United fan dominated the back pages. Then 17, Roy from South London was headline material for the *Mirror* and *Mail*: 'I don't regret it!' he told the *Daily Mail*.

' "It was a good laugh. I like a punch-up at a match. They're all nutters at Manchester United – and I'm as mad as the rest of them. I followed United all over the country because they're the best team in the land – but the game's not the same without a punch-up. It wasn't my fault with the sergeant. I had to hit him because he just powered into us. I'm a Stretford Ender and I jumped across from the paddock and ran over the pitch to join in the punch-up with City supporters. City had just scored and most of the lads wanted to stop the game and get a replay. We were going down and we didn't like it. They were giving us slag and shouting, 'You're going down the League' and when they do that you've just got to smack 'em in the mouth.
' "We do that with anyone who starts knocking United. You've just got to give someone a good kicking. There's nothing to touch us, and all the other clubs are

scared stiff of us. Next season there's going to be trouble and riots at every game because we don't like going down the League. We'll have a go at Carlisle, Oldham and everywhere we play. I don't think I've let the club down, everyone else was in trouble as well, and that's what it's all about."

'He was banned by his father from going to last night's United match at Stoke, but the teenager grinned and said, "There's a train going, and I'll be on it." '

More than twenty years on, Roy recalls being the first 'celebrity hooligan':

'I first started going up to Manchester on a regular basis in 1972–73, the year before United went down. On my fifteenth birthday, a mate of mine persuaded me to go up to Old Trafford. Up to that point I'd been to watch a few games at Millwall, Tottenham and Chelsea but nowhere regular; at that first game in Manchester the atmosphere just got to me, the noise was unbelievable. As soon as I walked in the ground, that was it.

'The aggro ballooned the season we went down. In those days there were more Cockneys going than now – nine out of ten were going for the aggro. That City game when we were relegated was pretty mad. It was all right until they scored: then there were about 2,000 City and they were giving it the big one. Once the first few went on the pitch everyone ran on. I was kicking someone on the floor and I thought it was a City fan. It turned out to be a copper and I was nicked. There were loads kicking him, but I was the only one who got done for it, the only one.

'After I was in the papers, people used to come up to me saying: "I've got your picture stuck on my wall." They banned me from going to United after the City incident and announced it on TV. United tried to stop me from going, they told me I was barred from Old Trafford. I got a letter telling me I was no longer welcome at the ground. It never stopped me going – they'd have had to have a picture of me at every turnstile. After the City game, I'd been kept in custody in Manchester the whole weekend. When I got out all the papers were waiting for me; I couldn't believe it. I left the court and all these reporters were outside, so I jumped in a taxi and went to the station. I wasn't the only one nicked but I must just have been the unlucky one. They wanted to make an example of me.

'I got thrown out of the supporters' club for giving it to that copper at the City game. Alex Stepney was the president of the London fan club, and he told them to throw me out – I was gutted. When I got back to London my mum was waiting. She whacked me from the train to the car, in the back of the car and when we got home. The City game was out last home game, and then we played Stoke away. My mum and dad told me not to go, but I just left a note saying "sorry" and went.

'I had no money so had to jib the train. I had my ticket from the last Manchester game and tried to use it, but the inspector was having none of it. I got off the train and loads of police were there. After getting forty yards down the platform, a copper grabbed my collar and nicked me for jibbing the train. They rang my dad and he told the police to hold me and not to let me to go the game. So they put me on the next train back to London. I was gutted, again!

'Next day, though, they got me to appear on the *Tonight* show with Eamonn Andrews. A limousine was sent to my house to pick me up. I wasn't meant to go on live. I don't think they trusted me, but one of the guests didn't turn up and I was bumped up to be the first person on the show. When he asked me why I'd hit the copper, I told him: "I thought he was a City fan." What I'd meant was that in the mêlée I'd just lashed out at this bloke behind me, not knowing he was a copper – but it didn't come out like that and people misunderstood.

'After that, Chelsea and West Ham and people like that were after me. Well, they never came round or anything, but I used to get letters saying: "You bastard, we're gonna cut your balls off and stick them down your mum's throat." We kept all the letters just in case something did happen to me

51

outside Chelsea or West Ham. I used to get threats that they'd cut me up: they were unhappy that I was from South London and going up to Manchester. The thing was that most of the Cockney Reds who went to matches were normal people during the week, but come the Saturday it was a different story. They went bananas. They wanted to chop people's heads off, kill someone, turn cars over – things like that. That's just how it was in those days.' – *Roy*

1974–75

It would be hard to over-exaggerate the unprecedented nature of the fall from grace suffered by Manchester United FC. To see that glorious, celebrated name itself confined within a Second Division fixture list was as incongruously jarring a sight as would be Wallace shagging Gromit. This wasn't just United's infamously arrogant self-regard; objectively, the sweaty morass of Division Two had claimed its most bejewelled victim. We were then the only European-titled club ever to go down, United first as ever with a new trend that would later account for Leeds, Forest, Villa *et al.* The only comparisons in the living memories of most were Chelsea and Wolves, last champions in '55 and '59 respectively, relegated in '62 and '65: mere morsels for this slavering beast of a division compared to the feast that was United. The media, who'd had a wonderful couple of years drooling over United's decline, found to their delight that the story still had 'legs' – the fun didn't end with relegation. Watching the regal Reds tiptoeing nervously around the rubbish of Division Two, holding their noses lest they breathe in the contaminating odours of the lower orders . . . yes, this could be the finest spectator sport for Fleet Street's sadists too.

To some extent, they had a point. McIlroy, Macari and Morgan all talked of the soul-draining prospects that awaited them from August, 'trips to places we'd scarcely heard of – Eastville, Bootham Crescent, Brisbane Road . . .' groaned Lou. City had revelled in this all summer; Malcolm Allison, en route to Division One's glamour parks, pointed at the frumpy Ninians and Frattons, shouting, 'Oooh, don't fancy yours much.' For every Houston and

53

Pearson who knew how to rough it amongst football's plebeians, there were both kids and superstars who'd known little but the flash smoothness, such as it was in the seventies, of the top flight. Still, at least no one had deserted the trenches after a summer of rumours muttered that the likes of Morgan and Macari 'wouldn't like it up 'em'; for *Dad's Army*, read Doc's Army. They had all, after all, learned as much about fighting for survival since '72 as any Latic or Trotter trundler they might face.

In truth, it was more a case of uncertainty than fear or loathing, despite the knowledge that they were all on a hiding-to-nowt with nothing less than instant promotion to suffice. No one knew quite what to expect from this new environment and that applied to the fans too – Andy Pollard vividly recalls waiting for the OT bus at Piccadilly wondering whether we'd even get 25,000 for the first home game. For the nation's scrap merchants and butchers, otherwise known as the Second Division chairmen, no such angst endured. A glance at the figures for the spring '74 travelling Red Army plus a quick calculation based on their own cheaper seats, half-empty stadiums and the lovely liberty of pay-at-the-gate meant that run-down boardrooms everywhere hummed with perspiring suits, revolving pound-signs replacing eyeballs. Every tin-pot outfit would be granted a simultaneous Cup Final and Lottery-winning bonanza-party.

Unfortunately for them, their party guests would have more on the mind than jelly and ice cream. Like Double Diamond and half-bricks, for example.

Brisbane Road, Leystonstone – 17 August 1974. Kick-off is supposed to be at 3 p.m. but parts of the 10,000-strong travelling Red division prefer two o'clock starts and promptly stage their own particular kick-off on the pitch. Any concerns about the response of fans to United's drop go straight out of the window, along with the odd turnstile section and makeshift javelin. Leytonstone, a grim but quintessentially English red-brick sprawl, isn't really used to this. As Orient's resident celeb Bob Mills has pointed out, pensioners doing volunteer work on the gates to escape a Saturday of Radio 2 are not exactly a match for thousands of jibbing Northern party animals. Poor Sir

Matt's appeals over the loudspeaker for calm go utterly
unheeded. It isn't disrespect as such; more the case that a
parallel universe has arrived with different laws of physics.
Or that playing 'All You Need Is Love' to All The Young
Dudes ain't gonna hit the spot if they're all tuned into
Iggy's 'Search And Destroy'. Especially when Orient is the
last stop on a summer itinerary of infamy that's just taken
in and taken over Ostend, Jutland and Copenhagen.

The twelve who legitimately took the pitch showed only
the last fleeting traces of Busby too. Stepney was now the
sole survivor of Wembley '68, Kiddo having been sold to
Arsenal. (Like every other United player sold against his
will – Law, MacDougall, McCalliog etc. – he would come
back to haunt us, at Maine Road in '77.) Of the other Busby
Boys, McIlroy was on the bench and Morgan unwittingly
about to start his last Red season in the celebrated Number
7 shirt. A retina operation in the summer after a tennis
accident would soon lead to Willie and the Doc failing to
see eye-to-eye (ouch).

But within twelve months, despite this dwindling physical legacy, Busbyism would be back in force spiritually.
Many on the terraces that day had spent the summer
watching their first ever in-colour World Cup on TV; I'm
certain ours wasn't the only household that took the plunge
with Rediffusion, all the better to see the luminous orange
and stellar skills of the Dutch. Total Football never did take
over the world. The German flirtation with it was over by
the time of their heinous crimes in Argentina '78 and the
rest followed negative suit – even, shamefully, Brazil. Only
Holland carried the torch until Platini's French were ready
to take it forward. Now although United never became a
Total Football side, they did still end up in a domestic
position analogous to Holland's worldwide: the sole
standard-bearers of pure attacking entertainment surrounded by hostile legions of defensive tacticians. That
afternoon at Orient, United took their first step back
towards a special kind of greatness that Sir Matt would
appreciate. As we shall see, by the spring United had
rediscovered a magic formula whose power still reverber-
ates at Old Trafford today.

Stuart Pearson, whose name and style carried more
happy Busbyish echoes of Stan, made his debut and

enough of an impact to suggest that McIlroy finally had the targetman foil he'd always craved. Supersam was not to miss a game, as content in his role of crack supplier as any of Moss Side's widest. Stewart Houston, glinting elegantly under the sun in United's lovely all-white away kit, wrapped up the points with a header, the ball nestling so close to the surging hordes behind the goal that you could taste it. Maybe this Division Two lark wasn't going to be so bad after all. The sense of relief amongst the players was tangible – so too the sense of mischievous discovery by fans that a series of tightly packed, atmospheric little hovels awaited invasion, undermanned outposts as vulnerable as drunken virgins.

By the end of August, United were top with a 100 per cent record and this wasn't the only refreshing experience that felt like new. Pancho Pearson scored on his Old Trafford debut to seal his instant-hit status, so different from the parade of stuttering anticlimaxes produced by all those post-'71 new faces. Gerry Daly got a hat-trick as United posted four goals – the first such achievements since September '71 and March '72 respectively. Daly's penalty-scoring was proving to be of Franny Lee proportions in both accuracy and frequency, except that United won theirs sportingly. He'd racked up four out of four in that month alone – the days of scrabbling around with Stepney were gone. Jim Holton and Martin Buchan, the latter making his 100th League appearance against Portsmouth, appeared virtually unbeatable at this level, giving us games to be won rather than saved. For most, the sheer novelty of seeing us playing well as a team and winning was delight enough after the First Division deprivations. Being caged in by the new Old Trafford fences would not suffice to cool the Red ardour on the terraces. 'We Hate Humans' sounded the ironic battle-cry from the Stretford End; if they were to be classed as animals, so be it. The wild jungles of Division Two would be United's for the taking in any event – claws out for the lads . . .

Not that this was to be a mere procession to the title founded on a series of dazzling displays, mind. United were still two or three steps away from their classic seventies incarnation, not to mention a vital tactical change. Those cast-offs in-waiting, McCalliog and Martin, still flitted in and out of the side; just one injury, such as Pearson suffered at Ninian Park, could badly disturb the equilibrium, whilst Morgan was increasingly turning curate's egg. More tellingly, the rest of Division Two immediately understood that taking on United in a battle of arts was suicidal – simple battle of attrition was a much better bet. Cardiff comprehended; our win there in a dreadful game was representative of a good number of joyless skirmishes that interspersed the epics we now remember. To be fair, performing stylishly in the war zone that was Ninian Park was a lot to expect. I use the metaphor of war precisely here. Some of the terrace fusillades displayed a tactical intensity reminiscent of El Alamein's opening and at least two Wehrmacht helmets were clearly visible in the mêlée. If 'Munich '58' was the cry from the scummier Welsh element, then Nuremberg '36 also sprang to mind.

So September had its grinding spells; McIlroy's late saver spared us a home defeat by Forest whilst hand-to-hand combat both on and off the pitch secured a three-point total from tough trips to Hawthorns and Den. But you were never more than a week away from a compensatory champagne supernova. A thrashing of Charlton in the League Cup began a campaign which Lou Macari seemed to take on personally; then Bristol Rovers were allowed to live to fight another day at 2-0 when ten-goal termination would have been just. Tony Dunne's Bolton merely proved that ultra-negativity could not always guarantee escape from Old Trafford, impaled three-nil upon Macari's stabbing volley and Houston's sword-thrust of a free-kick. Only at Carrow Road did we truly disappoint, outfought for the first time by this annoying bogey-team. Ted MacDougall profited from Pearson's keenly felt absence to grab the headlines, or so he thought: once he'd wreaked his revenge, Reds followed suit in the Barclay Stand and all the way down the riverbank. The impromptu car wash which several Cortinas and Triumphs received was probably a tad overdone as far as the owners were concerned. As in bottom-of-the-river overdone. Charitably viewed, an early example of environmental Reclaim The Roads activism?

We bounced back, as we always did, which is more than can be said for Norwich's cars. Still missing Pearson but revelling in McIlroy's blossoming, we beat Fulham and

Notts County, then got a point at Fratton Park in front of a trebled attendance; all efficient if not inspired. But then all the fans' and players' powers of inspiration had been centred on one almost extraterrestrial night sandwiched in between: we'd drawn City in the League Cup.

When a game has an extraordinary special meaning to it, you rarely hear it discussed in such terms beforehand; everybody just knows. Barely five months since Denis Law's back-heel, City were back at Old Trafford, the favourite and most rewarding hunting ground of their post-promotion era. But now they were coming as top-flight overlords, apparently Manchester's undisputed top dogs, determined to go all the way to make up for the disappointment in the Final of '74. After all, weren't they facing a very similar side to the one they'd beaten in April? So what if 56,000 were expected, a crowd the size they never saw at Maine Road lest we were the visitors? They'd turned over better teams and bigger crowds with depressing regularity at OT since '66; of course they were the favourites.

But this was no routine 56,000: this was a hyperventilating, rip-roaring, white-noise-blasting 56,000. This was the moment to serve notice that United were on the way back, that we'd be returning to the top to gain vengeance for all those derby defeats of the Allison era. And that an Old Trafford congregation, no matter the division, would always be superior to any Moss Side rabble. Andy Pollard has no doubts: 'Together with the Ajax and Barca games, that night against City was the greatest, most unbelievably exciting atmosphere I've ever seen Old Trafford generate.'

So much of the pre-match hype was of Rodney Marsh, who twice had the ball in the net from offside positions; but United's entirely unknown debutant Arthur Albiston produced the key moments. Clearing Tueart's header off the line saved our early Danish, allowing McCalliog, Macari and McIlroy the chance to spurn match-winning opportunities. After seventy-eight minutes of frenzy, fouling and frustration, Arthur went on one of his winging expeditions: Macari turned it on and young Jeff Clarke brazenly handled. Sammy McIlroy still recalls the knuckle-whitening intensity of the silent seconds that passed during Gerry Daly's spot-kick run-up; from bedlam to bead-sweat motionlessness within the minute – then to bedlam once more as infallible Daly scored. City were out and United were back: twenty years of Blue misery was just around the corner. The Old Trafford Derby Curse had been lifted, surely never to darken our doors again. 'Five foot eight, not much weight, Gerry Daly's fucking great.'

Just ten days after reminding City of our essential supremacy, United as an entire footballing movement held a weekend of celebration in Blackpool. Many had long since singled out this fixture as the awayday of the year, almost as if it were a Euro-trip. In 1974 the last great push towards continental mass tourism had only just started ('Y Viva España' still hovered in the chart's lower reaches); for many, Blackpool then was still both Pleasure Central and a place you could spend a fortnight's hols without people taking the piss. Every Red worth his salt had the same idea, with the result that at least 17,000 Reds were wedged inside Bloomfield Road, trebling the normal gate and gaining the temporary title Old-Trafford-on-Sea. Amidst carnival delirium, the team played their end-of-the-pier show to perfection, beating a good promotion-chasing side 3-0. Alex Forsyth hit a free-kick with an unbelievable speed and power that could lead to speculation as to the hallucinogenic properties of the local rock. Equalling him in showmanship was the unlikely candidate of Jim McCalliog, chipping fabulously home with vaudevillian panache. Little wonder that a couple of lads couldn't restrain themselves from coming on to the pitch for a kick-about during the second half. But the vision of the weekend, reckons Andy Pollard, was hundreds of goal-happy, fully kegged Reds on the beach singing themselves hoarse as they cavorted in front of bemused daytrippers.

It was noted at the time that the potential for violence was still frightening and this may have been so for some. Yet the beach setting conjures up images of the Mods and Rockers in sixties Brighton, which in turn offers an answer as to why so many now look back on the 'Reds Behaving Badly' era with something approaching fondness. The bank holiday beach mayhem was seen at the time as a threat to civilization yet now is a cause for mythologizing, humour and even celebration. There was something qualitatively different about it compared to, say, Altamont or mid-eighties Scouse hooliganism: you could never imagine a *Quadrophenia* being made either of the latter, could you? That is not to say that appallingly vicious and unforgivable momentary events didn't occur in mid-sixties Brighton or mid-seventies Manchester; of course they did. But there is undoubtedly a difference between the infamous Anfield dart-in-eye incident and simply generalized scrummaging outside any Maine Road derby in the seventies, just as there was between the stabbing of a Modette and a mere beach bundle in 1964.

To some, these are distinctions of tiny degree; to others, they are a world apart and speak of entirely divergent moralities. I appreciate that some would see this as a dangerous generalization but the vast proportion of Red Army disorder in this decade featured a roguishness and ritualism that separate it from the simply amoral viciousness of eighties razor gangs – certainly when all those involved were willing participants and accepted the basic code of 'the fair fight'. This particular kind of hooliganism clearly did not make the world a better place but neither did all its adherents deserve to be vilified as moral equivalents of SS commandants, as was the hysterical fashion of the day. This is not an apologia for violence but a tricky point which can be flippantly summarized thus: you can imagine a *Quadrophenia* being made about the Red Army. Tellingly, it'd probably be a big hit. Especially if Leslie Ash got her kit off properly this time . . .

Almost 49,000 turned up at Old Trafford to see Pearson's comeback against the Saints, the biggest gate of the League season yet. The Raging Bull came on a sub to score the winner; a week later, his overpowering hat-trick demolished Oxford. Any gripe-mongers' mutterings about buying an injury-prone striker were duly silenced; he'd only miss three more games that season. Still, even with Pancho back, we weren't quite right; with Greenhoff still getting up to speed, McCalliog merely ordinary and Macari looking to find a permanent position, the midfield remained V8 instead of V12. Half-baked cruddy defeats at Bristol and Hull followed, both places where no self-respecting Red wants to appear in the first place.

But at Old Trafford, the thrill-fest continued a-frenzy. More top-flight scalps in the League Cup as Burnley provided yet another rumbustious night of goalmouth ejaculations – Macari, yet again, was utterly inspired in a 3-2 win. Still visibly fizzing with excess panache three days later, United delighted 56,000 with a 2-1 victory over Villa in the pace-setters' crunch match. To win was enough; to do so in such rampaging style was another. The Scoreboard Surge that greeted Daly's roof-smashing goal was truly a sight to behold.

No wonder an English season record of near 61,000 turned up for the second table-top battle against the Mack-ems two weeks later. Thankfully, TV cameras were there to record an epic battle which, in Pearson's smashing strike, produced a defining image of United's flair and power that season. A 3-2 of archetypal classicism, full of fight-backs and swaying balances; that Sunderland fans dared turn up in some force and engage in a battle of vocal extremism with the Strettie simply added to the game's emotional force. Years later, players still marvelled at the blood-boiling excitement of being in the midst of such a mael-strom. In the afterglow, time too to reflect on the significance of United's line-up. Not Ron Davies' debut, newly arrived as swapsie for the hapless George Graham, but Macari finally claiming the Number 10 shirt from McCalliog which Lou would not relinquish for years. A perspicacious contemporary writer noted United's new 'dream midfield': the silky elegance of Daly, the leathery bollocks of Greenhoff and the unceasing bustle and energy of Macari. We were a step nearer to the Dream Team. But how to top such an immortal afternoon? That would take, ooh, all of a week.

Hillsborough, 7 December. At one end of the ground is what can only be described as a Red mountain, virtually the Stretford End transplanted cross-Pennines for the day. Their songs are echoed, however, on every side of the ground, the Red infiltration dominating every paddock and stand to make a total of 20,000 invaders. If that were not intimidating enough for Wednesday, United begin at a purr and Houston's free-kick missile has us one-up in seven minutes. A procession à la Bloomfield Road awaits; but one challenge transforms it into a battle and ruins a man's professional life. Jim Holton breaks his leg in the single worst moment of the season; the Owls rush into the gaping hole and score three inside 11 minutes. Few men leave such a void behind them as Big Jim, both in football and in life.

The biggest pitch invasion since the relegation clincher in April ensues, the first of three today, accompanied by fist-frenzy amongst unsegregated fans everywhere; again, this is quite clearly a concerted attempt to get the match abandoned. A white horse appears, conjuring up folk memories of Wembley '23 except that the flat caps have been replaced by flattened heads: 106 arrests, 51 casualties – no football could compete with that in the headlines.

Except that it did. Somehow, despite the Beirutian conditions and wrecked defence, despite playing into a gale, United stormed level by the hour after Macari poached and Pancho slammed. Sunley's fourth would, a year back, have finished United: not now. Macari scuffled home with nine to go, a goal greeted with every bit as much terrace gusto as Cantona's famous saver nineteen years later. So remarkable had been the performance that the press gave it equal billing to the violence; given the scale of the latter, which reached 'national scandal' proportions and brought forth a defining clampdown on travelling Reds, that was some tribute. It had been the one quintessential Red Army Years match, the one you'd take on *Desert Island Discs* if you could – the play as impassioned and reckless as anything Doc's lads produced, with terrace outrageousness to match. 'The Day All Hell Broke Loose!' yelled one tabloid screamer. For some it was; for others, it was more like heaven. Such is perspective . . .

After such a climax, some dozing in the wet-patch: Orient got the nil-nil they came to Old Trafford for, the day's best performer being an on-pitch stray dog (no, not Ron Davies). Yet again, First Division League Cup opposition in the shape of Middlesbrough resparked our initiative; yet again, Macari's outstanding crusadery brought forth 'Skip To The Lou' at max. volume. Any hopes that Wilf McGuinness, boss of our next victims, York, might've had of gaining some sweet revenge over his former tormentors were crushed under a weight of fear and loathing. The shed at Bootham Crescent was hastily rebuilt as a fortress, contractors all over Yorkshire enjoying a bonzer pay-day; that old Jorvik Viking spirit disappeared as the Red hordes and their swashbuckling team came roaring over the hills. Two impossibilities that day: a Red getting a drink any- where in the county and any chance that a timorous City might score. United fans snapped up the bundles of unsold tickets whilst the locals cowered behind boarded-up win- dows – the team won at a canter.

In festive mood 51,000 celebrated a Boxing Day beating of high-flying West Brom, little knowing that United's stratospheric flight was about to hit a bout of turbulence; Willie Morgan would soon discover his was the dodgy parachute covered in patches. For the time being, the Xmas X-rated display at Boundary Park could be filed away as the traditional seasonal upset. Pearson's spectacularly uncharacteristic open-goal miss was out-bizarred by Oldham's goal-that-never-was, the ball doing that annoying stanchion ricochet thingy which fooled several over- masturbatory refs in the seventies. Some of the 18,000 Reds who'd completely annexed the ground relieved the tedium by dismantling walls and chucking the debris at the poor sod in goal. Nowadays, tournaments get halted if so much as an empty Evian bottle gets within twenty yards of the goalie. Back then, judging the difference between goal- bound footballs and head-bound masonry was just part of a keeper's skill. (Save one, avoid the other – easily learned after a concussion or two.)

Getting knocked out of the Cup by Third Division Walsall was a tad embarrassing but beating the Owls at OT seemed to have headed off any crisis. The second goal of McCalliog's double, a crashing 50th-minute Scoreboard drive, was his last in a Red shirt; the post-match gush from him and Docherty about 'Jim being back for good' merely postponed for a month his inevitable departure. Far more significant was Martin Buchan's ridiculously overdue elevation to club captaincy, finally fulfilling Frank's old plan and further stoking the ravenous Rumour Beast's hunger for Morgan–Docherty fall-out stories.

It would have to be Norwich to intervene and throw us off course; I suppose these are the karmic paybacks when you trash someone's home. For the first time since '71, Old Trafford was in the grip of Wembley Fever – two legs with the tractor-fuckers stood between us and the League Cup Final. To the relief of the Metropolitan Police and Aston

Villa's fans, we wuz robbed. Fifty-eight thousand rose to salute Macari's majesty in the home tie; his outrageous overhead lob and juggling hooking volley on 53 and 75 seem to have given us victory. Lou had been undoubtedly the man of the tournament nationwide, a winner's medal the least he deserved. Yet instead of blowing for time as expected, the ref signalled a last-gap equalizer, MacDougall – who else – seizing upon a backpass which had expired in the mud. A week later on the wickedest wintry night, Kevin Keelan performed heroics and we lost to a grotty scrambled effort after a game of unrelieved brutality and foulsmanship. It could almost have been 1973 again.

As if the deflationary effect of defeat were not enough, Pearson had pulled up in the first leg. Chelsea's Tommy Baldwin rushed up on loan, a largely uncelebrated journeyman and deadringer for Ten Years After's Alvin Lee. Perhaps it *was* the whizz axeman, who hadn't been heard of since the Isle Of Wight festival; it would certainly explain why the stand-in looked so unlikely to score against Sunderland and Bristol City. To get a point at Roker in the face of the best home crowd Reds had seen was some achievement but to lose at home to Bristol in a game where only Steve James came close to scoring was wretched. Main scapegoat McCalliog never played for us again. The non-swearing song-sheets handed out pre-match by the do-gooders' fraternity were hardly the ticket for a performance that would bring 'bollocks' to a vicar's lips. (Not that vicars these days need much encouragement to get their mouths around plums . . .)

Worse was to come at Oxford – beaten by dullards we'd whupped only eight weeks before. Pearson, clearly unfit, struggled painfully; in truth, Buchan was intellectually outsmarted for the goal, as absurd as Churchill failing Common Entrance. More missile-avoidance practice for the Oxonian keeper ensued: 'We're a right bunch of bastards when we lose', goes the apposite Red tune. Ironically, this had been dubbed the 'Let's be friends game': Sir Matt had opened their new shed; locals hung out 'Welcome Reds' banners; cheap transport had been supplied to encourage 'nice' Reds to attend. Iggy Pop's composing royalties were clearly still mounting . . .

A brief respite for Hull's visit didn't convince. Sure,

Pearson was back against his old club and duly scored, ever a player with a sense of occasion, but had Houston not sucker-punched them after 90 seconds, we would have struggled. Nemesis of a sort approached: main rivals Aston Villa, en route to Wembley, at Villa Park. Fourteen thousand Reds doubling the gate couldn't save us from a deserved 2-0 thumping. Ron Davies slunk away, never to reappear, as Brian Little, Ray Graydon and Bobby McDonald garnered all the plaudits. Docherty wisecracked afterwards about the players' lack of precision, trying his best to hide his temper: 'One of the lads just tried to jump in the bath and fell out of the window.' But behind the scenes, he had lost patience with some whom he accused of bad attitude and general misbehaviour. Tabloid stories alluding to extracurricular naughtiness and player in-fighting painted a picture too close to pre-Docherty Old Trafford for comfort. On came a New Labour-style gag on players' pronouncements, with Willie Morgan portrayed as Clare Short – and in came Steve Coppell. The irony that two of Villa's stars had been Docherty signings hadn't escaped observers, who had suggested the time had come for some of that old black market magic. Coppell would be more than the cloud's merely silver lining: this was platinum encrusted with gold-rimmed diamonds.

Signing Stevie from Tranmere for £60,000 (£1.3m) proved to be 1975's first Cantona Moment, Gordon Hill's arrival being the other. United stormed through March and April unbeaten; five weeks after Steve's debut we were promoted, in seven we were champions, eventualities that appeared to be sorely in doubt on the way back from Villa Park. Yet, understandably, the Morgan Fan Club were horrified. When Coppell came on for Morgan against Cardiff, the boos and catcalls resounded menacingly; the fact that two of Coppell's first three touches produced the clinching goals in a 4-0 resurrectory win didn't stop a 'Save Willie' petition being mounted by Ms E. Wynne of Sale. But Docherty was to prefer 'Free Willie' – and it didn't end as happily as the film . . .

Resurrectory Easter approached and a sensational 25,000 Reds stuffed all four sides of Burnden Park, sensing that no '74-style false dawn beckoned this time. Pearson's header won the game but Macari's brilliance was the guarantor of the win bonus. Only idiots were still keeping their books open for Player Of The Year. Both Norwich and Bristol Rovers did their best to stop what Yanks call The Big Mo'. MacDougall was becoming a hate-figure of Shearer-like proportions with his Old Trafford point-saver deflating 56,000; at Eastville, a last-minute home equalizer was the final insult to add to the 15p (£3) hooligan tax imposed by the fearful club. (A United boycott limited our contingent to 4,000, thus probably wiping out Bristol's profit.) But in between came a vital 1-0 win at Forest as 10,000 Reds delighted in Daly's fantastic goal, the result of possibly the best one-touch move of the season. We'd be getting used to that sort of thing before too long. It meant that two Old Trafford wins over Easter would ensure promotion, bar a miracle. We didn't just find our way back to Division One that weekend. We found an Ideal For Living.

The simple facts are that we beat York 2-1 on Saturday with amusingly dodgy goals and should've scored six; then, on Monday in front of 57,000, defeated Oldham 3-2 thanks to Macari's naughty elbow and Coppell's first Red clincher goal on 74. An ebullient Docherty beamed afterwards: 'We've done it – there's just the mathematics to sort out.' However, we weren't just going back up as another decent team – we would be going up as something special. For Docherty played Morgan and Coppell as out-and-out wingers, with McIlroy and Pearson in the middle and Brian Greenhoff moving to centre-back; this, at last, was the pure 4-2-4 that Docherty had always desired, with the bonus that the 'Holton Gap' has finally been filled. And what results it had produced: mental chance-creation against York, then beating Oldham with extraordinary verve and flair. Andy Pollard cites this game as 'the finest display I ever saw from a Docherty team', which is clearly some accolade given that Andy saw all the classics.

The joy of discovering an ideal for the first time is always an ecstatic experience. For the next two seasons, whilst the personnel switched around occasionally, the system itself remained the guiding template, built upon the ever-present focal points that were Coppell, Pearson, Macari and the twin centre-backs. And there is only one way to maximize the benefits of 4-2-4: attack on all fronts. So, that Easter, United didn't just settle their immediate future status. The way they achieved it placed that 1975-77 side in a unique historical context. In United's tradition, it linked the halcyon days of the Busby Babes' twin wingers to the definitive Ferguson team of 1994, rekindling an old belief and keeping it alive in all our minds until the nineties. Watching this team shaped us all into believing that width, style and relentless attack will always be the United way; that in turn has placed demands on every manager and player since to live up to that tradition. Some will contend that to succeed in Europe these days, we will have to temper those beliefs but that is another argument for another book. One thing is certain. Had United come up in '75 playing in a different, tighter, more conventional way – similar perhaps to the rigid 4-3-3 Dave Sexton later imposed – the modern Manchester United spirit would never have developed in the fabulous manner which it has. The last day of March 1975 deserves remembrance for more than we realized.

April became an imperial triumph after that. Promotion was certified with a win at The Dell, the championship at a Red-hued Meadow Lane despite County's fightback to 2-2, so that 59,000 could then enjoy an angst-free final fling, fittingly against our October party-hosts Blackpool. The 4-0 victory reflected our overall dominance of the season; symbolically the scorers – Pearson, Macari, Greenhoff – were all key Docherty boys in the New Order. Of the *ancien régime*, Steve James took his last bow, Morgan having already done so against Fulham. Promotion had laid to rest the last ghosts of the sixties and its hung-over aftermath: of the eleven first-choice men Docherty took up with him, he'd given eight their debuts. With an average age even lower than United's '96 side, this was now undoubtedly a Docherty Team for a Docherty Era. The post-Blackpool pitch invasion, so buzzingly exuberant compared to that of a year before, made the point: the revolution is won, compadres. (And in time-honoured fashion, now was the moment for victorious Red Army revolutionaries to 'shag their women and drink their beer'.) The Red Flag was back in Division One.

⚽   ⚽   ⚽

November 1974 – and there's a couple of different Willie Morgan song mixes doing the rounds. On the Stretford, it still goes: '*Hey, hey, clear the way here comes Willie Morgan/Willie, Willie Morgan on the wing*' etc., etc. But out in a Manchester pub, frequented by a certain roly-poly Scot, they allegedly prefer: '*Willie Morgan on the wing/He's a cunt, I'm gonna sort him out/He'll be on the way out/Before the end of the season.*' And so he was: what a coincidence, hey?

History's conventional wisdom can be a right bastard. Because Willie joined just after one Wembley final and left just before our next, he'll be forever inextricably linked *solely* with United's Dark Ages; some cruelly dubbed him 'the poor man's George Best' and left him to carry the inferiority complex for the rest of his career. The fact that he won several supporters' Player of the Year awards, performed stylishly and effectively both on the wing and in central midfield, then captained our fight against relegation with real spirit, is apparently easily forgotten. Playing in an age before video-recorders, there's not much evidence left for modern Reds to reassess – no Cup Finals won with his goals or semis turned by his brilliance. I asked a kid I know what he'd learned about Morgan: 'Er, didn't he fill in after Best and before Hill?' was the reply. Whatever one's view about the nineties Morgan – and both his manner and hairstyle annoy many – that is scarcely a fair reflection of a cult hero's career.

Admittedly, he was never much of a goalscorer: thirty-odd strikes in nearly three hundred games looks poor next to Hill and Best's tallies. But then this was the norm for a proper winger in the old days – Best and Hill were freaks of nature. For Willie was a true provider, a furnisher of bespoke openings. Wilf McGuinness may once have accused him of 'dribbling up his own arse' (football's version of sucking your own knob, I suppose) but he soon shook off youthful affectations. By '74, he was enough of a team creator and all-round player to take a generalship role in the middle, his rectum now entirely free of saliva as even Wilf, an old adversary, would have conceded.

Willie was also cool. In a mid-seventies way, admittedly: next to sixties cool, as exemplified by Best, the image has never worn as well. But that goes for everything in life – Capri vs Mini, Steely Dan vs The Byrds, Lauren Hutton vs Jean Shrimpton. And by the height of Morgan's cultdom,

Best was fat, bearded and then retired. What else was there on offer to an impressionable Stretford End kid in 1974? The hairstyle, lovingly described by Jim White in his book, *Always In The Running*, was central to the image. But here is an indication of the naffness which has attached itself to even the coolest seventies artefacts – Morgan still has virtually the same style today. And he uses *a blow-dryer* on it . . .

Morgan recommended Docherty for the managerial job and praised him lavishly even when we went down. Here, one might think, was one Busbyite who'd made an accommodation with the Devil – and this is a player who'd had multiple run-ins with both Matt's successors. 'I am biased where Tommy is concerned and I make no apology for it. To me, the man is magic,' said Willie in '74. Hindsighted guffaws all round, of course. Tommy dubbed him 'the world's greatest right-winger' and sealed the membership of their mutual admiration society by making him captain. And thereby hangs a tale which twisted all the way to the law courts.

George Graham and Morgan were matey, all canny Scots together and so forth. Willie was surprised but pleased to be offered the captaincy, then horrified to hear stories that Docherty had told Graham he'd been begging for it all season. Whether or not that was true, he certainly felt his next encounter with George was hardly all kisses and hugs. For Morgan, here was your first *prima facie* evidence of Docherty's wankerhood. And perhaps Morgan was right, but he still took the captaincy despite this. Similarly, Morgan rails at Docherty for seeming to want to dump Tommy Cavanagh when he called Willie and Stepney in to discuss Cav's allegedly inappropriate industrial language with the kids. Yet as Willie himself reports the discussion, it appears more like a concerned boss garnering senior pros' advice, as he should, rather than some clumsy attempt at a *putsch*. No, the proper villainy was yet to come.

During the summer of '74, Morgan detached a retina playing tennis, a serious injury for a sportsman who relies on limb/ball/eye coordination. Docherty played the solicitous boss to perfection but Morgan soon felt more like Boxer in *Animal Farm*, a stalwart seen as damaged goods who'd be carted off to the glue factory on the slightest excuse. By late autumn, Morgan was the team scapegoat, the one who'd often get hauled off first and who heard he was being bad-mouthed off the record. Whispers around town echoed back to Morgan – Tommy was marking his cards. By January, Morgan was no longer captain; by March, his obvious heir apparent had arrived from Tranmere. Even if it were true, as Docherty alleged, that Morgan's eyesight was failing, here was some writing on the wall which even Willie could read.

There are those in the old Morgan Fan Club who'll tell you he should never have been dropped or substituted, let alone manoeuvred on to the transfer list; others, even Docherty-haters, will admit he wasn't hitting the peaks of yesteryear, despite the divisional drop. Certainly, he did himself no favours by reacting petulantly to Docherty's decisions, storming off AWOL at one point, refusing to warm up when he was on the bench at another. As others would one day discover, many Reds take the view that manly stoicism is the only permitted response in such scenarios: prima donnas belong at Covent Garden, or St James' Park. When Coppell performed brilliantly during his late-season run, any chance of a terrace revolution saving Morgan disappeared. The brutal unsentimentality of Old Trafford's faithful is a mighty force, too often ignored by self-absorbed players.

Still, as with Law, he hardly deserved what was coming. Docherty maintained Morgan had spent virtually the whole season asking for a transfer though perhaps that was just wishful thinking: certainly, Morgan would probably sue anyone who suggested this was the case. And, with a six-year deal and forthcoming testimonial in the back pocket, Morgan would surely have been a real footballing rarity to have looked for the exit, at least until Coppell's arrival. Come May '75 with Morgan showing no sign of wanting to accept the loaded revolver in a quiet back room, a touch of the Law treatment was clearly required.

Tellingly, Docherty skips this bit in his 1981 book. Morgan, however, told Jim White: 'Tommy came to me and said "I want us to be friends. Don't come on the Far East tour – take the family on a club holiday and I'll see you when I get back." The next thing I see is the front page of the *Evening News*: MORGAN REFUSES TO GO ON TOUR.'

Do you see a pattern developing here, dear reader? Tommy had secured the end-game; a couple of smart moves later, he'd pushed Morgan into checkmate and Willie was on his way to Burnley for thirty grand. Another Busbyite knight off the board – another enemy for life acquired. Many, even including David Meek, suggested Morgan had been disposed of too soon. Yet although we missed him for the first couple of months of 1975–76, when we could have gone straight to 4-2-4 instead of waiting until November, Morgan's departure brought Gordon Hill ever closer to Old Trafford. And the brutal terrace unsentimentalist in me says: that was a good trade-off. Filthy means produced worthy ends, as Sartre always said they would.

In June 1977 Morgan appeared on Granada TV one teatime. Bristling with righteous anger and burning with unrequited vengeance, he revelled in Docherty's imminent downfall. 'He's about the worst manager there's ever been and nearly all United fans will be delighted when he goes,' he declared. A month later, a writ for libel from Docherty's brief arrived. Suddenly, a new kind of end-game was on offer. And this time, Docherty's wizardry with the black pieces and the black arts would be of no use. For he faced an enemy of united forces, not vulnerable individuals; every recipient of the infamous Docherty Gambit would be coming out to play this rematch. And to switch game metaphor for a moment, this time *Willie Morgan On The Wing* would be replaced by Morgan as a fully armed and very pissed-off lethal centre-forward.

⚽ ⚽ ⚽

'*Hong Kong Phooey – Number One Superguy*
Hong Kong Phooey – quicker than the human eye . . .'
(Cue blue cartoon dog in martial arts outfit springing out of filing cabinet.) I was determined to get the seventies' silliest animated hero and his fab theme tune into this book somewhere. It has nothing to do with football, of course, unless you want to stretch out analogy comparing Phooey and his smarter sidekick to the Doc and Cav. But at least one newspaper used the cartoon's title to describe the

oddly smelling stories which emanated from United's 1975
Far East tour. For many, this particular Hong Kong Phooey
provided the first indication that life was not always sweet
even for Docherty's own chosen disciples.

Like many of United's foreign excursions in the seventies
– St Etienne, Tehran, Porto – this slog around Hong Kong
and Australia did not appear to have been planned with
much *savoir-faire*. It turned out to be a long, tiring, sweaty
and bad-tempered haul; worse, it was done on the cheap.
Two quid a day spending money wasn't enough even for
the kids – for the superstars used to the sixties glory days,
it constituted an insult. As United were playing to good
crowds, why the enforced impecunity? When sweat-soaked
players were informed they'd have to pay for their own
laundry at extortionate hotel rates, rebellion broke out – led
by the Scots, of course. Lou Macari, clan leader and already
a veteran of fights with the Doc, was minutes away from
getting on a plane back to Blighty. Only the mysterious
sudden arrival of Sir Matt and an increased allowance to £6
prevented melt-down. Grouchy players and management
staggered on to Australia, a battleground simply waiting for
a spark.

Bizarrely, a head-tennis tournament proved to be the
casus belli. Unbeknownst to the players, Docherty had
stitched up a deal months back which entailed United
providing a team of Greenhoff, McIlroy and Coppell plus
the management duo. The players would get about
Aus $150 each, but it has been suggested that a larger pot
was on offer. The three kids, doubtless chosen for their
naivety, had no idea of the score, and in particular that the
money should've gone into a player's pool; consequently,
they were rather taken aback and a touch terrified after a
chance remark alerted the older lads to the deal. The cowed
kids were left in the middle as the two warring camps – the
management versus Lou, Martin and Alex's troops – fired
verbal missiles at each other. Coppell, for one, was aware
that the kids' trio were seen as 'teacher's pets', as unpleasant a situation in the dressing room as in a classroom; he
had no qualms about chucking his cash into the pot.
McIlroy and Brian followed suit, though Sammy thought it
a rum do and finished the tour in as filthy a mood as
anyone on account of this 'surrender'. Poor Coppell, having

'betrayed' teacher to the class bullies, felt the full wrath of the Doc next day: 'You'll be out of this club before your feet hit the English tarmac.' Docherty was just warming up, however.

The touring party assembled in a hotel function room for what looked like a clear-the-air meeting, a description which proved to be a touch inappropriate given the foul insults that were to be hurled across the table. Alex Stepney thought the scene resembled something from a third-rate Western, which suggests the Doc to be the semi-hinged Ernest Borgnine figure who goes ape in the final reel. Michael Crick preferred the gangster image: Brando sorting out his feuding lieutenants maybe. Arthur Albiston was excused on the grounds of his youth – just as in classic butchery scenes, the women and children are evacuated beforehand. The players, emboldened by their collectivism, at least got their gripes aired. But in return, Docherty addressed every single player and lambasted him in as offensively vicious a manner as possible, all the while swigging from a full bottle of brandy. Stepney, in his autobiography, lists only two of the Doc's comments (telling Houston and Stepney how toss they were) allegedly because none of the rest is printable. Not, it appears, on libel grounds but because of the Obscene Publications Act. The air 'cleared', the Doc stormed off into the night.

Some will tell you none of this mattered, others that it was never the same again. Certainly, none who were there ever forgot it. And equally, the powers-that-be back home, be they 'junior board' or senior, heard all about it – hardly an exhibition of Busbyesque managerial class, was it? Chance for another turn on the knife-sharpener . . .

⚽ ⚽ ⚽

It is often said that the only good thing Frank O'Farrell ever did for United was to buy Martin Buchan from Aberdeen; if so, he still deserves a vote of thanks for his service. Because it could be argued that during all the Red Army Years, the only truly world-class artist we possessed was Buchan. He was already a Scottish Player of the Year, Cup-winning captain and international cap when he signed for £125,000 (£3.2m); by the time he led us to the FA Cup, colleagues could proclaim him the best centre-back in Europe without fear of ridicule.

You didn't need to know about his university-class mind and bookish pursuits off the field to recognize that this was a player of supreme intelligence, whose positional sense, timing and vision were virtually infallible. His character and style made him the obvious next captain of United, his leadership destiny as inevitable from the moment of his arrival as Michael Atherton's was at university. (Not that anyone would have dared inscribe 'F.E.C.' on Buchan's holdall, of course.) Alex Stepney, in a good position to judge, reckons we'd have won something in 1971–72 if he'd been signed earlier, such was his impact upon the defence. Later, next to Holton, he formed a Scottish central dream ticket, the only part of the team which could never be blamed for relegation. His indispensability became almost embarrassingly blatant; his injuries, such as the title-dooming lay-off during 1976–77, were as grievously damaging as any of Robson's or Keane's. It's a perverse but telling way in which to judge the true greatness of a player's contribution.

Docherty, perhaps badly advised according to Buchan, took time to overcome a lingering suspicion of him; but, as Martin drily notes, 'I won him over.' He did so partly by calling a bluff, agreeing to a QPR bid for his services after several dissatisfied weeks playing out of position. Within days, QPR had been told to sod off and Buchan resumed at Number 6: no one dared tamper with his status again, and he could continue being as single-mindedly self-possessed as he liked.

For Martin Buchan's 'otherness' is as legendary as his performances. Almost militarily meticulous, stubborn, rebellious in some ways, aloof, self-evidently superior . . . no wonder many found him intimidating. Even today, those who consider approaching him for interviews find the prospect pants-fillingly daunting. As Sammy McIlroy put it in that diplomatic footballers' code: 'He could be abrasive and didn't suffer fools gladly.' Doesn't need much translating – a Trevor Howard of the Forties could have played the Buchan role to perfection. Martin, rather amusingly, plays it down, suggesting that only his complete lack of interest in the card school and the gee-gees immediately marked him as a loner and outsider but he's surely being cute. As Graeme Le Saux would confirm, it's unusual to find footballers who are happiest brushing up their French and Spanish, perfecting suspended fourths on the guitar and disdaining the laddish banter in favour of weighty tomes.

The illustrative Buchan anecdotes are well worn: the journo asking for 'a quick word' and receiving the response 'velocity'; the refusal to hand over his passport to club safekeeping because that would be 'childish'; his one-man revolt against the Gola sponsorship deal because it 'would have been dishonest to take the money'; getting permission to nip off and see a pal in Oz, which turned out to entail a 400-mile expedition across the outback. He did his own thing, in his own way, no matter what the convention – it was a pattern he'd established long ago at school, battling against jobsworth teachers.

Some cite another example: his refusal to make a speech after the '76 Cup Final, to the apparent astonishment of all present. Old Trafford podium-watchers used to interpret this as a sign of residual anti-Docherty feeling but Buchan denies it; he simply hadn't been asked to do so beforehand and therefore certainly wouldn't be doing so off the cuff. That was not meticulous Martin's way. This was a man who, when in doubt, always plumped for the more formal and correct manner, blazer and tie beating T-shirt every time whether literally or in metaphor. In fact, as Jim White divined, wheedling Buchan into the factional intrigues of the time was a non-starter: 'Buchan did belong to a faction – the Martin Buchan faction, with a membership of one.' And it was a club with no vacancies, all the better from his view to guarantee it maintained its class perhaps, although room-mate Lou Macari did appear to receive an honorary associate membership. As long as he kept the practical jokery for others . . .

So Buchan steers a steady ship through the historian's more political questions. He won't directly diss any of the managers he served, finding something positive to say about each. If you touch upon the various conspiracies and factional fighting he knew full well were occurring, he'll refuse to name names: 'They know who they are,' is his stock response. This is simply well-judged discretion, not typical old footballers' air-brushed sentimentality.

Yet he can still display brutal candour where others would apply self-serving gloss. Why did he join United in the first place? No bullshit about 'life's ambition being fulfilled' – he looked at Liverpool's Smith, Leeds' Hunter and United's struggling Sadler before brusquely selecting his best first-team chance. How joyous was he at winning promotion? No stuff about phoenixes rising but a frank admission that he felt we had nothing really to celebrate, such had been the shame of relegation. Why did we lose the '76 Final? Because several young idiots let players' pool money and media slavering go to their heads. And 1979's? Remarkably, coughs Buchan without a second thought, 'Because I played the worst game of my life.' How refreshing that at an age when most pros indulge in self-justificatory padding, Buchan is quite prepared to remind us of something we'd be happy to forget, if it was ever true in the first place. He doesn't, however, boast about his own brilliance in the 1977 Final, a Cup-winning destruction of Keegan: that would be unacceptably flash.

Someone I know who recently interviewed the business-man Buchan described him as 'a bit of a cold fish', and in such a way as to suggest that the fish in question was a fossil frozen at the foot of the Pacific for a million years. So to my mind, all that does is make him appear even cooler, in the non-thermometrical sense. For in the mid-to-late seventies, to this young Red, only the Fonz could compete with Buchan for awe-inspiring cool. And though Henry Winkler's Harley was clearly more impressive than Buchan's Triumph Dolomite, Martin would surely never have hung around with such losers as Chochie and Ralph Malph . . .

         ✪   ✪   ✪

Red Army Despatches

Pre-season tours were becoming established as prime opportunities for laddish holidays and general naughtiness. Ostend away in August 1974 was typical:

> 'We'd gone over on the early ferry from Dover. I was eighteen at the time. Lots of younger United fans just

ran through British Customs and Emigration control to jump on the ferry – no one paid.

'We arrived on the Saturday morning; the game was taking place that afternoon. Everyone was pissed even as we landed in Belgium. We'd been doing the Duty Free on the way over – in those days I always used to drink a bottle of Pernod before the game. That or Clandew, a concoction of whisky and white wine that was popular with all the football fans because you used to get pissed out of your head on it and it was cheap.

'The bars in town before the game were fine; there was no animosity between the fans although there were loads of United over to see Stuart Pearson's debut. On the way to the ground, the seats got ripped out of the buses but nothing really serious happened. In the ground there was a bit of a stand-off between United and the police at half-time when United attacked about twenty of them, but nothing major; the real trouble came after the game which United won 3-0 with a hat-trick from Pearson.

'There were no buses to take us back to the town and it was a long walk back, similar to Montpellier. We got back into the centre of town to find lots of Belgian army lorries roving around. We were trying to find a bar on the far side of the bus station. As we crossed the bus station, about two hundred United fans started rocking a double-decker bus that was full of Ostend fans. As the bus started rocking, it fell over on its side with everyone in it. All the United fans shat ourselves and legged it. We dived into a restaurant and had a meal and tried to make out nothing had happened. For an hour or so we thought we'd got away with it, then three armed soldiers came in and arrested us. They said they had to arrest everyone from Manchester – the fact that we were from London seemed to make no difference to them. We got taken to a school gym and were kept there with another hundred or so Reds. Late that night a Belgian policeman came in and told us all that we were being charged with riotous assembly and would be in court the next morning. We didn't believe it for one minute: no way would a court open on a Sunday.

'First thing the next morning they brought us breakfast; then they started bringing benches and tables out
into the hall and the police officer told us they were
going to hold the court there and then in the school
gym. As some old bloke came into the "court room",
my mate Rhino piped up. "Who the fuck are you, you
old Belgian cunt?". Unfortunately for Rhino "the cunt"
was the judge and could speak perfect English. He told
Rhino he was going down for ten days – we couldn't
stop laughing. We all got fined about a tenner and after
they'd checked everyone's details out, the British Con-
sul arranged for a special ferry to take us back to Dover
that afternoon. There were no ordinary passengers on
the boat; the Duty Free was closed.

'When we got back to Dover, the press and television
were there trying to interview everybody. I just put a
newspaper over my head and to this day my mother
doesn't know I went to that game. At the time I was
living with a nurse who didn't know I'd gone to the
game; when I finally got home, it turned out she'd
spotted me trying to avoid the cameras on TV and
promptly poured a pot of lukewarm custard over my
head as I walked through the door.'

Residents of Leytonstone waking up on the morning of 17
August 1974 must have felt much like the Poles in September 1939. Overnight a blitzkrieg had taken place. The quiet
corner of East London surrounding Brisbane Road, home of
Leyton Orient, was already packed with United fans at six
in the morning. Hundreds had spent the night sleeping in
front gardens, doorways or any available space to be there
for United's first game in the Second Division for 37 years.
Any fears that support would drop after the tragedy of
April were quickly allayed. What followed over the next
nine months at football grounds as far apart as Blackpool
and Bristol, Cardiff and Sunderland, was probably the
greatest period of off-the-field anarchy in the history of any
football club.

Those Mancunians arriving at Brisbane Road later that
morning had already clashed with Arsenal at Euston before
wrecking the tube on the way to Leytonstone. Once at the
ground, chaos ensued. United broke down the gates and

police closed off the turnstiles in an attempt to restore order. Inside, things got even worse. An hour before kick off, United supporters invaded the pitch twice as fights between 'youths' and police broke out. At one stage Matt Busby came over the loudspeaker: 'I appeal to all Manchester supporters, behave yourselves for the sake of the game and the club.' The plea went unheeded and battles continued to break out around the ground. As United pulled lumps of concrete from the terracing, Orient keeper John Jackson complained about missiles being thrown into his goalmouth. United fans even got beneath the television gantry and tried to rock a terrified Brian Moore out of it.

It was all too much for United manager Tommy Docherty who banned his 18-year-old from travelling to watch United. 'I've refused to let him go, even though he says he'll steer clear of any trouble. Home games are different – there we can guarantee him a seat. But if he follows us away, there's just no guarantee of safety.' Orient boss George Petchey was even more forthcoming: 'They're like little Hitlerites, totally irresponsible, ruthless and unbalanced. If they're not stopped these louts will destroy the game.'

The following week United's opening home game of the season was against Millwall, already the most feared firm in the lower Divisions, as Jon from Kent recalls:

'When Millwall first came to visit Old Trafford, we'd been sharing a train up from London with them. There'd been no aggro on the train up: everyone knew that it would all happen when we got to Manchester. There were probably 150 Cockney Reds on the train. Millwall got on to the platforms at Piccadilly from where we chased them outside to thousands of waiting Mancunians. In the end, Millwall legged it down the back staircase to London Road and into the old fire station building across the road. Everyone followed them down the stairs and chased them into the fire station. Police came and stood between United and the fire station – Millwall just refused to come out. In the end they were put back on the train, and didn't get to see the game. I'll always remember one copper telling a

Millwall fan: "The next time you come to Manchester you'd better bring your mothers with you for protection." ' – *Jon, Kent*

The Millwall game also marked the first use of closed circuit cameras at Old Trafford, with United employing trained cameramen in an attempt to identify any trouble-makers inside the ground.

Already the tone for the season was being set. One week after Millwall's visit to Old Trafford, United headed down to South Wales for a meeting with Cardiff that looms large in United folklore. The press were in no doubt that this was going to be a biggie. Cardiff was described by the *Mirror* as a 'terror-ridden city' in the build-up to the game. City had spent five days building special barricades to separate the rival sets of supporters although it was already apparent that the hopes of a bumper 30,000 sell-out crowd would be dashed. The fear of hooliganism had knocked an estimated 8,000 off the gate at Orient two weeks previously and would have the same effect at Ninian Park. House-holders were warned to 'remove all breakable objects from their rooms and stand guard over their homes as fans pass'. There could be no doubt that trouble was expected: only twelve days some 137 Cardiff fans had been arrested at Bristol City.

'We were drinking at some leisure complex on the outskirts of Cardiff city centre. As soon as we came out the front entrance, it was well on us, with the local swamp estate boys. I got caught with a few smacks and kicks and was almost down when Maca saved my bacon. He pulled out a steel comb and got the main skinhead around the top lip; as his blood spurted out, it gave me room to get it together. Luckily one of them screamed, "They've got blades" and they give it legs. But there were more Cardiff around so me and Maca are soon getting legged past the complex into the swamp housing estate with a 20-strong crew in pursuit, who are screaming for others to get on to us. I grabbed a car aerial off and started using it like a whip to keep the first skinhead who'd caught up with us at bay. We clocked a main road and legged it on to a bus – the goon of a conductor was trying to get us off as we kept lashing out at this pursuing pack who were trying to jump on board too.

'Half an hour later we're back at the train station where we found a lot of Stoke and Brummie Reds who'd been wasted – they had the white flags up. Luckily, thirty minutes later all the Cockney Reds and Manchester service trains start arriving. The town centre pubs were either shut or had already been wasted. It's 1.30 and all the lads' reports were coming in – pure riots all over the gaff. Then the Manchester special pulled in; we know all the top lads are going to be on it. The noise coming off that train was spot on; first heads off it were George, Steve and Mick, all baying for Welsh blood. So the crew is now a thousand-strong and we burst straight through the police cordon into a massive pack of Valley skinheads. It was simply battles all the way to the ground, wasting anyone in our way, including every hotdog stand and off-licence, building the crew on the route up to 3,000.

'There must have been 10,000 Reds in the ground. Credit to Cardiff – they fought us toe to toe all the way through the first half. We'd steamed over the turnstiles and ended up in a corner, split by a fence. Every five minutes there'd be a bombardment of bricks and stuff from Cardiff. At half-time, we went to the bog; the gents had one way in and one out. Cardiff's boys were at the exit – ten of their main boys were at the front, in Bruce Lee poses (Kung Fu being all the rage in '74) with a massive crew stood behind them. They really looked the business. Me, Ashy and Maca happened to be first coming out of the exit when we saw this lot. I knew what a twatting I'd get off the lads if I tried to bail out of this one, especially 'cos Cardiff could then just pile straight in and have United over. I had no idea whether this guy in front of me could actually do his Lee stuff but in a split second I decided to give him one and landed a beaut. I just could not believe my luck when he dropped like a sack of shit. The United lads all steamed in ahead of me. At the time, I put it on a par with winning the pools. It's amazing how one divvy-punch can outdo a whole season's fighting. More so, as there's heads who've seen it, so it gets well spiced up!

'Second half: they start chanting "Munich" so we give it "Aberfan" which really wired the Valley lot out. The corner never stopped trying to break out and take their bit – the Old Bill were getting it from both us and Cardiff. But at full-time we still hadn't taken their end and you know that if you've not done that after kicking-off all day, then there's certain to be an absolutely massive kick-off outside afterwards. Dave smacked a copper to get in the mood. Sure enough, at the end of the street stood their mob. The charge was on. It took us five minutes solid scrapping to wipe them out: then it was loads of top singing all the way back to the trains and the *craic* was fierce all the way home.

'As usual, we were a couple of heads short on the way back. It turned out they'd had special court sessions that Saturday teatime. Then, on *News At Ten* they reported that Steve had got six months. In the papers the next day, there were top photos showing Cardiff getting a kicking outside the ground; some were in that *Clockwork Orange* gear.

'You never planned to do this and that as such in '74/5. You just got into Doc's Barmy Army and went forward with your own set of lads, linked up with the rest for a fight, got pissed, sang like fuck and then it was back to work – waiting for more the next Saturday afternoon.' – *Colin, Sale*

Reaction to the trouble at Cardiff was swift. Aware of the ever-spiralling adverse publicity United were attracting, the club invited 35 fans to meet their idols at Old Trafford the following day, with Alex Stepney asking them to 'tell the trouble makers we don't want them'. Skipper Willie Morgan even hinted that it could be a regular occurrence. (It wasn't.) Cardiff MP George Thomas wrote to Tommy Docherty claiming that the club had a 'moral obligation to pay for broken windows in nearly thirty homes along Ninian Park Road. They should settle this bill because this herd of young hooligans would never have come to Cardiff if they were not following their team.'

At West Bromwich on 14 September police set up 'instant justice courts' to deal with the 84 arrests at the Hawthorns. In a bid to combat the thugs, Smethwick Magistrates Court opened at 8 p.m. on the night of the game in time to deal with 16 charged United fans.

On Monday 16 September United played the return fixture against Millwall at their South London home, The Den. Legend has it that the special broke down outside Stockport and that the majority of United fans didn't make it to South London. Whatever the reason – delayed trains or the expense of a Monday night fixture only two days after an away game at West Brom – Millwall never got the chance to exact revenge for their humiliation three weeks previously. With only 11 arrests it was one of the quietest games of the season, United's small band of supporters being greeted with chants of 'Where the fuckin' hell are you?' from the South Londoners.

Not that absenteeism was on the agenda for long. One month later United went to Blackpool and turned the Golden Mile red. This was despite an attempt by the leader of Blackpool shopkeepers to get the then Prime Minister Harold Wilson to intervene and have the game called off. United fans started to arrive in the holiday resort at 9 p.m. the previous evening and by early the next morning the arrest count was already into double figures. Despite the rain, United set up camp on the beach as thousands competed with the donkeys for space on the sand, 'drinking, singing and waving their scarves' as the local *Gazette* put it. In total, 59 arrests were made out of a following of 17,000 but the police considered themselves lucky; a spokesman proclaimed that 'lashing rain drove the fans home early and prevented a clash with the illuminations crowd'.

At Hull, on 23 November, 27 United fans were arrested and ordered to pay fines totalling £1,357. By now arrests into double figures and more were the norm at United away matches, although games at Old Trafford remained relatively trouble-free. Anyone looking back at videos of the era will note that whilst it was commonplace for United to take a following well into five figures to away fixtures, visitors' followings at Old Trafford were seldom more than a few hundred. Fear of the fate that awaited visiting fans was usually more than enough to put off most supporters. When Notts County visited in mid-October, the *Daily Express* correspondent wrote that a visit to Old Trafford was 'akin to being thrown to the lions. The awesome baying of the famous Stretford End is having a distinct unsettling effect on visitors which United are quick to turn to their advantage.'

Sunderland, who came to Old Trafford for perhaps the most memorable game of the season, were an exception to this rule – though this didn't exempt them from the treatment United were doling out away from home, as Harpurhey John remembers:

'United were all outside the Scoreboard End and after an afternoon on the piss, we were queuing up with the Sunderland fans to get into the game. Roy told us all to be quiet: there must have been about three hundred Sunderland fans in front of us as we came down the tunnel on to the terracing. We starting giving it "You're gonna get your fuckin' heads kicked in". I pulled a can of Ronson lighter fuel from out of my back pocket and set light to this Sunderland fan in front of me. One minute, he's thinking about what Bobby Kerr might do in the game, the next his red cagoule's on fire. After that, it just kicked right off – real toe to toe fighting, some of the worst I've ever seen inside the ground. After a couple of minutes, Sunderland ended up running out of the Scoreboard, across the pitch and, because the Stretford was fenced in then, into the back of the A Stand.' – *Harpurhey John*

The following week United went to Hillsborough for a game that epitomized the season – a classic 4-4 draw on the pitch, and 106 arrests and 51 casualties off it. Wednesday's dismal average attendance of barely more than 12,000 was boosted by nearly 20,000 United fans in the 35,000 crowd. The *Sheffield Star* could not hide its contempt:

'Sheffield Wednesday's Hillsborough ground erupted in violence in the city's worst ever outbreak of soccer violence.

'More than 100 youngsters had been arrested by the time the game with Manchester United ended in a 4-4 draw. Another 60 had been injured in vicious fighting and 11 were in hospital – one Salford youth with a suspected fractured skull. Last night Wednesday secretary Eric England said: "It's a tragedy that people cannot come to enjoy the game in peace. There was an element in the crowd who had no intention of watching the match." Police expected trouble among the 35,000 crowd – Hillsborough's largest of the season – but it turned out even worse than they feared.

'Right from the start a steady stream of fans were being taken off the Spion Kop and arrested. Several more were carried out on stretchers by St John Ambulance men. But the violence really erupted after 30 minutes when Wednesday went into a 3-1 lead. Massed fighting broke out between rival supporters on the Kop.

'For several minutes it looked as if the game might be called off. Dozens of United fans jumped over the barrier at opposite ends of the Leppings Lane End and raced across the pitch to join in. Wednesday goalkeeper Peter Springett fled from his goalmouth as the scarf-waving youngsters charged across his penalty area. Fighting spread on to the corner of the pitch as scores of police, some on horseback and others wearing white crash helmets, battled with fans. At one time, more than a dozen fans were lying injured on the grass waiting for stretchers to take them to the first aid room. As the trouble reached its peak South Yorkshire Chief Constable Mr Philip Knights left his seat in the directors' box to take command. Immediately another 80 policemen were called in to reinforce the 100 already in the ground, and a small knot of Wednesday fans who had been standing on the Kop were evacuated to the safety of the stand.

'For the rest of the game, police stood shoulder to shoulder keeping the chanting, jeering fans off both ends of the pitch. Chief Supt Rod Jones, the man in charge of police operations at the stadium, said later: "We called in men from their meal breaks and traffic duty outside the stadium to contain the violence and arrested 105 fans."

'Most of the injured were suffering from bruises, sprains and cuts: "You name it, they had it," said a St John Ambulance spokesman. "We were kept busy all afternoon. It's the worst Saturday I can remember in Sheffield."

'The Manchester fans – referred to in court recently as "the scum of hooligans in this country" – have a habit of causing trouble when they cross the Pennines. In September 1968 they wrecked seven out of nine coaches on the special train taking them home from a match at Hillsborough. Ten youths and a girl had been arrested even before the kick-off. In April '72 they ran riot in the city centre after a game with Sheffield United. Six months later 68 were arrested when they were back at Bramall Lane. And in March this year – their last in the First Division – they smashed shop windows, damaged cars and kicked pedestrians. Police arrested 48.'

[A week later the *Star* reported on the court proceedings that followed.]

'Sixty-eight Sheffield Wednesday and Manchester United fans were fined more than £4,000 yesterday when they appeared at three special Sheffield magistrates courts in the aftermath of the Hillsborough riots.

'The courts sat for a total of nine hours, dealing with cases involving more than 100 adults. Twenty-four juveniles were dealt with separately. A special statement was read to all three courts in which the prosecution claimed that, of 30 arrested on Saturday December 7th, United outnumbered Wednesday supporters three to one.

'It soon became apparent to police officers that a large proportion of United supporters were determined to occupy both the Spion Kop and Leppings Lane terraces and were quite prepared to use violence to achieve their objective. There was a serious risk of the situation getting completely out of hand and for the first time at Hillsborough mounted police were used to restore order. Such is the reputation of a section of the United supporters that some people stay away from the

Best back from AWOL: drinking in the Last Chance Saloon, again.

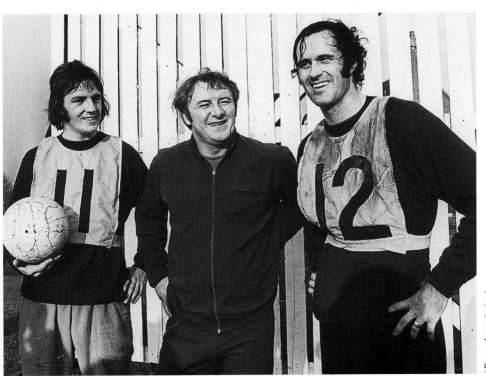

The Tartan Terror continues . . .

. . . but the original Scottish King is deposed.

23.4.73: Another Old Trafford adieu.

'Skip to the Lou Macari.'

*'Five foot eight and f***ing great.'*

27.4.74: (Above) The Thick Blue Line.
(Below) *'Division One can kiss my arse . . .'*

(Colorsport)

*'Willie, Willie Morgan
On The Wing.'*

(Syndication International)

Pancho.

17.8.74: Quintessential Englishness, '74-style: queuing up politely to demolish Brisbane Road.

31.8.74: Ninian Park, pre-battle.

31.8.74: Ninian
Park, mid-battle.

(Press Association)

(Colorsport)

Stevie – the only welcome import from Merseyside since Busby.

7.12.74: The Hillsborough Invasion.

26.4.75: Champions, of a sort.

game, shopkeepers shut up their shops, publicans close their doors and extra police are put on duty.

'At the height of the violence 213 police were on duty inside the ground and 60 people received first aid treatment. The most frequent charge, 88 in all, was that of using threatening behaviour, many of the offences being committed in and around the ground. Magistrates dealt severely with these cases imposing the maximum fine of £100.' – *Sheffield Star*

The rioting at Hillsborough brought the then Sports Minister Denis Howell to the fore. His plans for United away games to be made all-ticket with a limit on the number of tickets going to United were not adopted wholesale but were a forerunner of the schemes that would come in two years later.

The historic city of York was next on the Red Army invasion list and the good burghers of that city adopted a siege mentality at the prospect of the visiting hordes. The club invested the then princely sum of £800 in an eight-foot-high fence to enclose the section in which the United fans were to be housed, though the fear of trouble once again left the home club with unsold tickets – the York City secretary George Teasdale publicly destroyed 400 unsold tickets. All public houses in and around the city centre were closed for the day. It was an almost surreal situation that greeted the more than 7,000 United fans who crossed the Pennines for the second time in two weeks. A well-respected doctor and academic who happens also to be a Red recalls what it was like to be tarred with the brush as an 'invader':

'York City away – the shame of it! Still, the Doc had rejuvenated the team and we knew United were going up. So, off up the A1 with a footballing mate whose tackles on opposing forwards had to be seen to be believed, oblivious to the fact that the local press in York had built up this game to represent the invasion of a fair and beautiful city by unwashed and violent barbarians.

'Soon after entering York, a local bus driver left us in no doubt as to the hysteria and fear engendered in the

87

City by the prospect of United fans coming to town. Admittedly, passing the daft old sod on a blind bend around which he was trundling in the middle of the road at no more than 20 mph was perhaps unwise, but the driver's reaction was beyond belief. He must have spotted the United scarves on the rear window shelf: whatever the reason, he shifted down a gear and gave chase while at the same time radioing back to base for reinforcements. He chased us for three-quarters of a mile until we pulled into a car park, followed by this madman and a police car. The stupid old fart – he must have been at least 60 – jumped down from the bus and started shouting incomprehensible nonsense. Fortunately, the policeman was open to reason and accepted our explanation of events. Meanwhile, the bus passengers were staring down at us with a look combining amusement and revulsion, seeing at first hand two captured members of the invading tribe. At this stage I lost it for a moment and asked the bus driver whether he thought he was the 'fucking Cisco Kid' and told him where he could shove his sodding bus, passengers and all. The policeman advised restraint: the bus driver pissed off and we walked into town. What a farce.

'What follows is no exaggeration. Two men nearing 30, fairly well dressed and wearing United scarves, walking down a main road in York. People stare and point; women gather their children to them and cross the road. Worst of all, pubs are out of the question – either locked or with monsters blocking entrances and under instructions to keep the hordes at bay. After a long drive and our encounter with the lunatic bus driver, the last thing we needed was gloating faces staring at us from pub windows as we rattled locked doors and argued in vain with gorillas. In short, two mostly reasonable and peaceful Reds were gradually being transformed into homicidal maniacs! Eventually we persuaded a truly monstrous bloke, who fortunately had a sense of humour and a kind disposition, to let us in a pub provided we concealed our United scarves. He was impressed, and probably pleased, by my assurance that we were hardly likely to start any trouble if the sanction was having our heads torn off by his good self.

'Many pints later, into the ground. Well, not quite. First, a thorough search outside and then inside, the policeman inside the ground insisting he must confiscate the car keys, saying he'd 'be around' after the game. After much discussion, the keys and we were allowed in. Caged: steel mesh used to reinforce concrete floors was all around. Reds surging down the terraces and up to the rusting wire, howling and growling at the apprehensive York fans in the seats to our left, some of whom clearly believed that their last hour had come. As for the game, I think we won one-nil.' – *Doc Zed*

Whilst crowds at away grounds often failed to reach the giddy expectations of many a club secretary, at Old Trafford they continued to grow as the thrill of watching Docherty's young side and being part of the most vociferous and active supporters in the land took hold. United's opening home fixture of the season against Millwall had attracted just over 44,500. By November the biggest crowd of the season in England, 60,585, was swarming through the Old Trafford turnstiles to watch the Sunderland match. Over Christmas another fifty thousand-plus crowd watched the Boxing Day clash with West Brom; then in early January the first leg of the League Cup semi-final against Norwich drew more than 58,000 to Old Trafford, the biggest crowd ever for a non-Final match in the competition.

The second leg a week later at Carrow Road saw a return to the violence of before Christmas. After the one-nil defeat, United fans threw missiles at the Norwich keeper Kevin Keelan and overturned cars outside. Remarkably, there were only ten arrests.

'We were by now so infamous that I remember the Norwich fans jumped on to the pitch and running track and went out of the far end of the ground just so that they could avoid coming out near us. Outside things were not much better as a Norwich fan tried to drive through the United fans outside the ground in a MG soft top. As he did so, four or five United fans jumped on to the roof of the car and the soft top just collapsed around his head. I have this ridiculous mental image of his head poking through the cloth of the soft-top. Next minute, another group of United started pulling him out of his car, to kick his head in – which was lucky for him really, because the next minute his car blew up.' – *Collyhurst John*

The trouble at Norwich came only days after United had returned 2,000 unsold tickets to Sunderland for their top of the table clash at Roker Park, where the local paper was pleased and no doubt surprised to report that: 'Sunderland police commended the good behaviour of the 45,000 football fans at Roker Park. There were only six arrests and no reports of damage to property.'

After the riots at Norwich, the university city of Oxford decided on a different approach to try to appease the Red Army. The elaborate 'peace plans' started the day before the game, when Matt Busby opened a new section of the ground. On the day of the match United laid on cheap transport to the game and stands at the ground were emblazoned with banners proclaiming 'Welcome the Reds'. It was all too much for some United fans.

'Their supporters were clapping in the road as we arrived. They had banners proclaiming "Oxford United fans welcome Manchester United supporters". They were so pathetic, you wanted to puke. It was like the Vichy French – they couldn't stand up for themselves so they thought the best way to stop us wrecking their town was to creep up to us. The only boundary behind the away end was a corrugated metal fence: we soon pulled that down and most of us got in for free. Everybody was scared shitless of us in the Second Division, but Oxford were pathetic.'

Fourteen days later thirty United fans were arrested after wrecking a train on the way to Aston Villa. At least they missed the defeat. But the visit of Cardiff to Manchester on 1 March threatened a repeat of the previous August's South Wales riots. However, Cardiff City fans were advised by their own supporters' club chairman not to wear any colours and had managed to curb some of the hooligan element amongst their own supporters with a membership scheme under which those supporters under seventeen had to have a letter from their parents explaining why they couldn't accompany their children!

At Bolton the following week, estimates of the number of United fans amongst the 38,152 crowd range from 15–25,000. Once again, trouble flared as 75 were ejected from the ground in which United had fans on all four sides and 37 were arrested. United had rampaged through the town before the game, breaking shop and pub windows before fighting with Bolton fans on the terraces at Burnden.

In Nottingham the local Licensed Victuallers' Association sent a circular round to all its members recommending that they board up their windows and close early for the visit of 10,000 United fans on the 22 March, whilst Bristol Rovers imposed a special 15p hooligan levy on United fans to cover the cost of extra policing for their game with the Reds at the end of the month.

By now the team were well on their way to securing promotion and this was done at The Dell on 5 April, the United contingent of 7,000 invading the pitch at the end of the game, as they did in even greater numbers at Notts County when a 2-2 draw secured the Division Two title. The final game of the season brought a party atmosphere to the Stretford End, with manager Tommy Docherty calling them 'the best supporters in the world'. The Red Army might have 'brought shame on the club' up and down the country but its intimidation of visiting teams and their supporters had helped United to 17 home victories and only one defeat that season. The average attendance of 48,389 set a record for Division Two, was the highest in the entire Football League and was the last time a team outside the top division topped the attendance table. If United's fans, like their team, had used their spell in Division Two to train themselves up to top fighting form, then Division One would be, as the Chinese say, in for interesting times.

Pre-season trepidation: remember that? You probably had a touch in the summer of '86 but that's about it. Every other August kick-off has been glad confident morn once more – even '89, when the Knighton-shining-armour's gleam let us forget the woes of the previous campaign. Not so in the 1970s, of course. Quite the opposite in fact: only August 1976 was truly nerve-free. In August '75, the excitement of the Red Return concealed the normal fears of every promoted club. As most players admitted, no one was sure how good we really were. Beating top sides in the '75 League Cup was one thing: doing it routinely every week was another. David Meek predicted a mid-table finish; others at Old Trafford talked of 'honours within three years'. The assembled smartarses of the First Division were waiting, arms folded and lips a-sneer, for the Red balloon to burst. But it never did.

Checking out that first line-up at Molineux, you could see the critics' point. Any eleven featuring the podgy barrel-features of Tommy Jackson had a problem for starters. *Red Issue* later described the sight of Tommy popping up on the flanks as 'like watching a granny waiting for the 263 at the bus-stop'. The formation was a bit odd too, a misshapen 4-3-3 with only one proper winger. The team resembled an unfinished masterpiece, a Venus de Milo with one full arm – we were a Cantona Moment short of the full hour. Or a Camelot short of a Merlin . . .

So it was some achievement that for the best part of three months, this prototype was to have every Cassandra gorging on humble pie until they spewed. Sure, the sight of United at the top of the Division One table for the first time in four years still led some wiseacres to dust down their old quotes from Christmas '71: 'false position', 'they'll get found out', 'don't get carried away with these kids' and so forth. But most observers were happy to delight in the return of simple, almost forgotten pleasures. Virtually every match report of the time marvelled at the spirit, the attacking verve and the collective pace of Docherty's apprentices. They may, supposedly, have been heading for a fall, but what jollies the audiences were getting from watching the sparkling dash to the cliff's edge.

For those who were paying attention, those opening 2-0 wins in the Midlands were full of symbolism that boded well. Ageing, long-ball Wolves were destroyed by slick passing and with late goals that were absurdly overdue. Coppell's almost sadistic demolition of Bob McNab was a microcosm of United's new power – precocious youth taking the merciless piss out of a once-respected, rugged veteran of Arsenal's Double-winners. Lumbering boring dinosaurs out, sharp young punks in: United were about to be to football what the Pistols were to music. At St Andrews, so recently a graveyard of survivalist ambitions, Bob Hatton shattering Stepney's jaw was simply not allowed to matter. Greenhoff, taking his Mr Versatility reputation to extremes, settled into the gloves and defied all-comers for the entire half. The rest of the team responded to this apparent disaster in the fashion that was already becoming their trademark – by attacking even more. (Some fans took this as a cue too, running the infamous Brummies ragged and terrifying London Transport into planning a strike for the Red's next visit.)

A subtle point already made became explicitly and rampantly obvious to the nation after our first home game back at the top. It would be hard to over-exaggerate the impact that afternoon against Sheffield United had on all who were there and on all who watched *Match of the Day* that night. The Blades were still regarded as a smart outfit, sixth in 1974–75 and featuring in Currie and Colquhoun two class operators whom Docherty had courted hard in the past. How sweet are life's reversals; after the drubbing they received that day, neither would have been taken even on a free. Currie, a Shearer figure of his time for his apparent snubs and catty remarks about United, received special Strettie treatment all afternoon. And Division One hadn't heard anything like it since the late sixties: 56,000, trained up in Division Two, let rip the notorious aeroplane take-off barrage, a decibel level that equalled anything on offer at Ringway. The poor sod in Sheffield's goal, a Scottish international called Jim Brown, virtually admitted afterwards that he'd completely crapped his keks as he stood quivering before the Stretford End. In the worst Scottish keeping performance until the reign of Leighton, two goals were directly due to his nerve-ridden blunderings. United won 5-1, interspersing each goal with taunts of 'Currie, Currie what's the score?' As the Reds sauntered off, the Strettie sang 'champions, champions' – technically true of Division Two, now dreamtastically possible for Division One.

Currie, yer archetypal long-hair girlie-star who could've moonlighted as stunt double for the Sweet's lead singer, still managed to wrest headline inches: 'United have no flair,' he pronounced, 'and are two years from being anything special.' (Better that than being one year from relegation, you might think.) Currie was barely heard of again as the Blades plunged to the bottom. The man who had outclassed him, Lou Macari, fired back succinctly: 'Currie fannies about, all for nothing: give me Gerry Daly any time.' Sheffield United would not be the last mid-seventies 'big boys' to find that little Lou and dainty Daly could be too much to handle.

By the time Spurs came to Old Trafford on 6 September, we were still unbeaten, the win at Stoke – fifth last season – as impressive as any. That afternoon of madness, cock-up and terrorism was close to being some Pythonesque riff on the good old days: 'Eh lad, we saw twenty goals, six missed penalties, four broken legs, the main stand blew up and we still 'ad change from a threepenny bit.' We won 3-2: Spurs missed a penalty, rebounds and ricochets flew goalwards from every direction, poor Jimmy Nicholl virtually gave away two goals on his debut and at the moment the ground was supposed to explode with an IRA bomb, the crowd exploded at United's equalizer. Like good sex, top footie leaves you in breathless exhaustion. 'Was this what it was like in the sixties, Dad?' I heard a youngster ask. 'Yes, son,' beamed proud father.

94

The three best sides we'd played were next: QPR, Ipswich and champions Derby. And although we only beat Ipswich, United still emerged with reputation enhanced. Cynics who'd thought we'd fold when behind admired our fight to the death at Loftus Road; only Alex Stepney's last-gasp blunder prevented us sharing the points at Derby. Don McKay admitted we'd played them off the park for an hour – Daly's 84th-minute goal deserved to be the saver. Those who complained that Alex was getting too long in the tooth clearly didn't realize who lurked in reserve . . .

The Maine Road derby, full of battling on pitch and in stands, was yet another throwback to the good old days. After years of grim-death nil-nils and one-goal scrapes, here we got four shared strikes (three in two minutes) gilded by own goals, line clearances and fantastically awful open net howlers. For Niall Quinn '95, read Alan Oakes '75. Add to that the bonuses for the lads – 133 ejections, 28 arrests and a Civil War re-enactment outside – and for the lasses: Lou Macari's bum on display as he changed shorts. (In a Take That/United line-up of the seventies, Lou was very much the Mark Owen; pocket-size pertness and all-round cute cheekiness, at both ends.) But even the spurting thrills of that afternoon were to be topped a fortnight later.

In the annals of darkest symbolic United disasters, one of the most anally painful had been the rogering Leeds gave us in 1972. That 5-1 humiliation spoke, or rather yelled, volumes about our respective positions – Leeds approaching a kind of perverse perfection, United exposed as tired has-beens. Within two years, they were en route to a European Cup Final, playing for *our* trophy; we were in Division Two. But this October afternoon marked the moment the trans-Pennine pendulum swung back in our favour, never to return bar a few desperate days in '92. Eight thousand 'official' Reds plus at least another two thousand amongst the heathen had been active since the early hours. Local shopkeepers opening up at eight were amazed to see hordes of battling lads roaming around, breakfast bacon butties and cans scattered everywhere. Remarkably, there were only 75 arrests, which tells you what a shower of fat wheezers the WYP were. Later, much was made of the 'aggro badges' Reds were wearing, 'I Hate Leeds' being one of the more printable maxims. From the fuss the tabloids made, you'd be forgiven for thinking that these cloth fancies were offensive weapons in themselves. ('Ban These Aggro Badges!!' screamed one sub-ed; had he been threatened with a particularly menacing double-stitched patch?)

Leeds preambled with 'Where were you in '74?' and 'Second Division Shit!' but by four o'clock it was United who could sing 'What's it like to be outclassed?' Two outrageous Sammy Mac strikes, the second apparently defying laws of aerodynamics, capped a display of total confidence and vigour. Leeds' sole tactic had been up 'n' unders to exploit our supposedly aerially weak centre-backs: this was the *modus operandi* of a morally bankrupt team. Slow, tired and stupid, Leeds must have felt that their Euro final seemed so much more distant than a mere five months. The press revelled in this dethronement of football monarchs who had been barely as popular as Kings John or James II. And the momentary impression turned out to be enduring – a '77 Cup run was all that Leeds managed for the next fifteen years. Fittingly, that too was destroyed by Red Devilry.

When even bogey teams like Arsenal get a pasting, you know you're on a roll. Brian Kidd received full Stretford End honours on his return but Pearson's fabulously vicious goal in a 3-1 win demonstrated that the succession to Kidd had succeeded. Defeat at a then title-chasing West Ham to a late Bobby Gould strike was lost in the uproar over the terrace battle; the world now looked on United as genuine title contenders and handily placed in the League Cup too, thanks to a smart, well-paced win at Villa. But that was October. On November the first, Paddy Roche trotted out on to the pitch; by the 22nd, his efforts had seemed to ensure that United would not be troubling the Football League medal-forgers on either count.

The scenario is *El Mariachi* by Tarantino's mate Rodriguez. A bloke walks into a Mexican town at a vital moment for the inhabitants. He's dressed like a hitman, he's carrying a gun case and everyone assumes he's the real thing. Turns out he's actually a two-bit guitarist and social misfit whose blunderings cause about twenty deaths and he barely escapes from the last reel alive. So: poor Paddy walks on to the pitch under the glowering gaze of a dropped Stepney. He's wearing a green jersey, he's carrying goalie's gloves – *ergo*, he's a competent top-flight keeper, right? Instead, three cataclysmic nights at Anfield, Maine Road and Highbury reveal him to be a monstrous bogey man for every young Red's nightmares – 'the most repellent collection of DNA ever assembled within a green shirt', says my mate Ged, and he saw every Jim Leighton game. A recent *Red Issue* contributor wrote of how his bedroom walls were then plastered with United team pics; on every one, Paddy's face had been scrawled out and stabbed repeatedly with blunt implements. Today, people can laugh and sing ironic songs about eighties disaster Ralphie Milne. But Roche's name will forever go unsung.

We beat Norwich 1-0 on his debut but he'd not had much to do. When even Tommy Jackson is an offside decision away from a goal, you can appreciate how one-way was the traffic. And a fortnight later, after a bus strike forced many of the 52,000 to walk to OT in torrential rain, a similar dominance accounted for Villa by two goals to nil. By then, Roche was already the villain of this November panto-mime. At Liverpool, as 6,000 Reds groaned behind their Anfield Road steel partition, Roche cost us the game with throbbing cock-ups for their first and third. That first goal, when even the fans could hear Greenhoff shout 'Leave it!' only to see Roche come barging out into collision, set the tone for the fortnight. The press raved about the entertain-ment but United could hardly do anything other than attack full-pelt given the disarray behind them. Keegan, at his most smarmy and patronizing afterwards, lauded United for the way they played, doubtless slyly realizing that such kamikaze awaydays could hand the dull Scousers the title. Four days later we suffered a Maine Road League Cup defeat I refuse to discuss in case of traumatic flash-backs: Roche had all the domineering goalmouth presence of a fart in a canyon.

At Arsenal came merciful release. Alan Ball wasn't as stupid then; I bet he couldn't wait to get near our box and have a go. Twelve seconds gone and we're one-down – 15,000 Reds experience the kind of heart-sinking that can only be matched by vomiting over the girl you've just pulled. Despite McIlroy's injury and the nerve-jangling state of our defence, we fight back. Pearson's cracking volley takes us to 1-2; with a minute to go and United looking for the break, Roche punches into his own goal. After such a catalogue of infamy a keeper at, say, Grampus 8 would surely have immediately retired to the dressing room with a large machete and a bowl to catch his intestines.

Unbelievably, Roche didn't get run out of town but was to return to the team one day; for the time being, however, Docherty had no option but to bow to the howls of derision and reinstate Stepney. Poor Paddy: probably a nice guy, did his best, just happened to make a lifetime's worth of errors in fourteen days against three of our four most hated opponents in crucial, honours-deciding games. ('Happens all the time, son,' says Mrs Leighton.) In his book years later, Sammy Mac couldn't help himself: 'If we hadn't conceded those goals, we'd have won the title,' he bluntly but truthfully reflected.

We haven't had a paradox for a bit so try this one: November '75 was both the most destructive and creative month of the Docherty Era. Admittedly, we didn't feel the effects until December, after the Roche contagion was eradicated, but when Merlin arrived, Camelot was complete: two months of legendary magic immediately ensued. Gordon Hill's signing from Millwall in mid-November meant that Docherty's 4-2-4 dream team was permanently in place at last. The vision glimpsed so fleetingly over Easter matched for legendary impact Jesus' post-resurrection walkabout as far as Red worshippers were concerned. In this instance, the second coming had only been a six-month wait. With Tommy Jackson making way and safely sealed up in the tomb, we now had two out-and-out wingers, that extra starburst of flair and an unexpectedly gushing source of goals.

More than that, Hill became an icon. To me and many others who were young and idol-hungry, Gordon Hill stands as the single most representative figure of that Docherty team. Young, flash, intensely exciting, a bit crap defensively and undeniably 'cool' – that was the United of 1975–77 all over and Gordon Hill to a tee. If popular culture's two greatest forms are football and rock – and of course they are, if you're under fifty and haven't got your head stuck up your arse – then November '75 stands as one of pop culture's defining moments, especially for a Mancunian: Gordon Hill signed for United and the Sex Pistols' first, infamous, nationwide tour began. The results? United's 4-2-4 relit the torch of wing-driven attacking panache whilst the Pistols gave back pop music to its rightful owners – the revolutionary young. All United sides since, and those who aspire to Unitedesque ideals, can be judged against the ambition and purity that lay behind this 4-2-4 team. In Manchester particularly, it has resonated in the twenty years since; even City took up the challenge with Barnes and Tueart and have tried, during those rare seasons when they've not been a complete joke, to live up to these standards. Both clubs had been in danger of abandoning their late sixties legacies but between '75 and '78, both equipped themselves with a modern touchstone which our generation could relate to and remember.

As for the Pistols, the stunning influence of the legendary Free Trade Hall gig later in their early career has directly produced Joy Division, the Buzzcocks, the Smiths and in turn New Order, the Stone Roses, and Happy Mondays. (The only other such moment fit to be mentioned in the same breath is November 1992, when Eric signed for us whilst Suede's bedlam-inducing first tour broke the grunge/dance dominance and released the new guitar generation.) Late twentieth-century Manchester is going to be remembered historically for just two products – its football and its musical culture. So remember, remember our seventy-five's November?

This is no nostalgic exaggeration: every one of the eight League games we played in December and January was completely and willy-wobblingly enthralling. Hill took just three November games to click into connection; then on 6 December he was man of the match at Ayresome Park in the best goalless draw of the decade. Hill scored in the 4-1 drubbing we gave Sheffield United next; the acute angle finish, though driven rather than caressed, reminds one inescapably of Cantona's crucial winner at Upton Park '96. (The press broke off from their United-worship just long enough to note that the Blades were obviously going down: now what had Tony Currie been saying back in August?) Pearson's double added to the Pancho-for-England clamour which would eventually be rewarded in May; Greenhoff,

Coppell and Hill would not be far behind. Seven days later, Wolves came to Old Trafford to frustrate. The build-up of tension and anticipation was excruciatingly pleasureful, like the longest period of foreplay imaginable. Three minutes into injury time and still nil-nil as United pile forward rampantly – you've been there, haven't you, the moment when you only need someone to breathe on your helmet and it'll explode like a goddamn tidal wave? The ball falls to Hill, unmarked, 14 yards out in the Stretford End box. He twats it with absolute abandon into the roof of the net. Orgasmic is the only adjective to describe the flow behind the goal. That was the best sex you could get for 70p anywhere in 1975.

The juices never stopped flowing either. It was already wet enough at rain-drenched Goodison as 11,000 Reds doubled the usual gate for Doc's third anniversary game. The lights may have gone out for 15 minutes ('Why don't you pay yer bills?' sang the Reds) but no floodlight ever shone as brilliantly as the brilliance of Macari's goal: Andy Pollard reckons that the juggling overhead scorcher was the best he's ever seen. Top of the League once more, no Morgan-inspired early goal was going to deflect us against Burnley. In yet another in the endless series of minor classics against the whippet-shaggers, 60,000 greeted Macari's 80th-minute winner with a primal roar that no one ever forgot. Even the normally phlegmatic Stepney eschewed his usual seen-it-all-before demeanour to marvel at the ear-splitting din produced by the Stretford End that day: 'It really was like the best of the sixties,' he admitted. It would be seventeen years before United again went into a New Year on such a wave of emotion and excitement as that upon which we surfed so stylishly in 1975–76.

By five o'clock on 10 January, the deafening chorus of 'We're gonna win the League' which shook Old Trafford was no longer tongue-in-cheek; the wishful thinking of August had been transformed into hard-headed if dizzying reality. At ten past three, such an outcome had seemed improbable as Don Givens put QPR one-up with a glorious goal. Symbolism ahoy. Rangers had always been sniffily unimpressed by the United Revolution and ex-Red Givens in particular had snorted the most snottily in derision. Two hours later, Dave Sexton reflected on the 2-1 defeat and

scarcely bothered trying to conceal that United had outclassed his own title contenders. 'United are the best side
we've met – tremendous pace and such persistence,' he
gushed. Stan Bowles, once a tormentor, had limped off
after half an hour, Gerry Daly rising to the occasion to
dominate the midfield with total assurance. Hill's oppor-
tunistic blast into the Strettie goal had presented United
with the match on a plate and added another tier to the
legendary pantheon we were building for the magician.
Seven days later, he scored straight from a corner at White
Hart Lane – the last Red shirt seen pulling that trick had
been Best himself. Seven goals in five weeks from outside-
left – wasn't this against the laws of seventies football? Two
walls of my bedroom were by now already solely devoted
to the man; my local barber in Flixton offered a Hill cut at
kid's prices for all us impressionable ten-year-olds . . .

The Spurs match finished 1-1 but had been stupidly
exciting; someone calculated that the teams averaged a
chance between them every 90 seconds. The traditionalists
and purists, thrilling to this exhibition on *Match Of The
Day*, pulled their collective dicks out of their pants. And
for a fleeting period that winter, you actually felt United
were popular. What a different world that was, hey? I
vividly remember other teams' fans not being ashamed to
admit United were the second favourite team – and the
press simply couldn't get enough of us. We were young,
innocent and hadn't won anything yet, so perhaps it was
still safe to like us. But even the dreaded Red Army was
receiving condescending – and amusingly premature – pats
on the head. At Spurs, there were no transport strikes, no
Army call-outs, no thermonuclear devices on standby; the
tide of violence was supposed to have been turned. Articles
appeared lionizing United's support, repeating the not-
entirely-true assertions that the 'hoolies' were a tiny minority, and crediting the fans with rejuvenating the terraces. In
mediaspeak, we were a 'good-news story'. That also meant
setting your watches for the countdown to backlash, of
course, but for the time being we were in the slightly
unnerving position of having everyone in Britain wanting
to kiss our bums. (Had they seen the state of the Stretford
End bogs?)

Perhaps we shouldn't have been surprised. After years of

Leeds representing the flower of English footie, no wonder we were welcomed with such open arms and flies. Who wouldn't prefer roses to poisonous cacti? When Peterborough came up for a bit of a thrashing in the Cup fourth round, United having previously disposed of Oxford, a poignant contrast flickered in the closing stages. Three-one up at a canter against Noel Cantwell's boys, some Redshirts started taking the piss on the pitch. Now, doing so when, say, five up in a Premiership game is one thing: against plucky minnows managed by an ex-Red is another. Fans, even those in the Strettie, started grumbling, the odd boo distinctly apparent. Leeds United may well have found this sort of piss-taking amusing during that infamous 7–stuffing of Southampton but that's Yorkshire for you. Old Trafford still had a humanity and sense of decency that the Revie regime had long since cauterized out of Elland Road. Arrogance is a tricky customer. Modern United fans love our own swagger and that of Cantona – it has helped define our identity in this decade. But overplayed, however slightly, in the wrong circumstance and it easily translates into a disgusting, proto-Fascistic oppressiveness. Modern supporters sometimes seem to forget that arrogance loses its power if entirely unleavened by patches of humility. Old Trafford that afternoon still understood.

At the end of January, United remained top, level on points. On a frozen OT pitch against the Brummies, little Lou had donned a smart pair of trainers and duly sneaked in for a sly second, Forsyth's rasper having scorched even this chilled turf for the opener. We won 3-1. Forsyth won many a man of the match award, the full-back now firmly re-established having learned the hard way in the stiffs that he'd better get used to liking his defensive role. Any sulks Alex might once have had about his lack of involvement were duly put into perspective by the fabulously unhinged tantrum Brum's Archie Styles had at full-time. Purple-faced with fury, his bawlings into the faces of bewildered officials were funny enough; when not even his team-mates could prevent him whirring frenziedly around like a Gallagher, you could anticipate the first sub's appearance by a straitjacket. A tremendous end to the day's entertainment.

After two months of carnal delights, February became a post-climactic pause for breath: I think the women's mags call it refraction time, the necessary period of dozing and ciggies whilst you wait to get it up again. Nothing as damaging as Black November, of course, but dropped points at Coventry and at home to fellow title-chasers Liverpool and Derby took the edge off our surge. Defeat at Villa, during which Pearson and Macari were crocked, highlighted the problem: wear and tear with too many players needing a rest and carrying knocks. United's only weakness was that we had no squad to speak of – had 'rotation' been an in-vogue concept back then, we couldn't have indulged anyway. Our reserves were ropey to say the least and only finished mid-table in the Central League. Thankfully, the top eleven still managed to pull one win out of the bag, at Leicester in the Cup fifth round. Once we'd shaken off these late-winter malaises and sniffles, we'd be ready for a dose of Wembley Fever.

Annoyingly, Maine Road was already fully in its grip. On the 28th, while we entertained and thrashed West Ham 4-0 to place our title challenge back on course, City were winning the League Cup in the capital with an admittedly lovely Tueart goal. The thieving bastards had copied our 4-2-4 style and won a trophy with it, pinning our own fourth-round scalp to the ribbons. However much Reds' dads chirped that this was 'good for Manchester', it grated. But within the fortnight, trivialities such as the League Cup were forgotten: for us true contenders, the only talk of the town concerned the Double.

The FA Cup sixth round: for proper clubs, this is the point at which you're allowed to contract Wembley Fever. (City have special dispensation to indulge from Round Four, such are the rarity of their appearances beyond the Third.) Nowadays, Wembley Fever barely exists in a recognizable form for United. Repeated Wembley appearances have acted as a successful vaccine, diluting the delirium to such a point that 'Fever' has become 'Mildly Excited Interest'. We are so worldly-wise, smug and blasé now. This familiarity with glory has its obvious benefits but the contempt it has bred is regrettable. No such concerns in '76: only one FA Cup semi in a decade (1970) had left us parched, thirsting for any drops of immortality that the venerable old pot could offer us. Wolves should never have escaped

Old Trafford with a draw. That they should have led for eight minutes was almost insulting, Daly's sumptuous 15-yard drive the least we deserved in response. Nevertheless, Molineux on a Tuesday night awaited. Those who were there never forgot it.

'Wolves were one-up in 19, scored a second two minutes later and, worse still, Macari was taken off injured. The match seemed over – but only to those who did not know United. That night at Molineux was to exemplify the spirit of a United side for whom opposition goals were only an incitement to play even better. For United fans, it stirred memories of the 1960s glory days.' – *Michael Crick*

'To tell the truth, we weren't really bothered about being two-nil down. Really. We just knew we were better than them.' – *Steve Coppell*

'What can the marauders of United do to follow that? Win the Cup, take the League and toss in the Boat Race? Anything seems possible with United in such irresistible, aggressive mood.' – *Derek Potter*, Daily Express

Of course, coming back from two-down to win in extra time despite injury, tiredness and ground disadvantage is the very stuff of the Cup, no matter what the club. But add to that the extraordinary night-time atmosphere of a packed, pre-Taylor historic venue, dominated by up to 20,000 travelling Reds, watching a contest fit to live in the folk memory alongside Molineux's 1950s European specials: surely you can understand why all who were there place it among their top five experiences. Michael Coughlan remembers it well:

'I'd been forced to go on a school trip to the Science Museum on the day of the Wolves replay but I'd legged off and hitched a lift from the London Wolves Supporters Club to Molineux. There were 44,000 inside with 10,000 locked out and I had to go in amongst the Wolves fans. No sooner had we kicked off than Wolves were 2-0 up; it seemed to happen that quick. All the

Wolves fans around me were patting me on the head telling me not to worry but I felt sick. But never let it be said that during the seventies United support wasn't the best. Although we were two down, the South Bank, a mass of red, white and black-clad bodies, never stopped singing. The support that night was truly magnificent. Pearson pulled one back, Brian Greenhoff popped up for the equalizer. No smiling Wolves fans now, no more pats on the head!

'Any doubts that the North Bank was the right place to be disappeared when Sammy Mac tucked away the winner and came running over in my direction. As if by instinct, I jumped over the wall to help Sammy celebrate. Embracing like two lovers, we were joined by the rest of the team; when the players returned to the pitch, I fist-clenched all those baying Wolves fans before being escorted away by the police. But instead of arresting me, they walked me over to join the 20,000 Reds singing, "Two-nil down, three-two up – now we're gonna win the Cup!" What a great feeling afterwards as we sang our way through the streets of Wolverhampton. I walked confidently towards my busful of angry Wolves fans; I wasn't scared of them – I had to face my dad and headmaster next day ...'

– *Michael Coughlan*

The foibles of February were forgotten; that night to remember lifted the curtain on a three-and-a-half week period which stands comparison with any before or since for blood-pumping excitement. The five games that followed formed the nexus of this golden age, when you truly believed United could achieve anything, when you understood that this was how football should be. Despite the Doc's efforts to dampen expectations, Double talk was everywhere. Liverpool had shockingly lost at home, placing us effectively level, although we had games rather than points in hand. Our pairing with Derby in the forthcoming semi already bore the billing of the season's true final as excitable hacks foretold a Double for the winners. (Southampton and Palace were in the draw solely to make up the numbers, of course.) You can keep yer 'April in Paris': March in Manchester was the most beautiful spring experience known to man. Had we really come so far since '74?

Leeds received our answer, four days after Molineux. For those who'd missed the symbolism of October's Elland Road predecessor, here was a repeat message, twice as loud and in-yer-face. The volleys of meat pies – a comment on OT's catering as well as the opposition? – which greeted the Leeds coach turned out to be our only act of generosity that day. Virtually 60,000 witnessed the kind of abattoir slaughter that was once the speciality of Revie's destroyers. The record books detail a close 3-2 result but no one was fooled by meaningless late consolations. As every paper reported on Sunday morning, one of football's geological periods had come to an end: time-served observers struggled to recall any humiliation such as this during those eleven dark years of Tyke pre-eminence. A glance at the state of the defenders said it all. Whilst Houston and Forsyth marauded about up front, making and scoring goals, a wretched Norman Hunter ended the game dazed and confused, blundering about his box and roaring to the Fates who'd deserted him and his unholy kind. The Doc's pre-match mind games, in which he taunted Jimmy Armfield about what he described as his team's savagery and general grottiness, had been unnecessary: no amount of kicking and screaming could save Leeds from being entirely outclassed. Houston, Pearson and Daly's goals had finished what Sammy Mac started in October – the dethronement of footballing monarchs. The Red revolution, it appeared, was virtually complete.

End-to-end humdingers followed at Norwich (1-1) and Newcastle; the latter, as Andy Pollard reports elsewhere, is now notorious for being one of the moodiest days-out of the seventies but stands on its own in football terms as the ultimate seven-goal thriller. Never have so many defenders appeared to be on drugs; never has an away team attacked with such outrageous confidence. Middlesbrough, Old Trafford's visitors a week later, simply didn't have a chance with United in such temper – three-nil flattered Boro as United gave an all-round demonstration of 4-2-4's perfect brilliance. No finer preparation could be imagined for 3 April's appointment at Hillsborough. If only it had been at Wembley; if only the season could've ended just there . . .

I must have watched my videotape of that Derby semi fifty times. It still never fails to rattle the spine as Hill's glorious second flies in, as he is captured chest bursting out of shirt in one of the decade's iconic images. Derby simply never reached our level as United continued where they'd left off against Boro, apparently nerveless assassins paying no heed to 'champions' labels. Like Leeds, Derby were merely more old reactionary farts to be stood against the wall as the United revolution drove on to the capital. (Gordon Hill as Trotsky is an analogy that has more legs than you think: cf. Dave Sexton's ice-pick . . .) Yet even more riveting is the footage of the Red Army that afternoon. There are few sequences like it. The uncontrollable passion, the sheer joy of the historic moment and the colour-drenched vibrancy of the legions flare out of the screen as shockingly as a Panavision fireball. It looks as fresh and exciting as if it happened yesterday. That was the Spirit of '76, wasn't it?

So Derby sank into submission, as all teams did when we were on song. Leighton James, hyped as the canny creator who'd undo us, spent most of the second half keeping out of the way, chatting to Alex Forsyth about the weather and the birds. 'When I saw that, I suspected we might win,' remarked Steve Coppell drily. Bruce Rioch, sensing his last Wembley chance disappearing, took the opposite approach. Snarling and hacking at everything that breathed, his assault on Supersam enraged several Reds sufficiently to entice them on to the pitch at full-time. (Who is that man on the video attempting to twat Rioch whilst handicapped by a nasty red jumper? Looks very like a certain fanzine editor actually . . .) Nobody cared who'd won the other semi. Hadn't this been the real Cup Final?

And then, as so often in our pre-Fergie history, it all went pear-shaped. We're used to ruthless finishing these days: when we go for trophies, we almost always get them. Certainly, we never lose semi-finals anymore. Yet it used to be a case of winning trophies in spite of our habits. All those runners-up spots in the forties and fifties, all those lost Cup semis under Busby and Wilf, all those last gasp failures in Europe . . . that was part of United's perverse charm. So here we are in April '76, six games from a possible Double and with the FA Cup at least seemingly a cert – and we lost four of them to end up with nothing. 'You get nowt for coming second,' as Billy Bremner always said; not strictly true. We'd have our Cup of Tears, a place in Europe and a realization that, back in '74, we'd have sold our grannies to have witnessed such a season.

'We never stopped fighting,' remarked a still-proud Doc after April's drubbing at Ipswich (and that was true of the Red Army that afternoon too). But we'd certainly stopped being lucky. Steve Coppell's injury came at the worst possible moment; every fifty-fifty decision went opponents' ways; run-in nerves took a toll on raw players. Four games in seven days hardly helped either. Hairy victories over Everton and Burnley served only as preludes to bitter Midlands nemesis. Stoke broke away to score the only goal at Old Trafford on a cruel, quivering night – what a time to lose an unbeaten home record. Hopes of winning the title against City, the ultimate dream scenario, faded with the floodlights; Leicester finished the job on the Saturday as Peter Coyne became a pub quiz statistic. So the Doc had been right all along; the seasoned veterans of QPR and Liverpool had enough to outpace us and perhaps that extra man in the squad. But there was no time for mourning, even if it had been appropriate – which, after such an astonishing effort, it certainly wasn't. We had an FA Cup to collect in seven days' time, didn't we?

It would be hard to over-exaggerate just how much the nation at large took United's forthcoming 'victory' for granted. The only question was how many we would score and what degree of wing-driven brilliance we would attain. Papers puffed Hill and Coppell, predicting annihilation for Southampton's ageing defence; in fact, more column inches were filled with debate about United's fans than this foregone conclusion of a match. Frank McGhee in the *Mirror* had suggested we be denied tickets to prevent trouble, sparking days of dissection as to what constituted the Red Army and how its troops should be dealt with. (The answers ranged from the birch and/or National Service to medals and acclamation. Admittedly, the latter tended to be postmarked Salford.) Rent-a-quotes from Wembley's environs queued up to voice their fears that United's boys would put London to the torch: 'I just pray United win,' ran the common refrain. But, of course,

United were guaranteed victory, weren't they? So there was nothing to worry about . . .

Modern readers will be amazed at this hubris. We're now well accustomed to the phenomenon of crap overcoming class at Wembley: Sunderland, Southampton, West Ham, Coventry, Wimbledon, Everton in '95 . . . But in 1976, the historical perspective was very different. Back then the commonplace wasn't 'anyone can win on the day': rather, it was received wisdom that the pitch and occasion always brought forth the cream. Since the war, there'd only been one genuine Cup Final shocker – Sunderland's beautiful kippering of Leeds. That had only been three years ago. To warn that this once-in-a-century cosmic upset might happen again in '76 was solely to invite ridicule. I went to bed the night before, unable to sleep with the Christmas-like excitement, singing stupid made-up songs about the European Cup-Winners' Cup and chanting 'Four-nil', sad twat that I was. Or am.

Years later, Martin Buchan snarled: 'Too many of our players thought all they had to do was turn up to collect their medals. And they did – losers' medals.' (So we fans hadn't been alone in our pathetic over-confidence.) But for every flash harry who would discover the proverb about nemesis following hubris, there was a player who couldn't handle the expectation. Coppell and McIlroy both noted years later that the blasé blatherings had got to some of them. 'What if we didn't produce Wembley's greatest show and win 4-0? What if it all went wrong? We were still on a hiding-to-nothing, however good we were,' remarked one. And as United put press backs up by allegedly over-milking the players' pool arrangements during Final week, you could hear the knives being sharpened.

The '76 Cup Final wasn't just a new experience for the kids in the team. For my massive 25–40 generation of Reds, 1963 was history book stuff; this '76 Final was our initiation into a glorious ritual to which we would soon become so smugly attached. Joyce Woolridge, *When Saturday Comes*' resident Red, remembers being young, female and pissed on her Wembley debut:

'1976 was a very special year, even though the Reds ended up with no trophies. We were young, we were happy, we had wingers and we were on our way to Wembley. For my birthday I'd been given the team's hot 45 "We're Manchester United" (worth it for the flip side alone: our multi-talented skipper's composition, "The Old Trafford Blues", which contained immortal lines like "then there's Alex Stepney, the granddad of the team, he's been playing football since 1917"). But it wasn't this song of genius that accompanied me on the great day out at the twin towers.

'As I weaved along Wembley Way with my brothers, my feet killing me in my platform sandals, a slurred voice began to serenade me. "Kiss my arse, my arse," he crooned, to the tune of "Que Sera, Sera". "Come on, love," my fellow Red cried, "loosen up, have a drink!" This man was a real "Tet", as we used to call them. The crack in his backside, clearly visible, was big enough to keep a pasty warm until half-time; his arms were enormous from pushing at the back of the Stretford End terrace. He was carrying that staple of the seventies football fan who was in for a long journey – the Party Seven with two holes punched in the top. Not that I'm a snob, but I was a bit reluctant to partake as the top was covered in slabber. Then his friend came to the rescue. He battered Mr Party Seven around the head with a rolled-up copy of the *Manchester Evening News*' "Wembley Souvenir Issue".

' "YOU ****ng animal, you complete ***ing animal! Offering a bird beer! I've got something for you, darling," he went on, pulling one of those "it's all right, officer, it's only orange squash" bottles from his pocket. Well, I couldn't refuse, could I? And as I opened my mouth to take the smallest possible sip from the lighter fuel mixed with Jeyes fluid that was in there, his tuneful friend helpfully tipped it up so that most of it poured down my throat.

'Five minutes later the scene began to swim before my eyes. I suddenly wanted to sing. "Kiss my arse, my arse . . ." I strained, hanging on to my eldest brother's sleeve in desperation as the bodies surged forward. My middle brother was limping strangely in the Jake The Peg fashion that had to be adopted by anyone attempting to smuggle a flag with pole into the ground by sticking it up the inside leg of their baggies. He was to put his future ability to father children in serious doubt by jumping up in celebration when he managed to get past the security, sending the pole right into his gonads. Thus we were both incapable of watching the first minutes of the match, but for different reasons.

'I had been given the seat ticket, having drawn the short straw, supposedly among the Southampton fans – but, naturally, all of the seats in our section bar two had been filled at inflated prices by United fans. I'll always remember the two blokes who looked after me that day. They'd paid fifty quid each for their tickets (and in 1976 a dear LP was £2.99), hitched down and slept in a ditch by the motorway the night before. Because I looked a bit lost, though in reality completely paralytic, they bought me the programme, some peanuts in a paper bag and a cup of tea. The two empty seats were eventually filled by businessmen who got their tickets free and had been too busy enjoying the hospitality to watch the match. They lit up big cigars, announced that Southampton were bound to win, and before you could say "offside" the ball was in the back of the United net. I don't know if they left the ground alive. By that time I had unfortunately sobered up completely.

'Despite the disappointment, it was still a great day. The noise we made, even when the team went up to collect their losers' medals, was terrific and though we were beaten, we were still unbowed. This was the "Spirit of '76", when the football was played with a bit of a swagger and even losing could be enjoyable when you were with fans who knew how to enjoy themselves and knew what football is all about.'
– *Joyce Woolridge*

They dubbed it the Cup of Tears; few can forget the image of Brian Greenhoff, inconsolable as he trudged off the drought-parched turf. At least eighty per cent of Wembley's inhabitants that day had witnessed their most bed-wetting of nightmares. Being beaten by a blatantly offside goal, having been denied what would've been a floodgate-opener by the crossbar, was bad enough; to have performed so abjectly against such a team of trundling uglies added objectionable insult to injury. That our hero and inspiration Gordon Hill should've had a stinker at such a moment; that the nerveless assassins of Hillsborough should so chillingly have frozen inside such a blistering cauldron . . . football scripts are simply not supposed to pan out this way. Look at the wretched cast of that Saints team. Peter Rodrigues, a moustachioed full-back who looked 45 and as though he'd be more at home in a San Franciscan disco; Ian Turner, who in a decade famed for its ugliness stood out for true kiddie-frightening hideousness, a case of lacking oxygen to the brain when a foetus if ever I saw one; Jim McCalliog, a journeyman United reject who actually made the bloody goal . . . Twenty-one years later and it still astonishes. And still hurts.

The next day, the team did a tour of Manchester in an open-top bus, Lou Macari waving a silver cardboard cut-out of the Cup that was supposed to be ours. Estimates of how many Reds stuffed the streets vary from 100,000–600,000: assuredly, no city in Britain will ever see such a turn-out for beaten finalists again. A couple of players admitted to feeling humbled; they felt they'd let us down, yet here we were in party mood to lift their spirits. Surveying the scene, Pancho mused aloud, 'Makes you wonder how many would be here if we'd won.' Could Manchester have coped with any more? Surely, that afternoon wasn't really about the Cup Final: it was a thanksgiving service. We had a team and club to be proud of, no matter what had just occurred.

The Doc duly made his famous promise, that United would return the next year to go one better. Of course, that is what they all say at such a moment. And a Tommy Doc promise is – how can I put this non-libellously? – not something you'd bet your mother's life on at the best of times. As Buchan, McIlroy, Coppell and others all later admitted, most players thought the opposite: that they'd blown their one Wembley chance and the crushing disappointment would take some time to overcome. Again, football life seemed so different in '76. United had taken thirteen years to reach a Cup Final and many assumed it could be a decade before we returned. Most players of that era got just one chance of a winner's medal – the multiple

Wembley visits that became so common since for Arsenal, United, Spurs and the Scousers were highly unusual back then. You were disappointed to see us lose to Everton in '95 but you knew from experience that we'd be back within a dozen months. You were devastated in '76 because you felt it could be a dozen years. For Docherty himself, now tagged a Wembley Loser after repeated defeats, the burden as he set out to lead the 1978–77 campaign must have been onerous indeed. Enough to drive a man to drink, or adultery perhaps. How remarkable it would be if the shady old sod could actually keep a promise for once . . .

Three days after the Cup Final, we played our postponed derby match: City fans sang 'Show us yer trophy'. Two outstanding goals later, we could sing 'We'd rather win the derby than the Cup' but that wasn't the real point. As Reds invaded the pitch, it was the scarcely credible transformation in feeling from the last derby-day invasion that really mattered. Glory had replaced shame; hope for a gleaming future displaced doom-ridden despair. City had their poxy League Cup and the moment of *schadenfreude* grace of Bobby Stokes – but no Red would have swapped places with the beaten Blues that night. Our football club had rediscovered the spirit of Manchester United and no silverware was needed to validate that essential truth.

⚽   ⚽   ⚽

Tommy Docherty once called Lou Macari the Number One Poison Dwarf – and indeed, he was more popular in every way than diminutive rival, *Dallas*'s Charlene Tilton, with the possible exception of the breast department. Actually, it wasn't a particularly apt description. Not only were the rest of the team hardly giants in comparison but the point about Lou's individuality was that he remained completely poison-free. He didn't smoke, take drugs or drink at all, he was an excellent trainer and a guy who watched his diet long before it was fashionable. In fact, his only naughty habits were the horses and practical jokes – the vice of kings and the affliction of idiots respectively – though in Lou's hands the buffoonery often had an intelligent edge which almost excused the inherent Beadleness. And if it is true that his persecution-by-jape of Mickey Thomas helped end the Welshman's United career, then one can only be grateful.

Lou was a handful both on and off the pitch, a bundle of energy, fiery temper and righteous stubbornness which made him the archetypal Mighty Atom, a one-man awkward squad. No wonder Martin Buchan liked him, and that Docherty was irresistibly attracted to him. Tommy knew there'd be trouble down the road: but when Celtic looked like they were going to sell their established star striker to Liverpool, Docherty had to move in. Not for the last time, Macari's stubborn streak and love of a challenge worked to United's advantage. Feeling he had been manipulated into accepting Shankly's embrace – and that Liverpool would be too easy a ride – he opted to join a team going nowhere and a manager with a controversial history. The trophy bonuses he missed in so doing would have financed many an accumulator but Lou has never expressed a regret, not even when his tempestuous affair with Docherty reached the separate-bedroom nadir.

It was probably a good thing for all concerned that the inevitable clash of egos and ideas came early; it cleared the air, redefined Macari's destiny and helped transform the team. Lou had largely been shit since he arrived, unhappy at playing as an out-and-out striker. The Stretford End were grumpily underwhelmed by this £200,000 (£4.5 million) misfit and few complained when Docherty dropped Macari. But when Lou discovered he was then expected to play alongside a bunch of youth-teamers at Mossley, he 'went into one'; a public barney ensued, and Macari found himself fined and on the transfer list. He immediately admitted he'd acted incorrectly but never accepted that he had the fundamentals wrong – and when Docherty eventually acceded to his demands to play in midfield, the results were sensational. Wisely, Lou kept any 'told you so' crowing to himself; the Doc was big enough later to admit his initial mistake. Two supporters' Player of the Year awards and a good tilt at the national title underlined the point quite sweetly enough.

Lou had proved himself all over again, climbing up from training-ground transfer-list reject to Stretford End hero, just as he had risen to the heights in Scotland to collect three title medals after much of a childhood spent at a football-free school. He was nothing if not a fighter. He could always talk a good fight too, whether spelling out home truths in the dressing room, sometimes leading players' revolts (cf. *Hong Kong Phooey*) or acting as players' spokesman to the press. Match reports when Lou was 'on duty' were never dull: he spoke like a fan, full of stuff 'em combativeness and a readiness to defend anything Red to the hilt. His spirit of indomitability on the pitch, bolstered by phenomenal stamina and vitality, could have made him a captain if Buchan hadn't been around; his imagination, touch, originality and passion made him close to the complete player in any event. But he was also a model pro, 'sound' enough to please Sexton every bit as much as he did Docherty; somehow he had developed a perfect combination of being a '110 per cent' team-man *and* an individualistic artist simultaneously. When he was on song and in your starting eleven, you wouldn't want to bet against us. Unless you were Lou himself, of course. (Tee-hee. Only kidding, Lou.)

⚽ ⚽ ⚽

Red Army Despatches

The return of United to the top flight set the turnstiles moving at record pace, both at Old Trafford and throughout the First Division. At home the Reds were the best supported club for the ninth time in twelve seasons, their average of 54,750 a massive 13,000 ahead of Liverpool's. Away from Old Trafford too, United attracted the largest crowds, averaging just over 37,000.

United's opening fixture took them to Wolverhampton, where 12,000 Reds sang 'United are back, United are back' from the old South Bank at Molineux. Hundreds missed the game after a typical British Rail fiasco which saw those who took the football special re-routed via Stafford and Birmingham; they had to walk the last two miles to the ground, just in time to hear the final whistle being blown. The press were in no doubt that the return of United was not a cause for celebration. 'They're back . . .' screamed the *Mirror*, 'the hooligan armies, punching and hacking their way into Soccer's Hall of Shame.' At Molineux police had fought a running battle with United fans for 90 minutes; 86 were arrested and 14 stabbed. The main police station was so full at one stage that outlying nicks had to be used to hold fans before they could be charged. 'We've never seen anything like it,' said a police spokesman. 'God knows what would have happened if United lost.' Not that United were the only soccer armies causing mayhem on that third Saturday in August. At Leicester, a Birmingham fan was stabbed in the neck with a bottle. In Southend 200 Sheffield Wednesday fans went on the rampage after losing 1-0, whilst at Sunderland 25 arrests were made at the game with Chelsea.

Sports Minister Denis Howell had spent the summer formulating a plan to combat the hooligans, relying heavily on a scheme whereby soccer specials would arrive as close to kick-off time as possible. But by the first night of the season, much of his plan lay in tatters. Even the non-arrival of the United special had not quelled the violence, supporters having shown that they were prepared to arrive early and by any means.

After a midweek trip to Birmingham during which a further 26 were arrested, club secretary Alan Instone jumped on the United-knocking bandwagon. Unhappy at a gate of only 33,177 when he'd hoped the Brummy coffers would be swelled by over 40,000, he complained that 'thousands of Birmingham supporters stayed away because they didn't want to risk getting involved in the hooliganism which follows United around'. Not that United's support was going wholly unrecognized for the positive effect it was having on the team, as this piece from the *Daily Mail* for the opening home game of the season against Sheffield United indicates:

'Football's current sick joke is that Manchester United lead the First Division with six points, 14 stabbings and 110 arrests.

'In the last week, I have seen them win all their points and have seen many thousands of their supporters who have never even thought of stabbing anyone. At Wolverhampton, at Birmingham and finally at Old Trafford, I have watched them doing what they enjoy most – encouraging United, mocking the opposition with passion that no other supporters can match. They are warm, lively and humorous. All of that is no consolation to the victims of the stabbings or the shopkeepers putting in new windows or to the London tube drivers planning an unofficial strike next month when United visit QPR. Well this is how I saw their match against the Blades from the Stretford End. Well, "we murdered them", and like my pal Roy kept telling "that fairy Tony Currie", there's only one United. Must admit, I'm not usually a Stretford Ender, but it's the best 65p worth of football I've had for a while, and I can't really understand all this talk of caged animals. There was a bit of spitting at the coppers' backs but if there is any aggro it's down at the Scoreboard End where they let their fans in. The only time we told Sheffield they were "going to get their heads kicked in" was when they scored. And since we'd played them off the park by then, we weren't really serious. But back to my pal: Roy Potts is his name, he's 18 and an apprentice engineer. Met him in the queue going in. He was still a bit mad about being pelted with bricks and bottles by Wolves fans last Saturday.

' "We can get nicked for wearing a scarf and they get away with that," he said. "It's better at home. No trouble and the atmosphere's fantastic." You can get a bit hoarse chanting "Champions", "You'll never walk alone", and "When the Reds go marching in" all afternoon. But we still had the strength to jeer "Currie, Currie what's the score?" near the end. Perhaps we were a bit greedy shouting "We want six" after Gerry and Super Sam had scored a couple more. But at least we stayed on the terraces. Not like one nut who dashed on the field after No. 5. I'd like to think it was him we meant when we were singing "Spot the loony".

'It wasn't though. It was that Tony Currie again.'
– Daily Mail

Stretford Ender Pete from Miles Platting confirms the galloping hoarseness:

'We used to queue to get on the Stretford from late morning. If you weren't in the queue down United

Road by 1.30, you'd be lucky to get in. We'd spend the time between getting in and kick-off singing ourselves stupid, the Left Side trading insults with the Right Side and the Tunnel. By the time the players came out at five to three we'd almost sung ourselves hoarse. I can remember going home after a match and not being able to talk for the rest of the day, my throat was that sore.' – *Pete, Miles Platting*

Pleasant as the Stretford End experience had been for that *Daily Mail* reporter, members of the train drivers' union ASLEF on the London Underground voted to strike on the Central, District and Metropolitan Lines for United's 13 September visit to QPR. Fear of football violence was now spreading beyond the football stadium. British Rail refused to carry the travelling Red Army and the police bill for the match came to £5,000 with 250 policemen on duty, more than double that for any previous fixture at Loftus Road. Not that the shutdown was confined to locomotive transport; bus services operating within a two-mile radius of the ground were also halted. United's supporters club ended up hiring nearly 100 coaches to bring the army down for the 1-0 defeat, which ironically passed off without much incident.

United's next trip to the capital, to take on West Ham, would not pass off as peacefully. We reprint here the thoughts of *Red Issue* on United and their journeys into the East End.

'Nothing enrages more than the media cliché. Tired and emotional hacks who can't be bothered finding the news, the truth or even an original metaphor all too easily dip their gin-soaked hands into the bag of Media Myths, ready to slap on the page and fill another column-inch. Reds know them all too well; the witty sporting Koppite ready with a song and a smile; the eccentric surrealist humorists that are the "true Mancs" on the Kippax; and West Ham as a welcoming, family club, preaching the best traditions of the game in a luvverly East End atmosphere. Stick Trevor Brooking on the Beeb, refer to Saint Bobby Moore every other sentence, show a couple of Alan Devonshire

118

goals and, strike a light, West Ham are the nation's fave Cheeky Cockernee Chappies.

'Any Red attending virtually any Upton Park game since 1967 will find such myth-making a vomit-inducer of the highest order. Admittedly, we have to hold up our bloodied hands as the instigators of this particular vendetta. In May 1967 United travelled to West Ham seeking, as is well known, a win to clinch the title. What is less celebrated is that this day marked the first full-scale Red Army operation in the capital. Previously, all northern clubs had trod warily in London, especially in the docklands where Millwall had already established their fearsome reputation. By 1967, United's travelling forces had swelled to such numbers as to breach the banks caution had imposed; a tidal wave of Red swept through Upton Park, including 500 who'd occupied the North Bank. Aggro both inside and outside the stadium resulted in 20 hospitalizations and banner headlines in the Sunday press: "Soccer's Day Of Shame" blazed the *News Of The Screws*.

'What an epochal day 6 May 1967 turned out to be. It was to be the last title-winning day for us for 26 years; it kick-started the rise of the Red Army; and for West Ham, it was a day of humiliation never to be allowed again. In particular, the lovable dockers retained a fierce animus against the Reds. Not only had we caused their loss of face, much to the delight of the psychos at the Den, but we would always be seen as the most threatening of all the northern hordes who would henceforth be descending on the East End. Later, of course, the ICF and their hangers-on would export their violent parochialism to away games. Long after Reds had ceased going down to West Ham intent on causing trouble, this "family" club continued to treat our visits as a declaration of war.

'In the run up to our game at Upton Park on 25 October 1975, the "Hoolie-Hype" was in full swing. The London press was full of blood-curdling predictions mixed with the usual mock-horror sanctimony. The tabloid press in particular bear more responsibility for soccer-related violence than they would ever admit, of course. The undertone of the coverage was

119

clear: the Red Army were "top of the league" following their exploits in Division Two: they'd shown up London fans at Millwall and Orient; now West Ham could put the northern yobbos in their place on behalf of the capital. The press are always first in the aftermath of violence to yell "String em up" or "Bring back National Service/the birch/summary execution" but fail to recognize how much they'd helped create an atmosphere of conflict in the first place. So it proved to be this time. The press had set up the fight, provided motivation and then exploited the events to a maximum for the benefit of their circulation figures. Pass the sick bag Alice.

'United lost the game 2-1 and were knocked off the top by QPR, but all the headlines were devoted to the riot. Fans arriving in London had been told that the Underground had gone on strike rather than take Reds to West Ham; several hundred had to walk miles to the ground whereupon many found themselves locked out. Moods were not helped when it was learned that the tube had been running after all. Naturally Reds were attacked on the way to the stadium, outside, inside and on the way back to Euston. During the match itself, Reds on the South Bank were assaulted on three sides, forcing thousands on to the pitch and stopping the game for 20 minutes. Stretchers and police were everywhere. The final tally: 102 injured, 9 in hospital, 38 arrests and 132 evictions.

'Predictably the London media had a field day on Sunday. Almost without exception they blamed "United hooligans" for the disruption. It was lazy journalism at its most catatonic. United had the reputation so why look any deeper? If they'd bothered to do so, they'd have found that 70 per cent of the arrests and 90 per cent of the ejections had been Hammers. Even the local police, who have a tendency in these matters to blame the visitors, had to say: "Blame does not appear to solely rest with the United fans." Well, thank you PC Plod. The London edition of the *Sun*, pandering to its audience on Monday, stepped further into the world of the absurd by roaring in its headline: "The day the Terrace Terrors were Hunted and Hammered!" There followed a gleeful account of how West Ham crews had "routed" the Red Army – with not a hint of condemnation. Naturally there was no mention of the fact that the vast majority of Reds had had no intention of kicking-off. The numbers and the terrain made a Red victory unlikely from the start.

'Since that day, not a visit to Upton Park has passed without some form of incident, usually taking the form of isolated Reds being waylaid in true Scouser style by a pack of East Enders. Such episodes rarely reach the pages of the papers, presumably because it contradicts the "salt of the earth East Enders" image so beloved by the West End-dominated media, just as Koppites still get the benefits of their 1960s image enduring in the minds of the nation. The Hammers and their psychopath cousins at Millwall still milk the Second World War vision of blitzed Cockneys, epitomizing the strength and decency of working class England. As we all know, in reality Hammers fans exemplify everything about the modern East End: that it's full of fat, jewellery-laden racist wide-boys who've managed to create one of the ugliest, most hostile environments in urban Europe. Despite the club's efforts to create an atmosphere for "family values", what can actually happen is this: if you're not from the same street, you've an excellent chance of winning a free knife in your belly. Of course, if you're not the same *colour* then don't bother trying for life insurance. The East End welcomes its coloured brethren with the greatest selection of racist graffiti in Britain, often backed up by a personal welcome from your local BNP activist.

'Indeed, of all the disgusting facets of the Hammer, it is the racism that has been the most enduring. Banana sellers can still do good business there on a match day, as Incey recently found out; the Nazi paper *Bulldog* was freely sold around the ground for a decade. Throughout the late seventies, Hammers could be seen proudly wearing West Ham/NF shirts. But hey, the Hammers don't discriminate; they still hate Jews just as much, as any Spurs fan will tell you. This is presumably some weird throw-back to the days when Oswald Moseley stomped around East London in his puffy jodhpurs. Of course casual racism has always existed at footie grounds, Old Trafford included, but only four clubs have managed to elevate football racism to a sort of art form, to a level where it became almost ineradicable – and West Ham are first among that quartet. For this reason above all, let us hope they return with their jazz-funk CDs, crappy souped-up XR3s and chunky bracelets to their natural home that is the Endsleigh Division One.' – *R. Kurt*, Red Issue *1996*

'This was the one game that United got battered at and if anyone tells you any different, they're lying. United were all on the South Bank when one of their stewards opened a side door to the United section and all their boys were just stood at the back for a while. Then they came down and leathered us all over the place. We all jumped on to the pitch and finished up in the Chicken Run. There was no United left in the South Bank after that. We all left the game early and waited for them outside the gates to the South Bank. As they opened the big wooden gates, 500 United piled into them and did to them what they'd done to us. West Ham got a right good hiding. They all thought they'd got a result but we got our revenge in straight away.' – *John, London*

Segregation plus more effective policing and ticketing policies were starting to have an effect on the Red Army as Christmas and New Year came around. Liverpool erected a five-foot metal fence and put segregation zones into their Anfield Road End for the first time at a cost of £8,000. Everton too took the then-unprecedented step of making their match with United all-ticket, allocating a specific 'away end' to the 16,000 United fans. For the first time at English football grounds, segregation was becoming the norm; the lessons of Upton Park were being learnt. Indeed United's fans were starting to come in for faint praise from the most unexpected of sources, with both the Middlesbrough chairman and Cleveland police writing to United to credit the good behaviour of the 5,000 Reds at Ayresome Park on 6 December.

In the FA Cup, after polishing off Oxford, Peterborough

and Leicester, United faced Wolves in a replay at Molineux with a chance to make it to the semis for the first time in six years. As Michael Coughlan remembers elsewhere in this book, that fantastic night was typical of a Cup run marked more by terrace celebration and ecstasy than by aggro. But at Newcastle in the League later that month, there was a return to violence – although once again, the blame appeared to lie mainly with the Geordies. Of the 54 arrests made, the vast majority were from Newcastle. Having said that, there were those amongst the United contingent of 7,000 who were not *totally* blameless:

'The police tried to lock us in but there were just these little gates. So when Newcastle started throwing things United started rocking the gates. Well, there was a loud ping, and a big bolt came off the gates. All of United charged out and ran into 'em, then joined together and ran 'em everywhere.'

Andy Pollard's memories are rather more typical of a particularly 'moody' day out:

'One of the most popular questions fans used to ask each other was which was the most intimidating, violent ground they had visited. If a poll had been conducted back then, no doubt Stamford Bridge, Upton Park, Anfield and Elland Road would all have figured high on the list; but there could have been no doubt among the 7,000 who made the trip to Newcastle that St James' Park was the worst. In those days, the sight of *any* visiting fans at that ground was as rare as a cup in City's trophy room, so much so that there was no visitor's enclosure. Because of United's vast travelling support, a temporary wall was constructed down the middle of the Gallowgate End, the Reds occupying the left side.

'To reach the ground, United fans had to run the gauntlet of large groups of Geordies who had lined every pathway to the stadium. Yours truly got a good kicking in full view of the police who promptly did bugger all. Once inside, those footie-loving Geordies spent the entire game baiting United's vast following, thus missing most of a thrilling though mistake-ridden match. At regular intervals, empty bottles of Newcie Brown were lobbed over from the home section towards which all United fans kept one eye directed. The one moment of light relief came when a flock of seagulls flew over; thinking they were another bottle barrage, thousands of Reds swiftly ducked!

'After the match, the Red Army were kept behind; from the back of the Gallowgate I could see what must have been over 10,000 Geordies waiting for us outside. After an hour the police eventually led us across the pitch and out through the old Leazes End; even then, packs of Geordies were still lurking about and more scuffles broke out. Finally, we did get out of Newcastle but not before every window in virtually every coach was put out.

'Soldiers get medals for fighting in famous battles; I reckon every one of the Red Army who travelled that day should have got one too.' – *Andrew Pollard*

Back in the FA Cup to Sheffield for the semi-final – and portents of the disaster thirteen years later could be seen with overcrowding in the United section leading to some fans sitting on the edge of the perimeter track throughout the game. Whatever the original allocation, United's turn-out was twice that of Derby County with United fans occupying both ends of the ground.

'With a minute to go, McIlroy was on the ball in the left-hand corner of the field when Bruce Rioch came through with a scything "tackle". Even before he connected with Sammy, we could tell he was going to take him out: it was an awful challenge. As Jack Taylor came over to reprimand him, he must have seen the thousands of United fans clambering over the barriers on to the pitch; he promptly blew the whistle and pointed to the tunnel. One United fan came over and booted Rioch up the arse and a few others of us followed up too. I ended up carrying McIlroy back to the dressing rooms with about a dozen other Reds.'

The final game of the season – the postponed derby match

– marked the last ever sanctioned end-of-season pitch invasion, fences going up along all four sides the following summer. The first United fans headed over the barriers with two and a half minutes to go and though the police managed to half clear the pitch, the announcement that the referee had called a finish to the game brought a sea of red and white on to the pitch and into the main stand, from where the Doc and his players took their plaudits.

But before that swansong, United headed for Wembley. Some leading journalists believed United should not have been given any tickets for the end of season showpiece and the *Mirror*'s Frank McGhee caused a storm when he called for the FA to ban United fans completely from the Cup Final:

'A visit by Manchester United to any town, any city in this country should be an occasion for joy. Nowadays it isn't. Don't kid yourselves about that. Publicans, shopkeepers and cafe owners who ten or twenty years ago would have been rubbing their hands together in anticipation of their profits nowadays tend to close their doors, board up windows, opt for a day off. Extra police are drafted in for overtime duty and parents who care about the physical safety of the young fans in their family go somewhere else. That is one of the thoughts which prompted me to suggest that the more difficult it was made for Manchester United fans to get tickets for next week's Cup Final, the better.'
– Frank McGhee, Daily Mirror

In a season during which the behaviour of the United fans was acknowledged to have been a great improvement on 1974/75, chairman Louis Edwards was quick to spring to the defence of his supporters. With an average gate of over 54,000, United's main problem was the allocation of only 25,000 tickets. An estimated 10,000 were expected to make the journey without tickets, with touts demanding and getting £40 for £2.50 stand tickets. George from Collyhurst was luckier than most:

'I was working at Edwards's the butchers; everyone in the company got two tickets, and I went to the game

125

with Wills. He hadn't got a ticket for the game, so when I turned up on the Friday before the game with a ticket for him, he was in tears. We went on an over-night trip with Dave Smith's supporters' club; he was running two coaches, one with sensible lads on it, the other with all the nutters like myself. When we got to London, he'd booked us into a different hotel from the others round the corner from the FA at Lancaster Gate. We got into our room and we must have been given the wrong key because it was obviously occupied – by some Canadians judging by the stickers on their lug-gage. On the bed was one of the earliest video camera so we all stripped off and made a blue movie. All the lads took their clothes off and started doing daft things, mooning and the like. We put everything back neatly, realizing that if we robbed anything the front door staff would know who'd done it. It's always tickled me to think of those Canadians getting back to Toronto or Vancouver or wherever, and there amongst the pictures of Trafalgar Square and the Houses Of Parliament are half a dozen naked Mancunians waggling their dicks at the viewer.' – *George, Collyhurst*

Despite the Final defeat, which passed virtually without trouble, the Red Army was determined not to let the season pass without further celebration, pornographic or other-wise. The following day, 20,000 fans packed into Albert Square with estimates of several hundred thousand more lining the route to the centre of Manchester. Tommy Docherty appeared on the balcony of the Town Hall and proclaimed 'We'll be back' – and so would the Red Army.

1976–77

In those last pre-handbagging years that witnessed the collapse of Butskellism, Britain was still the most resolute of patriarchies. Macho flying pickets battled burly moustachioed coppers with not a miner's wife nor WPC in sight. Feminists disrupting Bob Hope during Miss World produced outrage rather than empathy. Angela Rippon and Mrs Thatcher were thought to be tokenistic rule-proving exceptions in their respective worlds. When the former flashed her bikini-line on the *Morecambe & Wise Show* – not something you'd imagine Kate Adie doing – chaps' smirking nationwide didn't require much translation. This was still, obviously, a bloke's world.

In such an environment, the image to which every public figure aspired was avuncular. Uncle Jim presided over our national decline from Number Ten, personally popular until the end; Uncle Denis Howell, Drought Minister throughout that absurdly hot summer, was the Brummie version of Jim except you could actually trust him to get things done. Later, when the Red Army rampaged across East Anglia in search of blood rather than water, it would be Denis to whom a terrified nation would turn for help. And at Old Trafford, we had Uncle Tommy. Too much of a rogue to be your dad, clearly, but a man who brought the feelgood factor to everything he touched. Every family has an Uncle Tommy at Christmas, the one who'll crack the filthy jokes during the Queen's Speech and smuggle sly sherries to the kids. Sadly, the age of these bouncing, cheery middle-aged geezers was coming to an end – and Docherty would be the first to go, under circumstances that made him appear more like the twisted uncle played by

Keith Moon in *Tommy* itself. A harsher age approached, peopled by slim, grim assassins such as Keith Joseph, Norman Tebbit and football's monetarist equivalent, Dave Sexton. But what a last hurrah – one final vaudevillian season, full of slapstick, passion, naughtiness and drama.

All right, I don't suppose the good burghers of Amsterdam would've used the adjective 'naughty' to describe Red behaviour there pre-season. If that trip to AZ Alkmaar, Nuremberg and SV Hamburg had been a fact-finding mission for the club, then several discoveries were indeed made in advance of the UEFA Cup campaign: continental police alsatians have a bite worse than their bark; Brit squaddies based in Germany need no encouragement from Mancunian tourists to batter local youths; chucking plastic bottles in the Olympic Stadium is more fun when they've just been used for urinary relief. The club also picked up a handy tip: blame everything on 'independent' fans and claim the 'officials' were faultless. (That this may well have been true at the time hardly justified years of enforced travel monopoly two decades on.) The Amsterdam police chief, surveying the scene, admitted that he was 'quivering in fear' at the prospect of United coming to Ajax in September; this wasn't taken to be a reference to Colin Waldron's 'prowess' at the back . . .

There was to be more August quivering in the British Midlands. The last time Brum's Archie Styles had been seen at OT was whilst being hauled off for a Care in the Community consultation. Returning rehabilitated, he opened our first game with a cracker into Stepney's goal. The hundred or so Birmingham fans who'd braved Old Trafford's 59,000 quickly decoded the crowd's response to their knock-kneed cheer and were never heard from again. Two-two at half-time, the familiar Brum steel curtain descended; the only Red who ever looked like piercing the defence was new-boy sub Alan Foggon. Now there's a sentence you'll never see again. Foggon truly made an instant impact – one look at him and we stuck him on a train to Sunderland.

Fifteen thousand Reds descending upon Highfield Road on a Wednesday night put more than the shakes into Sky Blues; 10,000 of them simply didn't turn up, sending an added frisson of horror through the division's chairmen.

Bad enough having the Red Army turn up at your gaff, Party Sevens under arm, without losing the one consolation – bonanza paydays. On a balmy, sultry night, United coasted home 2-0 and thoroughly enjoyed the red card shown to notorious beast Larry Lloyd for his savaging of Pancho. As if it were not warm enough already, Reds set alight much of the foliage behind their end, this perhaps an unforeseen psychological side-effect of the drought.

That the mother and father of all battles would surely follow on Saturday at the Baseball Ground was blindingly obvious, despite which unsegregated spares were sold to Reds on the day. Five thousand Derby fans had bottled out but many of the remnants seemed intent on securing some sort of vengeance for their Hillsborough humiliation. Lost amidst the acreage of hoolie headlines was a very good match. Few missed the significance of the appalling refereeing, however; Daly's tremendous 78th-minute 'goal', disallowed for non-interfering offside players, hardly improved Red tempers. Nor did Roy McFarland's treatment of Pearson, the like of which you simply do not see these days – he would've lasted precisely 60 seconds under David Elleray. Notwithstanding the wretchedness of officialdom that day, it should be noted that referees were largely superior in the seventies, certainly in comparison to the martinets, totalitarians and blatant incompetents who've wheedled their way on to the Premiership list. They whinge about scrutiny by TV today but one appalling decision in the seventies and your hapless ref could be responsible for hours of rioting. Must have concentrated the mind somewhat, don't you think?

The clarion calls of 'Bring Back The Birch' and 'Call In The SAS' echoed over the days to come, with Uncle Howell once again the focus for entreaties to 'do something'. Any solution – bar water cannons, of course – would have been accepted in this fevered atmosphere. One look at the forthcoming away fixtures stiffened the sinews: Newcastle, Ajax, City and Leeds – a veritable knuckleduster's delight. Somehow, the Red Army escaped from the encircling forces; there'd be 6,000 at St James', 7,000 in Holland, 12,000 at Leeds and untold thousands at Maine Road. These are forces of the side deployed in the Civil War and in most of our pre-Elizabethan French campaigns.

Just how could anyone stop them anyway?

Laura Norder had a few days respite before all that. Tranmere held out for almost an hour in the League Cup before taking a five-goal pasting, a smart McIlroy–Coppell tactical switch unlocking Steve's old club. Spurs came, with no support whatsoever, to face Old Trafford's highest gate of the season – 60,723. Logic-defying stupidity and enormous entertainment ensued, as once was the right of a United–Spurs spectator to expect. At 3.45, with United two-up and rampant, a pressbox hack turned to another who was busily dictating the brilliance of Coppell's goal and slavered: 'This is the best I've seen since the Babes.' By quarter-to-five, United were three-two down and beaten. No one in the stadium could quite believe what they'd seen nor explain how it happened. A case for Michael Aspel's *Strange But True*: 'Tonight, a real game of two halves, Brian . . .'

Heaven played more tricks at Newcastle, of a rather more prosaic kind. Six thousand Reds stuffed into the open-air Gallowgate received as much of a pummelling as they had in 1975–76, but by monsoonian drenching rather than bricks. A paper noted the 'inclement weather affected the football', an understatement on a par with 'the space shuttle has malfunctioned'. Lou Macari, ever one to have the fans' interests at heart, later marvelled at how the Reds had stuck out the Tyneside Twister. (To be honest, there wasn't much choice, given the warm welcome the Geordies had prepared outside.) Admirably, the teams contrived to produce four goals between them to set Reds on their way to the subsequent city centre battleground. 'Footballers aren't fairies,' snorted the Doc when asked how the teams had coped: neither were the fans that afternoon.

As United's boys staggered back to Manc, or on to Amsterdam via the northern ferries, one Red hero was beginning his journey in the opposite direction. The previous Monday, Jim Holton had played his last game for United reserves against Huddersfield; Docherty then sold him to Sunderland. Within the month, Tommy would have some small cause to regret at least the timing of the move, if not the fact; in truth, Jim was never quite the same player he once had been. In some ways, United were lucky – necessity had mothered the invention of the celebrated

Buchan–Greenhoff partnership. Still, there are those who'll tell you that Jim and Martin together could have been unbeatable, giving us the added aerial strength that champions need. Whatever the hypotheses, the sadness remains that the Holton–Strettie love affair burned so briefly.

Admittedly, Ajax were probably not the sort of opposition Big Jim would have relished. Smart, lithe, quick to break and assuredly ground-bound, the fact that they were in transition didn't detract from the chest-swelling glamour and swagger of this tie. How to put this into perspective? Bear in mind Ajax had completed a Euro Cup hat-trick only three years before and constituted the ultimate in club football ideals – as a young Eric Cantona then appreciated – and that United had not played competitively in Europe since the spring of 1969. Imagine the buzz if we'd pulled AC Milan out of the hat back on our last Euro-return in 1990, then double it: that would be a fair approximation of the excitement engendered. Sure, City had pulled Juventus, but in '76 Ajax were the purplest of plums. And so, despite Manchester's economic depression and our supporters' relative impoverishment – and in spite of the pound going down Denis Healey's toilet faster than you could say 'IMF' – over seven thousand still found the means to get to the Olympisch Stadion. There, surrounded by fencing, spikes, foam-mouthed hounds and fomenting police, they witnessed a United performance that instilled only pride and respect. (Younger readers brought up on Nou Camp and delle Alpi must use their imagination.) We lost one-nil, to a fine goal that even some Reds applauded, but as Tommy Docherty taunted his opposite number: 'That won't be enough, pal.' Lou Macari had hit a post, Houston had a goal incorrectly disallowed for not crossing the line and Pearson was cruelly denied by a desperate goal-line clearance. To think that barely three years before, they had been conquering Europe whilst we faced relegation. Ajax may have been quivering with fear at the sight of our fans; now their fear would be facing our football at Old Trafford.

From the sublime to the ridiculous in 72 hours: Jack Charlton's Middlesbrough greeted us on our return to Manchester. The majesty of evolution displayed for all – Ajax's art at one end of the spectrum, Charlton's clogging packhorse chumpery at the other. I apologize for offending

Irish readers on two counts, but has anyone ever seen born a Charlton team that society would not have been better off aborting? They hacked, we fell: forty fouls and a deserved 2-0 defeat later, Charlton's players suggested Reds had 'over-reacted'. Much in the same way that a shot Reagan over-reacted by falling over a bit, I suppose. ('Stand up straight, canny lad, it's only a bullet in the brain.')

So it was twenty years ago; no reason to bear a grudge you might think. But here's our Oliver Stone theory: Jack Charlton's team's bastardry cost us the double in '77. (Introduce fast-edits, fancy camera-angles and swallowed dialogue to hide flaws here.) Coppell, Macari, Pearson and Greenhoff all came off with bad knocks. Macari and Pearson consequently started to struggle over the next month, Pancho missing a couple of games as he aggravated injuries whilst Macari lost form, both contributing to our forthcoming black October and November. More pressingly, Coppell had to miss the League Cup tie against Sunderland four days later. Gordon Hill gave away a goal after six minutes, was roasted by fans and players alike and duly disappeared for the rest of the match. Without both wingers, United were lucky to escape with a 2-2 draw, thanks to an 87th-minute own goal. Two draining replays were needed in October and took their toll, tiring our players who began to wilt in the weeks that followed. As we shall see, the consequences for our putative title challenge were lethal. So they can take their national hero Jolly Jack with his Guinness, Shredded Wheat and Revie-inspired hack-sides and insert them where the salmon don't leap.

All that misery – which included the Return of Paddy, horror-fans – lay unseen just around the corner. Typically, it would follow the best seven days of the season – outstanding matches at City and Leeds, with the Ajax return sandwiched in between. On the eve of the Ajax match, the pound collapsed: Denis Healey made his infamous retreat from the airport to Conference, the IMF arrived to stamp on the working class after bailing out the Treasury and Britain entered a period of acute, sustained, national embarrassment. Whilst the rest of the nation cowered in dishonour and penury, Red Mancunians fervently celebrated one of the best weeks in memory. What a shameless contrast! (By December, one savage Healey mini-budget later and with

United in 17th place, we would be back in miserable synch with the national psyche.)

That Maine Road derby must rank in the all-time top five, surely. To be a goal down in seven minutes, to lose Pancho after 13 yet still run out 3-1 victors after a game of pulsating blood-rushes was as delicious as Blue-roasting can get. Gordon Hill, cavorting past our section of the Kippax in ecstasy after laying on a killer strike, would be echoes by Giggs two decades later. Another theme later reprised in the '96 FA Cup tie – the malicious delight in seeing City's 'equalizer' disallowed after Buchan hacked the ball away from behind the goal-line, as Bitter-baiting as Eric's dodgy penalty. Months later we would realize that had City won this match, the title would've been theirs. Isn't football marvellous?

To top that buzz would be akin to following good coke with great crack: 59,000 at their Old Trafford best and an inspired tactical switch made it happen, burning up Ajax four days later. Those who were there will swear to you the atmosphere that night matched Barca '84 for intensity and volume. You won't be able to tell from the videotape of the match, of course. In those days, they would turn mikes away from the crowd and reduce the levels, presumably to safeguard delicate equipment and lesson the impact of 120 decibel swear-chants blasting into living rooms. Now they have fifty mikes keening towards the passive crowds, picking up every fart and burger-munch. Yet still nothing is produced to match the incredible rumble of the Old Trafford crowd rattling your telly speakers to buggery every time a Red shirt approached the Ajax box.

Pearson was injured and out; Macari chose to play whilst slightly crocked. The Dutch, featuring the acme of cultured footie Rudi Krol and the Socratean dead-ringer Hulshoff, played on the break and frankly looked like scoring the deadly away-goal every time they got forward. Fortunately, United's perpetual onslaught ensured that such chances were rare – and Stepney was at his '68 Eusebian best when they did come. How pleasing a contrast for every stereotype-lover that his opposite number 'Punchy Pete' Shrievers looked anything but the best. In classic sniffy continental style, he refused to hold the ball at any point, left- and right-hooking all over the shop with a vigour that would worry Frank Bruno. Naturally, when Hill's blaster just before half-time had to be held, he spilled it girlishly into Macari's path for 1-0. For the first time since Poland '73, we could afford to laugh at a funny foreign keeper.

Young readers, and possibly Alex Ferguson, will now be amazed to discover evidence of a cunning United tactical ploy in Europe that actually worked, an occurrence so rare it became dubbed the 'Ajax Plan'. The Doc pushed Arthur Albiston on for Daly, switched Houston to roving centre-half and thrust Brian Greenhoff forward. Ajax took ten minutes to work out where the hell everyone had gone, by which time we were two up. Greenhoff himself material-ized in the Strettie box as green shirts spun round franti-cally looking for non-existent markers; beating the faltering offside trap, he teed up Supersam for his criminally over-due first goal of the season. Sweet Stretford Bedlam. The rejigged back-line held on comfortably for victory – by the final whistle, we were looking for a third. Once again, Docherty and his boys had restitched a lost badge of honour to our colours – the 'Pride of All Europe', for one night at least. City had lost, naturally: their conquerors Juventus would be our next opponents.

Any suggestion of a post-European anticlimax lasted a matter of minutes at Saturday's Elland Road. We were not to be deflected, no matter how many boulders the sheep dropped on our coaches from motorway bridges. (Space Invaders had not yet arrived in Yorkshire, so this and burning crosses constituted youth entertainment.) By ten past three, United were two up through Coppell and Daly, the latter's luscious volley being particularly fantastic. What a never-ending nightmare United's top-flight return had proved to be for Leeds – worse was yet to come in spring. For much of the next 80 minutes, Leeds' fightback seemed from the stands to consist of studs-up assaults and general thuggery, intermingled with some cheeky United piss-taking. Pearson and Macari especially were taken out as efficiently as if in a scene from *Goodfellas* – they would miss the League Cup replay at Roker Park. Norman Hunter, in now traditional fashion, spent the latter stages being humiliated, then booked and taken off, a continuing sym-bol of Leeds United's death as a force in football. Docherty, points in pocket and top of the table, contented himself with some succinct post-match repartee about Leeds' animalistic stupidity. There were no need to over-emphasize what was obvious to the nation. They could have closed that club down and no one outside Leeds would've given a shit.

From zenith to nadir in thirteen unlucky steps, thirteen games to a grotesque League Cup knock-out and a position too close to the relegation trap-door for comfort. We were about to discover that we had a Bryan Robson in the team, a man whom we simply could not do without – Martin Buchan. All right, we had more problems than just his injury – sustained playing for bloody Scotland, natch – but Buchan's absence took on a totemic quality. No combination of Waldron, Paterson, Houston or Clark could fill the vacuum Martin left: three or more goals were conceded six times before Christmas. Brian Greenhoff took the captaincy but with all due respect, as the Yanks cried in '45, who could replace Patton?

The exhausting dénouement of the struggle with Sunderland already had us staggering. Two-all after extra-time at Roker, complete with last-minute equalizers and goal-line clearances, meant another battle only 48 hours later, eventually settled thanks to the resuscitated Ajax Plan and a one-two played with McIlroy's face. Unfortunately, Sam was one of our growing problems: to play up front and still not be on the League scoresheet by November required remedial action. Jimmy Nicholl, newly established at right-back, had his own dedicated boo-boy section inside the Strettie; Macari began to struggle as general confidence sapped away. Front and back pages carried variations on a theme – which would plunge faster, the Labour Government's tottering majority or United's League position? Out went the call for Messiahs: Labour, eventually, would be rescued by a Berwick Liberal in nasty two-colour shirts. We were to find our salvation much closer to the family home.

The worst was over first, at least. Being shat upon four-nil at a Giles-inspired West Brom was, said Docherty, 'the worst we've ever played'. What a moment to find every pub within three miles closed. Two-nil up at home to Norwich, we were eventually lucky to get a draw. Ipswich and West Ham both came to Old Trafford in order, frankly, to show us up and the 9,000 Reds at Leicester knew we'd robbed a point quite Scouseishly. Even when 3-1 up against Sunderland, with Hill sparkling and Brian Greenhoff marauding up front, we still contrived to let a point go. Paddy Roche was back, so no surprise in the next sentence from every match report: 'The goalkeeper was badly at fault for Sunderland's second . . .' Debutant Clark came on as sub, fucked up and allowed Alan Foggon of all people to set up the third. Fans who'd been at Villa Park and the Stadio Communale earlier in the week had now seen nine goals fly into our net in seven days.

Ah, Juventus: more continental clichés brought wonderfully to life. Hill's goal had beaten them at Old Trafford but, just as they had intended at Maine Road, Juventus had come for a 0-1 from the off. Appallingly dull blanket defence matched by a sly, bollock-scrunching, hair-pulling dirtiness had been their archetypal means to an end. Suddenly, Leeds looked quite cuddly in comparison. And there was no sense of irony in the Stretford End's hardier element chanting 'Animals!' at the Italians. Blimey, at least United fought fair. In Turin, it turned into men against boys, literally true given United's average age was less than our '96 side. Juve didn't score their second until well past the hour and only gained immunity from a possible away goal with five to go but no one could argue that the brilliance of Boninsegna and Benetti didn't deserve the tie. Tardelli, however, remained in everyone's mind the ultimate Italian psycho – a player who could start a riot in an empty stadium. This Juve side went on to win the UEFA Cup and provided more than half of the 1982 World Cup winning team – there'd been no shame in defeat, aggravating though it was to have smug City fans saying, 'We told you so.'

Just as a dying man has moments of bouncy lucidity, we'd enjoyed one great moment during this descent: a 7-2 League Cup thrashing of Newcastle, garlanded by a Hill hat-trick and a scarcely credible Nicholl dream-goal which helped bring him out of his terrace-induced misery. As there had never been so many Geordies inside OT before, what timing to remind them of their eternal inferiority. The first hot rash of Wembley Fever was not to live through that cold December, however. A quite devastating 3-0 home defeat by Everton appeared to bring us to absolute zero.

Without Buchan, Coppell, Houston or Macari, it was perhaps inevitable. Blood flowed freely in the Scoreboard End that night – the season had truly turned ugly.

What better time, then, for our most handsome and intelligent players – Jimmy Greenhoff and Martin Buchan – to ride to the rescue? Jimmy had actually signed in mid-November and already played against Leicester and West Ham, feeling his way in as low-key a manner as possible; this was not quite a Cantonesque impact. But the second great change of the Docherty era was at hand. By New Year's Eve, the classic 4-2-4 Mark II line-up would be in place. Gerry Daly's stinker against West Ham, combined with McIlroy's lack of goals upfront, had combined to settle Docherty's mind. What taste, luck and hard-headed judgement he displayed in adding precisely the right extra ingredient at such a critical juncture. However much one's view of Docherty has been coloured by his erratic behaviour recently, one must admit that each of his last five major purchases – Pearson, Houston, Coppell, Hill and Jimmy Greenhoff – was superbly timed, perfectly chosen and the resultant team adaptations remarkably well effected. Docherty has always argued that given another twelve months, he could have finished the job and made us champions. On such a roll of winning deals and team-shaping, who would dare doubt it?

McIlroy moved back into midfield, taking Gerry Daly's Number 4 shirt; Greenhoff J. slipped beautifully into the Number 8 inside-forward role. Subtle changes in playing relationships sparked across the forward section of the team, rejuvenating United for the New Year – politically, the ideal Cabinet reshuffle. Sadly, the Norman Lamont figure had to be Gerry Daly, who would soon fulfil the LBJ maxim about pissing on the tent from outside. Winning elections or cups is never without its victims.

Rebirth of a sort began at Highbury just before Christmas. We lost, as we always did – Coppell's injury perhaps the difference between the two sides – but few missed the signs of renewed fight and vigour. McIlroy, revelling in a new midfield freedom, celebrated with an outrageous goal, jinking past five Gooners in unearthly premonition of Wembley '79. We might have been losing 3-1 but the last minutes were filled with the sound of United songs – they knew what they'd seen. St Stephen's Day against Everton put the nation on notice that United were back – and better. For the first time, the Mark II line-up took the field: Stepney; Nicholl, Houston, Greenhoff B., Buchan; McIlroy, Macari, Coppell, Greenhoff J., Pearson, Hill; sub McCreery. You know it off by heart, don't you? Jimmy Greenhoff scored his first Red goal, United thrashed the Scousers 4-0 to dispel the memories of three weeks before and 57,000 looked forward to 1977 with rather more than a mere Jubilee in mind. God Save The Queen? God Save King Jimmy, surely.

'Whoa-oh, United are back, United are back, whoa-oh . . .' resounds around the beaten Aston Villa heads on New Year's Day, 1977. Now there's a chant you simply never hear at Old Trafford these days, unless you replace 'United' with 'City' and infest with heavy irony. If one state of terrace mind marked the seventies, it was that we seemed to be in a perpetual state of bounce-back: promotion following relegation, cup winners replacing runners-up, god-awful slumps transforming into tremendous runs. Nineties-style smugness and complacency had no place at United then. I'm writing this days after United have beaten Spurs 2-0 at OT, on an afternoon where the atmosphere reached an absolute all-time low. There will be great days and nights ahead at Old Trafford, of that I'm sure, but for much of the year we are condemned to pay the price of our sustained success. That is to go to Old Trafford expecting and demanding convincing victory – and, unless the opposition happens to be Leeds, 'Pool or the Toons, not getting particularly over-excited when the team duly delivers. Drama depends on the possibility of the unexpected and the emotional response which results: ironically, just at the moment when OT is physically at its most theatrical, it is largely bearing witness to the predictable competence of pre-recorded television. Perverse though it is to bemoan the by-products of today's routine excellence, the fact remains that OT's audiences have reacted in line with this metaphor. Where once our crowd behaved like seventeenth-century Globe-goers, robustly participating in and thus shaping a dramatic Shakespearian event, we now have a largely passive TV-style spectatorship, druggily hooked on a succession of seamless 90-minute productions.

In the seventies, no such comfortable security existed. Every trip to Old Trafford meant a step into the unknown. On 1 January 1977, for example, we'd just endured three months of cataclysm. We were about to enjoy three months virtually unbeaten but you had to be prepared for the possibility that shite could succeed sensation at any moment. More than that: Reds at games felt and truly believed that their vocal efforts would help script and direct the drama they had paid to see. A live event is defined, after all, by the interaction and even symbiosis between spectators and actors – in a sense, we are all participants. Sometimes, these days, you are entitled to wonder whether certain home fixtures can really be classed as true live dramas. When three-quarters of the audience appears to be dead and the routine superiority of the team remains entirely undramatic, who can blame you for hankering after those adrenalined afternoons of a pre-Thatcherite youth?

Macari and Buchan had been outstanding in the 2-0 win over Villa, the latter reducing Player of the Year Andy Gray and his vibrant skin complaints to the role of spectator. Tellingly, McIlroy had justified his place in the Mark II line-up at Daly's expense, equalling Macari for ankle-snapping busyness. Defeat at high-flying Ipswich would be the winter's last, to aggravatingly late goals; still, critics conceded that had Hill's scorcher not been criminally disallowed, we'd have walked it. Even when as dogturdishly bad as we were for Walsall's Cup visit, there'd still be a diamond to admire amidst the ordure, the flowing pitch-length move that produced Hill's winner as good as any that season.

Efficient, low-key wins against Coventry, Bristol City and Brum followed, St Andrews being particularly sweet for the 15,000 travelling Reds who'd not seen an away win since October. Granted, the football world was hardly spurting over us as of yore just yet. But all the ingredients were settling back into the mix. Lou's double against Coventry marked his complete recovery; Martin Buchan's earclipping of Hill demonstrated that our returning leader's velvet touch still concealed an iron fist; and the genuine warmth that greeted Jimmy G's first away goal spoke of an idol in the making. And if an iced-rock pitch reduced our Cup tie with QPR to farce, there was not a trace of Brian Rix in the superb move that created Lou's winner. United, undoubtedly, were getting it together once more.

By the end of February, the rest of Britain had taken due notice. A hat-trick of 3-1 victories sent us soaring up the table – in a title race that would be won with only 57 points, United were soon to be spoken of as contenders again. If we had laboured somewhat to beat Derby, then there would be nothing so horny-handed about the win at White Hart Lane: 'United are the best we've seen here,' marvelled Keith Burkinshaw, the brilliant ball-juggling of Macari and thumping power of Hill still brightly fresh in every spectator's vision. Better still was the crowning of Jimmy Greenhoff against Newcastle a week later, his hat-trick banishing memories of an archetypally dull 0-0 shut-out from Liverpool mid-week. 'Greenhoff for England', roared by the Stretford End at full-time, now signified Jimmy rather than Brian; that Mariner and Channon con-tinued to get the national nod tells you all you need to know about England '77.

The final terrace chorus that afternoon, however, had been a most heartfelt 'We're gonna win the Cup'. Wembley Fever in February? A round earlier than usual, admittedly, but then our opponents were to be Southampton at The Dell. A chance for our favourite dish: Revenge à la Rouge, served cold. The historic joy of following United is that we always seem to get the opportunity to bury the bastards who've done us wrong whilst the memory is still fresh enough to grate. Drawing the Saints drove the FA Cup to the top of our agenda – what more significant pairing could there be to illustrate the sense of mission every Red felt this Cup season engendered? If you're looking to regain lost honour, what better than to collect the scalp of those who once dishonoured you in the process? Two matches of unrelenting entertainment, intermingled with vicious bit-terness, ensued. Blood-boiling frenzy for the 7,000 Reds who beat the lock-out at The Dell: twice ahead, twice pegged back, then backs-to-the-wall skirmishing after Jimmy went down injured. United escaped; the Saints fans and local plod weren't so lucky as a ten-minute pitch invasion and all-in battle greeted the final whistle.

Ten days later, the Saints discovered the concept of karmic payback. One-down since the fifth minute and being completely outplayed, Saints grinned gormlessly as the outstanding Buchan was outrageously deemed to have committed a penalty offence just before the break by the loathsome Clive Thomas. As United battled throughout the second half to regain their rightful advantage, Jim Steele waged his own personal war with Jimmy Greenhoff to the increasing howling anger of the Stretford End. Such poetry, then, within a two-minute spell as Jimmy scored his second and Steele received a red card. This time there would be no offside winners, no cavorting collection of ugly cast-offs revelling in underdog sensationalism. And when Docherty picked Jimmy up off the floor in a loved-up bear hug, he acted for us all. Honour restored: and now Wembley was just three hours away . . .

If the ideal sausage sandwich is beating the meat between Misses Anderson and Zeta-Jones, then stuffing the Saints in between Saturday triumphs over City and Leeds must run it close. Watched by 60,612 – including 1,200 brown-trousered Tykes – United shagged the Sheep without even bothering to fire all cylinders. As for City, their much-vaunted and blatantly imitative 4-2-4 was abandoned for the visit to OT; we kept the faith and won 3-1, Stevie Coppell's soaring drive into the Strettie goal as unforgettable as any derby goal one could nominate. To see Jimmy Greenhoff constantly bamboozle Mike Doyle through sheer intelligence and cunning was delicious, while Macari's dominance of midfield was almost an embarrassment. City's title challenge, as the press honestly noted, had been exposed for what it was – a statistical anomaly.

By the time Aston Villa, League Cup Finalists, came to United for the FA Cup quarter-final, there was an irresistibility about us that seduced every observer. But Brian Little's stunning early goal coupled with Brian Greenhoff's injury left us on the precipice. Live, raw, unpredictable drama, with 57,000 extras. Houston's free-kick levelled on 25 but with Hill 'n' Coppell at their most idiosyncratic and Villa full of bloody-minded fight, an hour of classic cup conflict unfolded. Macari's sizzling drive after 77 minutes was enough to save us from a doom-laden replay.

March had been an unmitigated triumph for United, now joint third in the League and through to a Hillsborough semi, but not for Gerry Daly; Paul Collier carries a torch for a victim of our success:

'March 3rd 1977 is not a date which will instantly spring from the memory for members of Doc's Red Army, but for me it was a day of stunned disbelief and total heartbreak. Along with legions of fellow Reds, I will never forget Brian Greenhoff's tears as he trudged from the Wembley pitch after the Southampton Cup Final defeat of 1976 but this terrible news ten months on was, for me, on a par with the Saints defeat. "Gerry Daly has been sold to Derby County for a bargain £175,000." When I heard the news I was numb. It was beyond belief that the genial genius Irishman had gone from centre-stage to join the Baseball Ground Rams.

'One month previously I had stood and watched Gerard Anthony Daly on what turned out to be his farewell appearance in a United shirt, after being recalled to first team action following differences of opinion with Tommy Doc. Rumours had been rife that afternoon during the 3-1 defeat of Derby County that Daly was on his way out of Old Trafford and yet I hoped beyond hope that such a situation would never arise. Devastation, however, lay only 25 days away.

'His silky skills, neat passing and fierce shot had become an integral part of the resurgent Reds after the total decline of the early 1970s. The Irishman appeared lightweight but he was a true terrace hero. His ability to score penalties – he converted 16 goals from 17 attempts – was legendary. But I can even remember the one he missed against West Bromwich Albion in October 1976; I can still see John Osborne saving my hero's spot-kick. To make matters worse, we got mauled 4-0 that afternoon. When United beat the Moss Side Mob 3-1 two days after Daly's departure, I couldn't help but feel that he should still have been on the Old Trafford stage that afternoon as part of the United engine room. Instead, Gerry was to make his Rams debut soon after against mighty Coventry City in front of just 22,808 spectators.

'The reason for Gerry Daly's departure never became totally clear. Disagreements with the Doc certainly hastened his departure. When Derby sacked manager Murphy, they replaced him with Docherty; subsequently stories circulated that the Doc and Daly would be on collision course and a move back to Old Trafford for the midfield maestro could well be on the cards. My hopes were built up, then dashed as manager and player patched up their differences.

'Watching United with Daly was an honour; watching them without him was still a pleasure yet I could not help but feel us Reds were subsequently deprived, never to see Daly's talents in a United shirt again. The Eire international continued to ply his trade with lesser clubs and at one point even caused me to hit the panic button when he almost joined Leeds United in 1978 during Jock Stein's brief reign. I'm not sure even I could have forgiven Gerry Daly if such a move had come to fruition . . .' – *Paul Collier*

'April 'tis the cruellest month', wrote T. S. Eliot, I think: or perhaps a Norwich fan surveying the state of Carrow Road after the Red Army's visit on 2 April. What had the East Anglians done to warrant such Visigothian devastation, apart from the fact that their team had just ended our three-month unbeaten run? If March had been marked by United title-talk on the back pages, then April saw our return to the front covers – and, incidentally, the end of our League hopes. Apparently, the Red Army was now a cause for national mobilization. You could tell this was so by the reappearance of 'General' Denis Howell, supremo of the establishment defence forces. In place of water tankers and hosepipe patrols now came all-ticket restrictions and blanket policing. When Parliament is forced into emergency session to discuss United's fans, you know things may have progressed a tad too far.

For the next few weeks, the media's only talking point would be apocalyptic speculation as to what United's legions might do next – a proper away fan ban couldn't be achieved until 7 May at Bristol. The citizens of Sunderland, Middlesbrough, Sheffield and Shepherd's Bush quaked behind boarded-up windows as the tabloids curdled their blood with forecasts of doom: 'Two million Reds are coming to shag your pets and dissect your daughters,' etc., etc. Public transport workers, never slow when finding an excuse to strike in the seventies anyway, enjoyed the bonus holidays as they cut every bus they could on matchdays. Meanwhile, Reds faced several weeks of trudging about foreign estates on the way to watching some pretty half-hearted and half-arsed League footie: the obsession with the FA Cup became all-pervasive.

Admittedly, United produced a last League hurrah in the week after the 'Rape of Norwich' (*Daily Express*). A Hill double did for Everton at Goodison; the 38 Red coaches that received free bricks through the windows from generous scallies garnered scarcely a mention in the press, of course. Mustn't confuse the readers with life's grey areas, must we? Three superb goals beat Stoke on the Saturday at Old Trafford before the team virtually shut down and switched to auto-pilot. We won just two of our last ten League games: a 3-2 knockabout with Arsenal, and a last-gasp Macari dancing special beating QPR. Here were eleven anxious guys playing well within themselves, desperate not to get injured or suspended, worried lest the legs gave way before the end of May. After the trauma of '76, who could blame them? Any sign of a knock and off they came: Buchan, Hill, Brian Greenhoff and Pancho all missed games which, in other circumstances, they might just have endured. So, at times, it became ridiculous: we were hammered at Ayresome and Loftus Road, our central defenders stepping aside like golfers to say, 'Would you care to play through, Mr Francis?', midfielders tiptoeing around like waltzers on a first date. My guesstimate is that we dropped eleven points in those last two months which, without the Cup distraction, we would've won: we'd thus have finished champions on 59 points. Again, Docherty was right – with a final tinker or two, this was a potential title team throughout '75–'77.

For all that care and concern, disaster still struck. In a battle at Ashton Gate of all places, McIlroy got sent off and Stewart Houston broke an ankle; there were further horrendous scares over Buchan and Hill. Every minor outbreak of flu seemed like an ebola epidemic, every bruise a potential haemorrhage. Nowadays, this seems rather hypersensitive, so accustomed are we to challenging on all fronts with a mighty squad. But in '77 we had about twelve and a half good players, counting little McCreery as the half-pint, and faced eleven games in one five-week period; to be able to put out two decent teams for the Cup semi and final would be a major achievement. Consider, for example, the result of any injury to Stepney: Paddy Roche in goal at Wembley. *Apocalypse Now* or what? (Paddy actually played the last League game at Upton Park – he conceded four goals, reliably consistent to the end . . .)

Hillsborough, Sheffield, 23 April. United were at full-strength – in every sense of the word. How much significance and historical clout can be ladled into one match? Here was a fixture, Leeds versus United, that could not be over-hyped. If *Red Issue* had existed in 1977, let there be no doubt that their annual 'Most Hated Opponents' award would have been a runaway triumph for the Tykes. The 60,000-plus attendances that swarmed to every Old Trafford clash in recent years provided hard-currencied testimony to the intensity of the rivalry, leaving aside the impressive arrest figures every time we met. Second, United had a historic debt to settle. The 1965 and 1970 Cup semi-final defeats by Leeds amidst viciousness and cynicism, the former depriving us of a Double, the latter bringing poor Wilf and his P45 ever closer together. And third, United obviously had a promise to fulfil, a promise made in the heat of stinging, tearful disappointment but one that could now be kept – 'to return the Cup to the finest fans in the world', to quote the Doc. This was the ticket to kill or be killed for: no wonder several hundred fell for the dodgy forgeries in Manchester; no wonder several thousand braved the supposed Leeds' Penistone Road end with tickets touted from Yorkshire. (And no surprise too that over 100 arrests ensued, despite the presence of 1,250 police; with the Blakeys taking another day off, Sheffield became a pedestrianized war-zone.)

In the tunnel, Leeds towered over United. 'We'll crush the midgets!' yelled Gordon McQueen; McIlroy and Coppell's passion flared an extra degree or two. Howling wind and sporadic sheeting rain there may have been, but United roared out of their half with the fire of the Furies. They'd been here before and knew how to treat cocky, even-tempered old pros: burn them off from the whistle. That opening quarter-hour was as exhilarating as any seen since Benfica '66.

Only eight minutes gone and Houston's already up in the Leeds box, making trouble. His tortuous back-header panics Gray – Jimmy Greenhoff smacks home for 1-0. What had they been singing about 'Leeds Reject'? What sweet pay-back for a Barnsley boy. Leeds reel drunkenly as Macari and McIlroy seize control, the latter to the befuddlement of fancy-dan Tony Currie whose United nightmares are expanding geometrically. Once, Macari had spoken of pre-ferring Daly over Currie anytime; now Sam is proving to be the worthiest successor.

Six minutes later Leeds are the walking dead. Hill starts what seems like the twentieth box incursion already; then he's there for a lashing shot which Stevie Coppell pounces on for a superbly controlled drive into the net. Yes, you can smell those overflowing Wembley bogs already. Leeds' yellow shirts are fitting: a cowardly refusal to take us on at proper football results in a succession of hopeless aerial bombardments for Jordan and Clarke. Stupid, for the wind makes a mockery of their 'ambition'; stupid, because as Buchan and Brian have so often proved, intelligent positioning compensates for lack of height almost every time. An Allan Clarke penalty at least provides twenty final minutes of drama but the curtain-calls are ours alone. United are at Wembley once more – and history's final business with Leeds is done, for this generation at least.

At first, jubilant players in the dressing room thought we'd be playing Everton in the final, such was the news from Maine Road. Back-slapping all-round: that was a team we would beat without question. Hadn't we just sorted them at Goodison, after all? Instead, Liverpool slithered their way through to a replay, largely aided by their seemingly traditional 'benefit of the doubt' from officials. Choke back the vomit, Toffees. One 3-0 replay walk-over later and the harsher truth dawned: we'd be facing champions-elect and European Cup Finalists at Wembley. Opponents whom we'd beaten just once since 1969. To do so with a team that had largely frozen stiff on the big occasion twelve months earlier. Featuring a kid at full-back to face Heighway and Co. with fewer than thirty games under his belt. Clearly, there would be no danger of Manchester United losing the 1977 Cup Final through over-confidence.

For this Red, and for many others, the Man of the Match in the 1977 Cup Final was Arthur Albiston. Nineteen years old and largely unknown on the national stage, he gave an assured, flawless performance in the face of the canniest, most successful forward-line in Britain. One of the Final's biggest football stories soon became the tabloids' top human-interest tale too after a tearful dressing-room reunion with the man he'd replaced, Stewart Houston. Who better than Arthur to describe that glorious May day?

'As a kid, I didn't really grow up with the "magic of the FA Cup"; living in Edinburgh meant the Scottish Cup Final came first, of course. And the Hampden Final wasn't the biggest game of the year, to me anyway – that was England versus Scotland. We lived closest to Hearts but I used to go and watch Hibs, Rangers and Celtic a lot too – I was more of a football fan than any particular club's supporter. But I was at Hampden for the '68 Final to see Hearts lose and the '71 and '72 Finals to see Celtic win; Lou Macari was so impressive. Little did I suspect I'd soon be playing alongside him . . .

'When Stewart broke his ankle at Bristol, I didn't have time to think about the implications: we were just all upset for Stewart. But the boss came up to me on the coach and straight away told me I'd be in the Final, which was still a few weeks off. To be honest I was surprised because there were plenty of alternatives for the boss. Perhaps he was trying to help me by telling me early, to get me used to the prospect. (I wasn't sure that was such a good idea, actually!) And I know this sounds corny but I was still more bothered about Stewart missing out. I'd watched him help us through to the Final – he was one of our best performers during the run – and seen him score that vital goal against

Villa in the sixth round. He'd really earned his place, you see.

'I had been in the squad for the 1976 Final and felt the disappointment at close hand but I don't think we carried the burden into the Liverpool match. It was such a different situation, after all. We weren't hot favourites but underdogs, as we had been in the semi-finals in my opinion. They were going for the Treble and that took the pressure off us. I always preferred being the underdogs. Most of our best performances in those days were against the form book. And I always felt our fans were better when we were up against it – there'd be something extra in their support which you could truly sense.

'Some outsiders thought Wembley was going to be my first ever United game: they'd just never heard of me! And true, it was my first ever FA Cup tie. But I had already made 20 or 30 appearances and the thought of playing in front of 100,000 didn't worry me. There were 53,000 at my Old Trafford debut [v. Man City!] and people tell me that was one of the loudest United nights; I'd played in front of nearly 100,000 on our Far Eastern tour. My only concern was not to let people down – I knew I could cope with the crowd.

'I honestly don't think we felt intimidated because we were playing the champions Liverpool, despite their good record against us. Team spirit was good: we had a great Final week, laughing and joking, looking forward to the occasion. There was a bit of press hype about me being so young and coming in as a late sub for Stewart but I didn't let it affect me. I remember seeing one headline quoting me as saying: "I'll win this medal for Stewart", but I never said it: the paper just invented it! But I *was* conscious that I was there in his place and my sole aim was to make sure I played as well as Stewart did every week. Because I did feel like an impostor, taking Stewart's shirt after all he'd done that season.

'After kick-off, you just want a good early touch to settle you down. It fell luckily for me: some Liverpool player hit a long crossfield ball over towards Jimmy Case and I made up my mind to let him take it on his

chest before going in to claim it. It worked out perfectly, the crowd reacted well and I felt I was on my
way. If there were any concerns at the back of my mind
about me being seen by some as a "weak link" or
something, they didn't last. I seemed to spend a lot of
the game up against Steve Heighway and Jimmy Case.
Jimmy was a smashing bloke but a real battler – you
came off the pitch knowing from the aches and pains
you'd been in a tough game.

'When Jimmy scored their equalizer only moments
after Stuart's goal, there was no panic or sense of
dread. I know some might have thought "Here we go"
but whatever the momentary disappointment, I never
considered that the game had turned. We'd felt really
confident at half-time and I still knew that the Final
was wide open with a long way to go. Then we got our
slice of luck to make it 2-1; it was a hot day, Liverpool
were tiring quicker than us and apart from Ray
Kennedy's late effort, I never felt it was going to slip
away.

'The whistle went; I remember vividly flying
towards Alex Stepney who was closest to me, then
Stevie Coppell. Fortunately I can still recall everything
that followed, all those classic Cup scenes, especially
walking around the pitch with the Cup. You have to
appreciate how lucky you are to get to this position –
think of all the pros and famous names who haven't
been so blessed.

'Of course it was a very emotional moment. In the
dressing room, amidst all the champagne, there was
Stewart Houston on his crutches. I tried to give him
my winner's medal. He said: "Don't be stupid, you've
won the Cup – it's yours." He just wouldn't take it. I'd
done the easy bit, playing in the Final – Stewart had
done all the hard work and he'd contributed more. I
don't like taking something if I feel I haven't worked
for it whereas Stewart deserved it. Even at the post-
Final banquet, I still felt like a gatecrasher at the party.
Mind you, I enjoyed myself that night . . .

'The next day we had that fabulous open-top bus
ride around Manchester, an extraordinary experience
in itself. Many Sunday newspapers had pictures of me

above the medal story which they'd now got hold of; some match reporters were even calling me Man of the Match! I never felt I'd had an outstanding game, just that I hadn't done anything wrong to let people down. Having said that, when I watched the video for the first time ever with my sons last year, they were ridiculing me throughout for putting too many crosses into the crowd! But at least I didn't make any crucial, match-turning mistakes, which many people were perhaps expecting of me. When ITV's Martin Tyler asked me to come to the studio to do a feature and pick up some sort of Cup Final award, I couldn't do it. I didn't really want too much of a fuss, to be honest. We'd won the match, the team and supporters were having a tremendous weekend down in London and I'd done OK: every time I saw my picture in the papers, it just made me feel worse for Stewart, actually.

'I suppose that, under different circumstances, being on every back page in tears might have been the cause for some mickey-taking but the lads knew how I really felt. Even Lou Macari, who was the biggest piss-taker going, wasn't going to take advantage. In fact, Lou was always like an elder brother to me and was a great source of advice and encouragement throughout my Old Trafford career and he understood more than most how I felt.

'Winning the Cup gave us such confidence – it established us as a team in some ways. I felt when we started 1977–78 we would be in with a title chance; we had a good blend of youngsters and older heads who, as a collective, possessed all the right ingredients. Maybe with Alex coming to the end of his career, a new goalkeeper would've completed the picture. But it didn't work out for us that season. Gordon Hill was a great loss to us. I know some people used to joke that replacing him with a "hard worker" would save us left-sided players behind him from an early grave but you can't lose a twenty-goal-a-season winger who can produce chances out of nothing and just brush it off. I certainly didn't notice my burden of work being eased anyway!

'Looking back on that Final, I'm just grateful I didn't

let anybody down and that my late father was able to see me play at Wembley before he died. We'd been to see the Auld Enemy clash at Wembley a few times when I was younger which always seemed to end in a Scottish defeat so I was pleased that for once we both left the stadium happy!' – *Arthur Albiston, 1996*

To me, that was the Age of Innocence's last Cup Final. Yes, United fans actually chanted 'Liverpool, Liverpool' in magnaminity as the Scousers traipsed past on their own lap of honour. The arrest rate was negligible, the hatred confined to minority pockets. Pearson's goal is an unforgettable image yet the famous photo has a sepia-tinted feel to it, aided by the sunlight and parched turf, which almost consigns the moment to another era altogether. Arthur's story of underdog spirit and gallantry would seem out of place in these world-weary, cynical times. In those days, your pants were drenched with excitement at the prospect of a Wembley trip, you spent days making a 'witty' banner and you celebrated victory for a summer, not a week. Our words aren't up to capturing how the 1977 victory felt for every Red, so we won't try. But this book, which we conceived years ago, was postponed so it could appear for the twentieth anniversary; and I suppose most of it is a tribute to that classic side. Perhaps it's a small way for a couple of Reds to say thank you. I'm sure thousands of other Reds can, like us, look back to 4.40 on 21 May 1977 and recognize it as one of the most exhilarating moments of their entire youth. And however old and senile they get, here's a twelve-word litany they'll always be able to recount:

Stepney; Nicholl, Albiston, McIlroy, Greenhoff B., Buchan, Coppell, Greenhoff J., Pearson, Macari, Hill, McCreery.

The post-Final banquet mixed jubilation and relief in equal measure; if the event was tinged with anticlimax, it was in the Doc's demeanour. He was quiet, brooding almost: if one weight had been lifted from his shoulders, another appeared to have descended. Scarcely had the dregs from the Cup party bottles been swigged when the corrosive truth began to leak out with mercurial effect. It transpired that the Doc, already well established as a Falstaffian rogue of the first order, had been playing away – and it was the physio's wife who'd been coming on as sub for his missus. For many observers, first reactions were hilarity mixed with a grudging admiration. As a roly-poly middle-aged bloke in the most pressurized of jobs, he'd done pretty well to net a good-looking woman seventeen years younger than himself and keep it quiet for so long, hadn't he? But to our dismay, the affair was transformed from tabloid comedy to tragedy. The pro-Docherty school of historical revisionism posits the Doc and Mrs Brown as the Edward and Mrs Simpson of football – Docherty, the King of Old Trafford, was forced to lay down his crown for the woman he loved. Dave Sexton was to play George VI, of course – the shy, media-unfriendly successor who came to a premature end. But, to continue this analogy, who were the Stanley Baldwins, supposedly so jealous of the populist King that they seized the chance to dump him? These, to the Dochertyites, are the true villains of the piece. Others will argue that they, in fact, were the guardians of United's honour and integrity. But let us adopt Docherty's brief for argument's sake: this is roughly how the pro-Tommy spin-doctor would explain what happened.

'The Doc had, famously, made enemies at and around Old Trafford from the moment he arrived. No manager could act so ruthlessly in dismantling the old guard without doing so; naturally, few of the pre-1973 crowd have a good word to say about him. Some seemed to resent the bond that the Doc created with the fans, whilst others of a more moralistic hue found the Doc's personal style and idiosyncratic behaviour distasteful, especially when compared to the saintliness of Sir Matt. Docherty himself muttered darkly about the "junior board", the assorted Manc big-wigs, hangers-on and cronies who vulturishly circled the club in the mid-seventies. Having done so well to establish excellent personal relationships with the Edwards family and certain leading directors, it must have been most galling for him to be undermined by the whispering campaign mounted by these unelected, unrepresentative types operating in the shadows of Old Trafford.

'Warning lights flashed for Tommy well before the May dénouement. It came to light that he was being followed by private investigators, hired by certain Manc businessmen, who were compiling some sort of dossier on the Doc. The press too were on the trail, tipped off about his love affair and engrossed in preparing their tabloid scoops. Friends of the Doc feared that the "junior board" were preparing to move in for the kill, presumably in time to prevent the Doc signing a contract renewal which was due in June. They must have realized, when it became clear that the press were about to break the love story, that this was the perfect moment.

'On Cup Final night, as the players knocked back the celebratory bubbly, Tommy was out walking alone in Hyde Park, wrestling with his conscience. He had left his wife Agnes three weeks previously having conducted his secret affair for three years; by Monday, he was on the phone to the Edwards house to inform the chairman of what he had done. As Louis was apparently still "in drink" at this point, son Martin answered the call, told the Doc not to be worried and toasted his future success at United. When Derby County, who'd got wind of the story, approached United days later with a view to taking on the Doc, they were firmly rebuffed and left under no illusions – the Doc would be staying at OT. A public statement from the club declared that these were "personal matters". (Even as late as the day before Doc's dismissal, Louis Edwards was still telling the *Mirror* that sacking speculation was "a lot of nonsense"; a new contract containing a "good conduct" clause was under consideration.)

'Understandably, Tommy concluded that all was well; when Louis called to reassure him, saying that the affair was a private matter for the Doc, he felt confident enough to take a short break and go out with the youth team to Portugal. He had come clean, he had made the commitment to Mary and both the current and future chairmen had guaranteed his future. He

could now go on from the Cup win, pursue Peter
Shilton's signature and prepare for a serious assault on
the title in 1977–78.

'Ten days later, summoned to Alderley Edge, the
Doc was suspended after refusing to resign when
asked to do so. He had replied: "Why should I resign?
I'm not ashamed of my actions." He had every right
to take such a line – after all, hadn't the Edwardses
said the very same thing? On 4 July the Doc was
sacked after a two further board meetings for "breach-
ing the terms of his contract". One assumes there was
no clause saying "no shagging with officials' wives" –
so it was supposed his crime was to have "brought
the club into disrepute". What a delicious irony in
that reasoning! Presumably the United directors
didn't consider the following newspaper and television stories damaged the club's reputation: insider
trading, breaking company articles, front page reports
of Martin Edwards' later alleged peccadilloes, Ron
Atkinson's marital bust-up, players being convicted of
drink-driving, the *World In Action* revelations . . .
need we go on? The English are supposed to be
famous for their hypocrisy; here was a perfect illustration. Perhaps the prep schools which educated the
club hierarchy didn't do RE: the edict "let he who is
without sin cast the first stone" seems to have passed
them by.

'Admittedly, the fact that it was a club official
who'd been cuckolded complicated matters for the
board and certainly the tabloid front pages were
unhelpful, but it is impossible to believe that the
club could not have squared matters if they'd really
wanted to do so. It is hard to avoid concluding that
during those ten fateful days before that first board
ultimatum, the Doc's enemies both inside and outside the boardroom had worked their voodoo. The
other factor, cited in particular by the Doc, was the
all-pervading influence of Catholicism and, above all,
Catholic women. Whether this picture of Papist
harridans rattling rosaries angrily at contrite hus-
bands is a true one or not, surely the Catholic
culture of the club must have played some part in

154

the board's evaluation. What a pity that they couldn't have taken such a high-minded view during later scandals.'

There are grains of accuracy and specks of persuasiveness dotted throughout that case for the defence, admittedly. And for a couple of years afterwards, many Reds on the jury of public opinion were prepared to accept much of the rest as 'the truth'. But as Docherty continued his post-United career as manager-turned-pundit, he has managed to alienate huge swathes of former supporters and demonstrate the very character facets which so enraged his enemies in the seventies. The court cases of '78 and '81 did the initial damage; his later erratic public pronouncements, in particular during the Cantona Affair, turned many remaining Docherty boys off him for good – me included. Re-examining the defence pleas in a rather different light produces an altogether less favourable summing-up.

If his sacking was a question of morality, then let us get one thing straight: it had nothing to do with the edicts of Catholicism but the ethics of professionalism. There never was any evidence that 'the Catholic women' had anything to do with this whatsoever. They were easy culprits to finger, 'meddlesome women' being a good line to sell to the Stretford Enders. True though it might have been that the 'junior board' and a director to two, particularly Denzil Haroun, were outraged, they would not in themselves have been sufficiently powerful to overthrow the Edwardses' original judgement. No, surely the key moment came when the twin guardians of the club's honour acted – when Paddy Crerand phoned Sir Matt in Ireland, told him the score, and awaited Busby's return to OT on the first flight back. Not such 'easy culprits to finger', hey?

The issue, surely, was never adultery *per se*. As Docherty correctly guessed, the Edwardses would agree that this particular sin was hardly a novelty at OT and certainly not one over which they'd be prepared to get on their high horse. After all, 'it's been going on since Adam and Eve' was reportedly Martin Edwards' first shoulder-shrugging reaction. Instead, as Willie Morgan said, 'The thing that got him sacked wasn't the falling in love – it was making the physio reserve-team trainer, sending him on scouting trips and giving his wife one while he was away.' Docherty was manager, Brown his colleague and subordinate; this was a professional's betrayal of trust, an abuse of position and responsibility. How could it ever just be 'a personal matter'? If a lieutenant cheats with his corporal's wife, it is a regimental dishonour: the colonel has every right to have his officer horse-whipped. Laurie Brown had not only suffered a disaster in his personal life but in his professional life too – in turn, the club's honour and solidarity were at stake. How could we be Manchester *United* if such activities were in any way excused? If there was a moral point that exercised Busby, Crerand and all those who supported them, this was it. And in that judgement, they were undoubtedly correct.

As it happened, there was more to consider than simply adultery and the professional misconduct therein. The private investigations decried by Dochertyites had, *prima facie*, some justification as allegations surfaced about ticket-touting, incidents on tour and car crashes. Evidence of the sort collected by Willie Morgan for his libel case also reached the board's ears. At one point during the Alderley Edge meeting, Martin Edwards cited Docherty's Cup Final ticket scams as a contributory factor to his sacking. Docherty replied that he'd been doing it since 1959, had hardly been secretive about it, and could have added that United players had done the same in the past. Maybe so: but there's surely a qualitative difference between underpaid players of the past selling off spares and a manager inviting Stan Flashman into the directors' lounge for larger-scale trading! The barman on duty that day had the right idea – he tried to punch both of them when he saw what they were up to.

Clearly, one of them had to go, and there is a story which suggests United's board considered dumping Laurie Brown with a golden handshake and keeping the Doc; certainly some of the players expected it to pan out that way, according to Steve Coppell. Practitioners of cold *realpolitik* might have prescribed such a course – physios are ten-a-penny, inspirational managers a rarity. Thankfully, more morally sound counsel prevailed and I find it impossible to believe that either Sir Matt or Paddy Crerand would have stood by and allowed any such weaselry to pass unchallenged. For if, in brutal terms, the exchange United made of Brown for Docherty damaged our playing prospects, it did safeguard the club's soul. That is far more important, just as style means more than success on the field. Some will scoff that such concerns are hypocritical, given the minor naughtinesses that littered United's post-war years. But arguing that because Busby's United once allowed the odd irregular payment, the men of that era had no right to condemn Docherty is as facile as suggesting firebombing Dresden excuses the Holocaust's perpetrators.

Dochertyites often say that July 1977 was the Busbyites' last stand, their final revenge. Perhaps: but after making so many enemies so foolhardily and giving them so much ammunition, Docherty only had himself to blame. In any event, I would prefer to think of it as the last time the club made a stand for morality and decency, or at least those parts of the club's family which still believed in these Busbyesque ideals.

So forty-odd days after his greatest triumph, the Doc's reign was over. Derby County got their man after all, but Docherty never scaled the heights again. Eventually in 1988 he was free to marry Mary and had already begun to carve out a new career as a media mouth. As a 'personality' he had *seemed* ideally suited for a club such as ours. Anyone who saw his team at its best will always retain a place in their heart for him – or rather, perhaps, just for his footballing ideals – however badly he behaves. He played on the fans' every erogenous zone – he gave us a young team, predominantly home-developed, who truly believed in attacking football, who exhibited a never-say-die attitude and played with the flair, passion and skill for which United have traditionally stood.

As a man and a character, however . . . A United player once said: 'If Tommy said "good morning" to you, you went outside to check for rain clouds.' Cynical historians say he was 'perfectly suited for the Edwardses' United' – but surely not for Busby's. I suppose it all depends on how you saw the balance of the nature of the club in the mid-to-late seventies, torn between different moralities and schools of thought. Docherty might be charitably viewed as merely a victim of that existential conflict. One should be generous, maybe, and remember him for his team's performances, not his own deficiencies – just as one shouldn't dismiss the products of Wagner and T. S. Eliot simply because of their disgusting personal politics. Though I admit this can be difficult when you're listening to him spouting shite on Piccadilly . . .

⚽   ⚽   ⚽

United fashion-disasters of the seventies were legion. Two spring to mind from the darkest recesses most readily – those disco king suits before the '79 Cup Final and the rash of moustaches which infested the team after '77. Only 'Pancho' Pearson managed to sport one without looking entirely ridiculous, as befitting his spaghetti western gunslinger image and nickname. Someone once told me that 'Pancho' was actually a mishearing of 'Punch-up' which stuck long after his original temperamental reputation had been forgotten. But certainly his punch up into the air after scoring became the single most recognizable post-goal image of the seventies, a successor of sorts to Denis Law's shirt-stretching salute. Thankfully, as often isn't the case with our imported strikers, Pearson had plenty of chances to delight the photographers with his trademark pose.

We gained from two strokes of luck during his apprenticeship at Hull: both Tommys Cavanagh and Docherty had spells in charge of him, and a dream move to Manchester City fell through. Naturally, he was gutted at the time to lose his Maine chance but Reds can only be grateful he never teamed up with Tueart and Barnes – they might well have won more than a fizzy pop cup with Pearson as a spearhead. Instead, the Tommys agreed that even at a huge £200,000 (£4.8m) fee, Pancho was the solution to our painfully obvious goal-scoring problems. By the end of our promotion season, claiming a prize which would simply not have been won without him, we had our first true line-leading centre-forward since David Herd.

And how good we were for him, too. After years of Route One at Hull, where he was the first port of call for every forward ball and a punchbag for the entire opposition, Pancho was now allowed to display some subtlety alongside colleagues who were never slaves to the obvious. By

'76, he was twice the player Docherty had first clapped eyes upon in Yorkshire – an England call-up was his by right. They were very different times; I remember being stupidly proud that one of our lads had been summoned to lead our nation's attack, whereas now we see these stints of duty as tiresome intrusions. But his greatest moment came at Wembley for us, not England, in '77. Is there a better seventies goalscoring picture than the one of Pearson's Cup Final opener? The billowing net, bleached-out turf, a stunned Clemence – and Pearson's body at full stretch, the epitome of power, athleticism and concentration. Always evocative, always inspiring.

It was obvious that Sexton never fancied him enough. Once Jordan had signed, his prospects dimmed; injuries, always a problem throughout his career, removed him from the reckoning at vital stages. Missing virtually the entire 1978–79 season, including the Cup Final, only eased the management's delicate task in the close season of getting rid; a below-par contract offer, and only for one year at that, greased the exit door's hinges. In the event, Jimmy Greenhoff's injury meant we played the whole of 1979–80 a squad-man short upfront – and after we missed the title by two points, Pearson made a point of his own by picking up a Cup medal at Upton Park. Would it be too fanciful to suggest that he could have given us that title-winning extra touch during that season's leaner spells? His panache, drive, touch and sublime shot would have deserved such a reward.

⚽ ⚽ ⚽

Red Army Despatches

Pre-season friendlies had taken United to Hamburg and Alkmaar in Holland in search of much-needed European experience before their UEFA Cup encounter with Ajax. In Germany there had been trouble when squaddies had started throwing beer cans at locals in the crowd; in Alkmaar things got no better with the Alkmaar players having to flee a barrage of missiles as they paraded their trophy round the pitch at the end of the game. For the travelling Red Army, it appeared to be a case of *plus ça change*. And whatever the efforts of Dave Smith, Louis

Edwards and Co. to dispel the image of United as the most fearsome fans in the country, there could be no doubt in the mind of visitors to Old Trafford such as Jasper Carrott that an OT awayday in the mid-seventies was not one to be undertaken by the fainthearted:

'The nearest I came to getting into real trouble at a football match was when I went to Old Trafford. It was the first game of the 1976–77 season and Birmingham were playing Manchester United, and I thought I'd risk it – it's your life in your hands up there but I'd arm myself with a nuclear missile and I'd go. So a mate of mine and myself bought tickets at the Birmingham City ground and on this beautiful August day we bowled up to Old Trafford.

'The ground was absolutely jammed with people, 60,000 in the stands and another 2,000 outside. It was just a heaving mass, a sea of red and white everywhere you looked, and not a blue scarf in sight. Well there was one, but it had a Birmingham City fan dangling from the end.

'After about 20 minutes of the game, a minor miracle occurs, Birmingham score – away from home. This takes everyone by surprise, including Birmingham who were just getting ready to kick off again. But all the City fans – about 135 of us – who were sitting in one block of seats forget for a moment where we were and start cheering. For an instant 60,000 people stared at us. Then we started to get a bit of a reaction – like "You're going to get your fuckin' head kicked in" and so on. So all the Birmingham fans decided that they'd better cheer United and stay alive.

'Unfortunately my friend was something of a rookie football fan. He used to watch rally driving but had just changed to football because he liked the colours better or something. He was totally naive about the situation and after everyone else had gone a bit quiet he kept on bawling and shouting for all he was worth.

"Go on, City, shove it in the net, show them how to play the game!" I grabbed him and was hammering him in the face in as obvious a way as I could manage.

"Look, look!" I shouted to the crowd of hostile

observers. "I'm punching his face in!"

"What are you doing?" he was saying.

"I'm saving your life!" I replied. "You do *not* come to Old Trafford and cheer the opposition." ' – *Jasper Carrott*

After a relatively trouble-free trip to Coventry on the opening Wednesday of the season, United fans were once more front page news after their visit to Derby County's Baseball Ground, as Collyhurst George remembers:

'When we played Derby County in '76, Gerry Daly had a perfectly good goal disallowed. We were behind the goal in the seats above the Derby fans. (Ian Storey-Moore was in the seats with us – by this time he must have retired.) Someone threw a corkey ball up from below and it missed one of the lads' heads by inches. A United fan spotted the Derby fan who'd thrown it and pointed him out. One of the lads went to the front of the seats and jumped into their section to get him; that was it. Everyone jumped down and we must have been fighting for a good half an hour – it spilled on to the pitch and into the streets afterwards.'

– *George, Collyhurst*

From such tiny sparks ... The press, naturally, gave it the full eight-page treatment. 'BATTLING FANS RUIN SPECTACLE', 'DERBY DAY RIOT: "They are animals" roars County boss Sam Longson.' Chairman Louis Edwards was quick to put the blame on Derby County, however, with some justification. In an effort to control the anticipated outbreak of trouble, Derby had insisted on making the match all-ticket, but with thousands of unsold tickets burning holes in their greedy pockets they had sold those unsegregated tickets to United fans in the build-up to kick-off. This had been an obvious recipe for trouble. In the debate that followed, David Meek argued that it was 'time to put safety first – not cash', contending that the only way forward was to fence all fans in as United had done during the close season. The alternative, he argued, was to make all United away games all-ticket and refuse to put any on sale at Old Trafford. (Who'd credit it? David Meek, the accurate prophet.)

Not all solutions were so well thought out. For the ebullient Doc, there was only one answer: 'If that's what happens when we draw 0-0, what will those idiots do when we lose? I'm in favour of bringing back the birch. Then we'd see how brave they are.'

At Newcastle a fortnight later, United and Toon fans battled in the city centre for three hours, wrecking, pubs, cafes and parts of a shopping centre. But greater rivals awaited at Elland Road on 2 October, as one Red Army veteran remembers:

'As a proud member of Doc's Red Army, I'll never forget this day as long as I live. My three mates, Jock, Baz and Tony were already on the bus when it pulled up at my stop. When I got on, they all shouted: "Ere, look at this then." As I sat down next to Baz, Jock stuffed a newspaper in front of me. I filled up with excitement as I read the front page of the previous night's *Yorkshire Evening Post*. Jock's dad, who was a wagon driver, had picked it up on a drive to Leeds the previous day. In large, bold print, the headline read "Red Army Invasion". Almost all the front page was taken up with reports of shopkeepers boarding up their windows and landlords closing their pubs for the day, in anticipation of 10,000 Reds taking over Leeds. By the time I'd read it twice and taken it all in, the bus had approached Victoria Station. We jumped off at the traffic lights and hurriedly walked towards the station. There seemed to be thousands of Reds queuing up against the wall of the famous football specials. After what seemed to be ages we were told that all four specials were booked up, but there was a "service" leaving ten minutes after the last special. "Brilliant", we said, as we knew that all the police at Leeds station would have gone by the time we arrived. The plan went well. When our train arrived in Leeds we all piled off and raced down the platform. There must have been 300 Reds charging towards the ticket barriers. No one bothered showing their ticket; we had other things on our minds.

'When we got outside, there were about six coppers stood there, looking absolutely gobsmacked. We charged straight past them and down some steps on to the street. When we walked under the tunnel outside the station, the roar of "Manchester, la, la, la" was so loud that they must have heard it at Elland Road, two miles away. The lads at the front started running – they'd spotted a mob of Leeds up front. By the time Leeds realized we were there, it was too late: they panicked. There must have been a couple of hundred of them, but only about seventy stood their ground. The rest shat themselves and ran off towards the ground. The traffic came to a screeching halt as every United fan piled into Leeds. After what seemed ages, but was probably only thirty seconds, the Leeds fans gave up and legged it, apart from those that were laid out on the floor. We didn't bother chasing them as they didn't seem worth it. Just then Tony came running over and told us how he knocked one out in the middle of the road.

'When we reached the park, half a mile from the ground, we couldn't believe it. There must have been five hundred Leeds running towards us. Obviously those that we'd "done" earlier had gone for reinforcements. To be honest I didn't fancy our chances – we were outnumbered and they were getting closer. There were only a handful of coppers and they stood watching. Just then, this massive bloke – he must have been 35 and looked well hard – shouted: "Come on United, let's give 'em if they want it!" We all charged at Leeds who, seeing our actions, suddenly slowed down. By the time we were 50 yards apart they were having second thoughts, almost walking. We just kept running at them, they shat out again, turned and ran. We stopped and then suddenly, as if they'd had a change of heart, they ran back towards us. No one backed off, it was full-blooded, unadulterated violence. There were injuries in both sides but after a while we got the upper hand and Leeds backed off. Just then the coppers came from all directions, driving through the park in vans, cars and even some on horseback. We were rounded up and taken to the ground.

'During the game, which we won 2-0 with goals from Daly and Coppell, we all swopped tales of what we'd

163

seen or heard and agreed that it would be good after-
wards because Leeds would be really "mobbed up".
The game couldn't finish soon enough for me: Jock,
Baz and Tony had all managed to inflict some pain on
Leeds fans and I wasn't going home the odd one out.
The final whistle blew and the Red Army in all its
glory poured out of the ground.

'We could see Leeds being given a police escort up
Lowfields Road out of their kop, as if they were the
away team! United fans stood laughing at Leeds. Police
moved us along towards the city centre. Some of their
fans had broken free of their escort and were up front.
The Red Army charged through the coppers and
attacked. Leeds fought back and all hell let loose. A lad
next to me got decked when a half brick hit him on the
head. His mate picked it up and screamed "No prison-
ers" in a Cockney accent. The poor lad who'd been hit
by the brick was bleeding heavily and in a dazed
Cockney accent said: "Get into the Leeds bastards". I
owed it to him, as much as to myself, to hurt some
Leeds twat. I got my chance about 30 seconds later
when I spotted a Leeds fan trying to escape down a side
street. I intercepted him and without going into too
much detail, kicked and punched the living daylights
out of him. I'd got my result and it felt great. It took
three-quarters of an hour to get back to the station and
there was plenty of action on the way. Leeds mounted a
couple of half-hearted attacks, but we knew we'd got
them beat. It must have been a rotten day for Leeds fans.
Their team beaten by the old enemy and their fans
being run ragged and battered by the Red Army.

'I'll never forget the police reception waiting for us
at Victoria as we poured off the trains like a victorious
army returning to home soil after a gallant victory. One
old transport copper on the forecourt shouted: "You're
a bloody disgrace to Manchester!" Jock replied: "Fuck
off you blue bastard." We asked him how he knew the
copper was a blue; did he know him? He responded:
"He must be a blue if he thought today was a disgrace!" We all burst out laughing and headed for our
local to tell the other lads who couldn't get a ticket
what they had missed.

'The Sunday papers were full of it, how the Red Army had run riot in Leeds, and I was up at the crack of dawn to buy every paper that I could afford. I had many a similar day like that in those days. West Ham, Newcastle, Everton, Chelsea, Spurs and of course Liverpool. All fell victim to the Red Army, but for some reason that day at Leeds always stands out for me. I suppose it's because Leeds, at the time, were getting publicity themselves for hooliganism, and we went to their place and showed them we were the best.

'I'm in my early forties now and I hung up my boots years ago. I still follow United home and away but I don't get involved any more. After being nicked on four occasions in the past and losing many a job over my "tours of duty", I've settled down with a wife and two lovely kids – BUT I STILL HATE LEEDS!'

Over the next six months, United's arrest count seldom fell into single figures: Aston Villa 18 arrests, Birmingham 33, Tottenham 45, Southampton 54. At Arsenal, United made their by now annual attempt to take the North Bank:

'There was a big mob of United outside the North Bank: Bob, Will, Roy, mainly the Cockneys. We all went into the North Bank and stood at the front right behind the goal. Arsenal scored in the first half – in the seventies we always seemed to lose at Highbury – and as the ball hit the net not one of us moved: it was obvious we weren't Arsenal. Bob turned round and shouted: "Come on you Cockney cunts." Their boys all came down from the back of the North Bank, but we gave them a right hiding. In the end they all backed off and the police relieved them by putting a cordon around us for the rest of the game.'

– *Roy, South London*

However, one game above all others put the nail in the coffin of the Red Army. At Carrow Road on 2 April, the damage to the ground caused by some of the 7,000 United fans present could not be ignored. BBC *Nationwide* cameras were at the ground to film the Red Army in action; they couldn't in their wildest dreams have imagined the

165

feast United fans would serve up for the Monday tea-time audience.

'There'd been trouble at Norwich in the League Cup two seasons previously but I'd never seen anything like what happened at Carrow Road that day. We were occupying the Barclay Stand, though we didn't have the whole end. The thing was, there was no real violence at Norwich, not like at Leeds or Newcastle, just destruction. The Barclay Stand was pretty decrepit, a lot of wood and loose corrugated iron; it was ideal really for pulling bits off. When they went ahead in the first half that seemed to be the signal to start pulling the ground to pieces. I don't know how they got up there, but holes started appearing in the roof where United fans were ripping the corrugated asbestos sheeting off. Of course one lad fell through the roof and it was that piece of film that always appeared on TV. When he fell through the roof, he only just missed one of the barriers − if he'd hit it, he'd have broken his back. As it was, he only had a broken leg and was stretchered away, though as he was being carried around the edge of the pitch Norwich fans were laying into him. Like me, he was from Huddersfield and he appeared on local news the following Monday night. They interviewed him live from his hospital bed on *Calendar* local news and when they asked him if he had anything to say, he just said: "Yeah, the coppers were fucking wank" − no apologies or anything.
'Inside the ground, people were setting fire to anything they could, lobbing bits of concrete on to the pitch. I think one just missed Tommy Docherty when he came to try and calm things down. Everyone was just going mad. I remember coming out of the back of the ground after the game, and on the embankment behind the terracing there was scrub and bits of the ground, and that was on fire. It was like a film set scene, after a victorious army has sacked a small town: absolutely unbelievable.' − *Steve, Huddersfield*

United travelled to Everton on the Tuesday night following Carrow Road, with police putting special contingency plans into action for what was already an all-ticket game. United had seven away fixtures to complete and one of those opponents was swift to take action. Bristol City announced on 7 April that they would not be giving any tickets for their game with United to the visitors. It was a move then unprecedented in English football. Tickets would be on sale only in Bristol and the South West. On the same day, two years since the battles of Cardiff had first brought about talk of government intervention, Denis Howell acted. After their game at Sunderland on 11 April, United fans were to be banned from the terraces completely; tickets for away games could only be in the seats and even then, these would be at the discretion of the home club. With few clubs back in the mid-seventies having any sizeable allocation of seats, the government were effectively banning United from away matches. Furthermore United were told to discourage the recognition of a whole host of supporters' club branches from outside Manchester.

The press prepared for two final Red Army flings. At Roker Park on 11 April, there were wildly unrealistic predictions of a 20,000 turnout as Reds were expected to take advantage of a final opportunity to pay on the gate to see their heroes. But on the night, fewer than 5,000 United fans turned up.

A week later, United were back at Loftus Road and facing a bus strike yet again. Most of the Red Army were already in possession of their £1 match tickets from when the game was originally postponed on 4 December. The real implementation of the ban would have to wait until Bristol City on 7 May. (In the meantime, there was the small matter of a semi-final clash with Leeds at Hillsborough. South Yorkshire police deployed over 1,200 officers, a record for any match, but it still wasn't sufficient to prevent over 100 arrests as United piled a sizeable contingent of fans on to the Spion Kop.)

Bristol City v. Manchester United at Ashton Gate, 7 May 1977 – the beginning of the effective ban on United fans at away matches. What could have been expected to be a full battalion of 6–8,000 Reds was reduced to a few hundred who had managed to secure tickets by any and all means.

'We shouldn't even have been to Bristol. I can't remember how we got match tickets with us being banned and everything, but in those days a ban meant nothing. After the game we got back to Bristol station, and all the bars in and around the station were shut – you couldn't get food or a drink anywhere. After twenty minutes, an Inter City 125 pulled into the station and we thought that at least we'd be able to get a drink and some food in the buffet carriage. We got on but the buffet car was shut off. Some of the lads decided to dismantle the doors between the carriages; they got in and kicked the shutters in on the buffet bar itself. It must have been stocked up for the next day; by the time we got back to Paddington there wasn't a Penguin bar left in it, the windows had been put through in some carriages and even some of the doors were hanging off. We got stopped outside Paddington for an hour or so, no doubt whilst the Old Bill got on the case. We all thought we were going to be nicked, but as we got off the train – the police were on the platforms with dogs and everything – they just let us go. But the next week, the London Supporters' Club got banned by United from getting tickets for games when they found out we'd destroyed an Inter City train.'

So, whilst the police and opposing supporters had failed to stop the Red Army in its tracks, the government would ultimately succeed. With the ban on United fans now part of English law, the days of United taking away support in excess of ten thousand on a regular basis were gone. There would be a relaxation in the ban the following year, but opposing clubs were no longer afraid to refuse United tickets; Chelsea and West Ham were amongst many the following season who declined to give United any tickets. Others were more than happy to comply with the request that United only be given a small number of seat tickets.

For United fans themselves, even when an allocation was received from the home club, getting hold of tickets required undercover techniques which were early blueprints for the now perpetual struggle for away tickets. None of the out of town supporters' clubs was entitled to away tickets, and those members of the Manchester branch had to purchase coach tickets at the same time. United were setting a precedent even then for the 'some are more equal than others' syndrome which to this day dictates away ticket sales. Season- and LMTB-holders in the seating sections could purchase away tickets but those in the standing sections could not. It became a regular occurrence over the next season to see season ticket holders being besieged as they came out of B&C and G&H stands by crowds of Reds begging to 'borrow' their vouchers for the following week's away ticket. Sometimes, it felt as difficult as getting hold of a Cup Final ticket . . .

Like several thousand Reds, Billy J. found last-minute salvation from a Cup Final ticket fairy called Dougie. This is Billy's Cup Final story:

'A very eventful semi-final against the Sheep Worriers at Hillsborough left us with the mouth-watering prospect of playing the treble chasing Mickeys at Wembley. The scramble for tickets began with a phone call to my uncle Dougie, a Manchester club owner with plenty of contacts around town. Going directly through the club did not seem the best option and looking back it's funny how some things don't change. My partner for the trip was to be my best mate Howard, or Azey to his closest friends. Now, at the time of the '77 Cup Final Azey had until very recently been in the army. Unlike most grunts Azey loved his tours of duty in Northern Ireland and had become very restless after a long stint in barracks back in England. He had finally decided to get himself discharged by using varying degrees of bizarre behaviour to convince his officers he was unfit for duty. Azey's desire to land back in Civvy Street was quickly encouraged by the prospect of United showing up at Wembley for the second year running. Amazingly his deceptions worked and he arrived back in Manchester a few days before the game.

'Come the Friday morning before the game and there was still no sign of any tickets. I worried that I should have gone through the club and the prospect of "jibbing in" came increasingly to the fore. At about 11 a.m. Dougie turned up with two tickets priced £25 each and despite the high price found himself elevated to God-like status. By noon we were winging our way southwards in the company of a trucker called Bob from the estate behind the Kildakin pub in Salford. Bob regaled us with tales of sexual depravity in just about every town his shitty truck rolled through. That's right, Bob was one lying bastard. We spent the night in a truck stop motel that, like most of those gaffs, had seen better days. The "rooms" were made of flimsy plywood walls with a two foot gap at the top, and the regular sounds of hairy-arsed truckers farting set us both off with the giggles. Giggles that didn't cease despite various threats to "kick our childish heads in".

'Azey and I went down to breakfast about 6 a.m. to be met by a lot of stern-faced fellas in greasy overalls and no sense of humour. Bob had done one, leaving us the prospect of hitch-hiking the rest of the journey. After declining offers of lifts from various Scouse modes of transport (you know, like the Skelmersdale Community Bus etc.), we finally cadged a lift to the Greyhound pub near the stadium. The Greyhound had been "our" pub the previous year and this visit was no different. After a few beers at the boozer we bought a few cans each from a nearby shop and set off towards Wembley Way, but not before depositing a few cans under some advertising hoardings for consumption after the match.

'Now Azey wasn't behind the door when it came to the old fisticuffs routine and having spent most of the previous couple of years on active duty in Belfast, you could say he was up for it. On reflection, a Liverpool Cup Final was perhaps not his best introduction back into the joys of following United, especially after his really concluded career as a trained killer. However, we were there for the Reds and we were there for each other. Even in those days scarves and hats were not on the agenda. We both wore white Adidas short-sleeved shirts with red stripes on the arm. It didn't matter that the Scousers were wearing white that day because our swaggering demeanour gave us away as being different from the enemy.

'We were both now quite the worse for wear and a small scuffle with some mouthy Scousers just at the end of Wembley Way lit a fuse in Azey that was to burn for quite some time. After all, this is what he was trained for and ultimately this was what he was good at. We gathered a small band of fellow Reds and headed past the twin towers away from the United fans towards the Scousers end of the ground. High on drink and high on hope we chanted and clapped our way into enemy territory until the rest of the Red Army was out of sight and only our small band of about thirty remained. The first missile to land was a half empty beer can, quickly followed by more flying debris. This triggered the desired response from our intrepid little band – a few Mickeys were swiftly placed on their arses. This brinkmanship didn't last long as soon hordes of Scousers were running at us, throwing anything they could find. A few of our group broke away and started to retreat. This is where Azey came in handy.

' "You fuckin' shit-houses. Stay and fight or I'll fuckin' find you and knock you all out." (Honest, it was real *Boy's Own* stuff.) Eloquence was not Azey's strong point, but his outburst worked and we all stood our ground as the Scousers poured on. The sight of our small band of rabid Mancs smacking anything that moved and not running seemed to unnerve the Scousers and they turned and ran back up the grass embankment towards the turnstiles. At this point the Old Bill moved in and we were shepherded round to our own end. No real injuries and best of all no damaged pride: Mancs 1, Mickeys 0.

'The official attendance for that final was around the 100,000 mark, but if the Scousers were practising as many of the illegal methods of entry being used at our end of the stadium then the attendance must have been nearer 120,000. The usual pre-match entertainment of marching bands and dodgy gymnastic demonstrations was boosted that year with a display by the "Wonder-wings Aeronautical Display Team". This consisted of two noisy little remote-controlled planes decked out in the participating teams' colours. The planes took to the skies to the accompaniment of the *633 Squadron* theme tune, and proceeded to swoop and dive bomb each other above the pitch. This brought no end of amusement to the Scousers who predictably accompanied the display with various Munich chants. A volley of abuse back from the Red Army saw the level of animosity grow visibly inside the stadium. The two little planes eventually collided, leaving the White Scouse plane plummeting earthwards in a cloud of white smoke as the Red United plane continued to soar skywards in triumphant loop-de-loop movements. An omen, me thinks.

'Although not a classic game, any victory over the "Bag Snatchers" is to be celebrated vociferously, especially a Cup Final victory that stops them doing the domestic treble – ha! We watched United receive the trophy and headed out for a piss and some fresh air. We reckoned the walk back to the Greyhound was going to be pretty moody, but I think most of the Scousers got off quickly while we were still in the ground celebrating. Suffice to say, those that were left milling around afterwards seemed to have left that sparkling Scouse wit and overhyped sense of humour back in Doleville.

'We retrieved our lager and eventually managed to cadge a lift back to Manchester from a passing coach. The lads on the coach – who seemed to be under the impression that Azey and me were brothers, probably due to the matching Adidas tops – were quickly persuaded that a stop for refreshments was a good idea and we pulled off the motorway and headed into Dunstable. The coach parked up and we headed up the main drag looking for a decent pub. We eventually found one and tumbled in to discover just three customers and the ex-Scots Guards landlord who greeted us with: "I hope we're not going to have any trouble from you gentlemen, are we?"

' "Not if you keep the beer coming, tash face," came the reply. The original three customers thought better of our company and left the pub in our safe hands. A couple of locals then turned up who obviously knew the landlord and thought it would be good fun to attempt a quick bit of Manc piss-taking. The launching of a full pint of lager in their general direction made them reconsider that prospect, and with all the inconspicuousness of Bernard Manning running naked down Market Street on a Saturday afternoon, they left. A gang of girls on a hen night arrived and the decision to stop in Dunstable was looking a good one, especially when a couple of the lads even managed some sexual depravity on the empty coach.

'The first brick came through the main window, just where most of the hen night girls were sitting. Through the broken window we could see a gang of about forty local idiots, all decked out in the colours of various London teams. It seemed supporting Manchester United, drinking in their pub and getting off with the local totty wasn't going down too well with some of the inhabitants of Dunstable. The bricks and bottles kept coming until hardly a pane of glass remained. We all eventually broke out of the pub and to their credit the locals made the grave error of standing their ground. Azey was in his element wading into them like a man possessed and it wasn't too long before our attackers, whose lovely London footie shirts now carried varying degrees of blood and snot, turned and ran, splitting up into small groups pursued by the Red invaders.

'Things calmed down a bit and we headed back to the pub to check if the girls were all right. The pub was written off so it was decided that a helping of fish and chips was a good idea. As we headed for the chippy we noticed a tall skinhead staring at us from across the road.

' "Who's that cunt looking at?" said someone as Azey started off across the road.

' "What's your problem mate?" asked Azey.

' "I'm fackin' Chelsea," came the reply.

'Azey promptly nutted him squarely across the bridge of his nose and as he slid down the wall replied: "Oh yeah, well I'm Man United so fuck off." I even got a result in the chippy when the girl behind the counter gave me change of a tenner for a quid – yes! The coach turned up and the driver wouldn't let us eat our food on the bus, and as we stood debating the matter a coach full of Scousers pulled into the car park.

' "All right lads, what's the chippy like?" ventured the first one off.

' "Fuck off you Scouse bastard," was the general response; a large tray of pudding and chips was launched towards him as he scuttled back on his bus.

' "Come on lads, don't be like that, wish us good look in Rome eh!"

' "Fuck off you wankers," came the second general reply as a deluge of half-eaten food smashed against the Birkenhead Scousers' coach. They thought better of it and swiftly made a quick exit.

'I slept for most of the journey back to Manchester, whereas Azey glugged on a bottle of Teachers whisky that miraculously appeared from the wreckage of the Dunstable pub. "Billy, Billy you'll have to sort your kid out. The driver's going ape shit," said one of the lads as he woke me up.

' "Oh God, what's he done now?'

' "Come on you'd better look." One side of Azey's face was squashed against a piece of sodden newspaper that someone had wedged between his face and the window. He also wore a rather fetching newspaper bib that the lads had tucked into his shirt. This was catching the copious amount of yellow vomit that was regularly exiting his mouth. Next to him on the seat sat the now empty Teachers bottle. "Come on lads, you're home, it's Salford," someone shouted.

'I got Azey to his feet and escorted him off the bus. "Thanks boys, we'll see you again some time," I shouted as we stumbled down the steps. I'm pretty sure I heard a faint "Not if we see you first" as the reply. We were actually at the end of Princess Parkway in what I recognized to the Southern Cemetery and it occurred to me that perhaps we'd overstretched our welcome with our newfound travelling companions. I cleaned Azey up as best I could and prayed for a taxi to arrive. Eventually one did and I told him our destination as Azey lay sprawled across the sumptuous comfort of the black floor. After heading through Manchester city centre and up Bury New Road we finally arrived back at George Street. I got out first and reached back in for Azey, before dragging him backwards up the path towards the front door.

'"That's £6.50 mate," shouted the driver.

'"Yeah, right mate," came the reply.

'"Hey, that's £6.50 or I'll get the police."

'"Fuck off now or I'll shoot you," mumbled Azey as he slowly awoke from his drunken haze.

'As I closed the door I gave the driver a bit of advice: "I'd get off mate if I was you, 'cos he might just do it." We made a bad attempt at climbing the stairs and finally settled for a couch each in the living room. A loud rasping fart leaked from Azey's jeans as he whispered. "Good day mate, or what?"

'On 23 August 1979 Howard (Azey) died suddenly and unexpectedly in his sleep aged 24. He had been out the previous night with his dad Ted for a couple of beers and a chin wag. I saw him two days before he died and he looked the picture of health and good living. He loved life and most of all he loved Manchester United. I'll never forget that day in 1977 and I'll never forget Azey Parkes.' – *Billy J.*

1977–78

Dave Sexton – a manager granted so many prefixes in his four years at Old Trafford. 'Whispering' Dave. 'Deadly' Dave. 'Dickhead' Dave. 'Satan's Armageddonian Offspring' Dave. But, sadly, never 'Victorious' Dave. It's always a mild shock to catch sight of Sexton on TV these days, usually in the background of the latest England set-up, training under-21s. You mean he's still alive? And, more incredibly, still working in football? Somehow, like that other unloved ex-boss Don Howe, he has escaped the black hole that has accounted for all his flashier seventies contemporaries. No drink-sodden or scandal-ridden crises, no wasting away in minor punditocracy, no foreign banishment and early death – just good ol' Dave, reliably boring to the end.

Ain't hindsight wonderful? Within months of Sexton's departure in '81, every pro and manager in the land would claim how obvious his unsuitability for United had been from the start. But in the line-up of usual suspects for the job during that summer of '77, he stood out. In fact, even in retrospect, you'd be hard pressed to prefer another. Consider the other candidates: Terry Venables, the single most over-hyped 'talent' of the decade, whose arrival alongside the Edwardses would surely have constituted one wideboy too many; Lawrie McMenemy, amusingly first-choice, the ultimate triumph of image over reality; Don Revie, single-handed destroyer of what was left of English football's reputation; and Ian Greaves, the obligatory long-odds candidate. Dave had the kudos and track-record to trump the lot: purveyor of successful footie at Chelsea and QPR, an actual winner of trophies and a 'first-class coach', whatever that amounted to in seventies Britain. The man who'd once been Docherty's deputy at the Bridge would now, at last, succeed and surpass Tommy – so every pundit predicted.

Arsenal, who had hoped to lure him themselves, were apparently devastated to lose the tug-of-love with Old Trafford. Such irony of unrequited passion: how perfectly Arsenal and Sexton would have been suited, whispering sweet nothings such as '4-3-3' and 'offside trap' into each other's ear.

At that time there was already in the public domain a photograph which, within a few years, would have sufficed to ensure that Sexton never got near the shortlist. For in the late fifties Dave had been a member of the celebrated West Ham set, the group of Hammers who would meet near Upton Park over a cappuccino to theorize about football modernism. For years, no more modish qualification to be a manager was possible. These guys had the answers: in a post-Ramsey world, British football would belong to them and their arty Euro-inspired idealism. Now we know better. What a roll-call of ignominious failure: Malcolm Allison, Frank O'Farrell, Dave Sexton, John Bond, Malcolm Musgrove and Ken Brown. For some reason, almost all chose Manchester as their place to come and die professionally, as if commanded by a fatalistic anti-Mancunian conspiracy. (As every Red knows, never trust anything that's spent more than a day near the Upton Park infestation.) But back in 1977, before Allison's return and Bond's botchings, that photograph was still testimonial rather than torchable.

Much pathetic excitement, on the media's part at least, resulted from Dave's 'intellectualism'. Admittedly, his donnish bookishness was rare amongst seventies managers, most of whom graduated from the School of Hard Knocks and Groin Strains (probably a degree-awarding ex-Poly nowadays). Unfortunately, his interest in Chinese verse didn't produce much poetry in motion on the field and the frequent factfinding missions to Germany resulted only in United eventually resembling the Krauts of Mondial '78 – unloved, unattractive and unsuccessful. Whatever unusual intellectual gifts he possessed might have been invaluable twenty years later in dealing with Cantona and McClair. Faced with a no O-levels Norman Wisdom fan such as Gordon Hill, a nineteenth-century haiku poem was unlikely to be the ideal bonding agent . . .

There's nothing worse in football than the dead season, that empty futility of reaching February and March with nothing left to play for; you might even argue that it's better to be involved in a relegation dog-fight than be farting around mid-table for those final months of a campaign. One of the overlooked joys of United in the seventies was that although we won only one major pot, each season took us to the brink, filling Old Trafford with expectant faces well into every May climax. Except 1977–78, that is.

This book is full of stories and narratives following United's campaigns: two relegation battles, four championship chases, three Wembley runs . . . most may have had unhappy endings but only Hollywood's vulgarians believe that any good plot must have a saccharine-sweet resolution. But 1977-78 had no twisting tale to tell, no inherent drama hooking us until the dénouement. Instead, we were presented with a messy, injury-riven and often joyless pondering – cinematically, more Ingmar than Ingrid Bergman. Moreover, the hero 'died' before the final reel: what sort of tossy screenplay was the 1977–78 story? It was a season with straight-to-video written all over it.

Virtually all the hope, passion and exhilaration that the year had to offer was completely expended by the time the clocks went back; come March, one might have wished they'd been put back a year rather than an hour. How different life seemed on August's opening day as Birmingham were put to the sword. With Gordon Hill's supreme swivelling volley and a Macari hat-trick in front of jubilant Red hordes who'd spent the morning fighting Chelsea fans in Brum, we were simply carrying on where we'd left off. Lou Macari actually said the dread words after the game: 'For the first time, I really feel we have a good chance of the title.' Such fate-tempting comments after an opening day are now notoriously taboo, of course – except at Newcastle – alongside chairmen's votes of confidence. But didn't we all believe it? Sexton had talked of sorting out the defence as being the last tweak United needed; in this, he concurred with the Doc, who'd hoped the signing of Shilton would've completed the jigsaw. And hadn't we just shown twice at Wembley in the Cup Final and Charity Shield that we could comfortably live even with European champions?

(Twelve years later, after another opening day 4-1 festival, we'd once again fall for the fleeting beauty of the same kind of dawn – a false one.)

As it happened, Wembley's Charity Shield – a 0-0 draw with the Scousers, bookended by tribalistic aggro that would soon become a hallmark – did contain a true sign of things to come: Jimmy Greenhoff's 20th minute injury. He would make only 23 League appearances this season and would be too often joined in the treatment room by Buchan, Macari, Pearson and his own brother. United's run of good health was over and the paucity of the squad brutally exposed; the classic Mark II line-up were able to take the field on only three occasions. McCreery and McGrath received unexpected runs in the side, whilst Grimes, Ritchie and Rogers all got their first chances. But with all due respect to this quintet, their appearance on a team-sheet tended to dilute, rather than strengthen, our power. Here, then, was one major factor in our decline for which Sexton cannot be blamed. (Unfortunately.)

By the time City came to Old Trafford on 10 September, the optimists were still in the ascendancy, lavishing credit on Sexton for persevering with the 4-2-4 he'd inherited. We'd only dropped one point and had won well at Derby despite the reduced support. It seemed every attempt by Reds to hire a coach, car or bicycle to beat the away ban resulted in a government threat to call the troops out. Had Denis Howell himself appeared on the motorway in helmet and khaki to bellow, 'Get back to Manchester, you vermin', it would not have surprised. For the Red Army at least, little had changed – and, as they were about to demonstrate, not without good reason.

But City frankly thrashed us 3-1, with Kiddo making his particular point twice, to go top of the League. The minorest of consolation was that the only goal you ever get to see from this grim afternoon is Jimmy Nicholl's unbelievable 35-yard cracker; just as with Mark Hughes in '89, we still contrive to steal a smidgin of glamour from the gore of defeat. A week later, during the 90-minute cessation of hostilities between Chelsea and United fans, a 90-second goal beat United at their least imaginative; a good point gained at Leeds on a day where all eyes and TV cameras were on the terraces was soon forgotten as United lost five

League games by mid-November. Champions-to-be Forest would only lose three all season; we'd lost seven already. An injured Lou Macari would now have ample time to eat his August words.

And yet, amidst such increasing concern, despondency and anger on the terraces ('Sexton Out!' chants being quite audible during November), United somehow, and quite typically, managed to provide one afternoon and three evenings of sheer class. The 2-0 defeat of Liverpool on 1 October stands out for many reasons: the uproarious fervour of the Stretford End, rarely surpassed since; the first defeat of these new European kings; Sammy McIlroy's instant crackling finish for the second. A historic delight, too, in Alan Hansen's awful misjudgements and missed challenges that led to both goals. (Recite 'Now that's dreadful defending, Des', in a Scottish accent.) But above all, it had been the scale of the destruction; this was no Cup Final knife-edge win but a comprehensive battering, a rarity in Scouse–Manc battles of the last twenty years. This had been my co-scribe's debut in the Stretford End proper: some baptism. These are the days that hook you for life.

The bristling aggression and pumping adrenaline easily survived a four-day hiatus and 200-mile trip to Plymouth for the St Etienne return match in the Cup-Winner's Cup. The riot in France and front-page furore which ensued does not obliterate the memory of United's performances against the svelte French. There's a good argument to be made that this stands as one of United's finest ever Euro ties. After all, St Etienne had made the European Cup Final only sixteen months before and been unlucky losers; and only Scouse romantics truly believe they deserved to lose the infamous '77 quarter-final against Liverpool. (That David Fairclough, quintessential Scouse urchin, should have triumphed over the glorious Bathenay and Rocheteau ... *Incroyable Mais Vrai*, as the French TV show has it.) No amount of French offside-trappery and disallowed United goals could stop us.

The 2-0 'home' win in particular showed United's potential in Europe, given a fully fit Mark II eleven; sadly, in Oporto for the next round, that eleven never had the chance. Infamy is too weak a word to describe the scandal of the Iranian Injection Affair. In a display of cretinous

cowardice, the club allowed themselves to be cajoled into
sending the lads to Tehran on 24 October for a British Trade
Exhibition friendly. In order to help the Labour Government suck up to the shitty Shah, soon to be justly deposed,
virtually the full first eleven would play – and all would
need anti-cholera jabs at least a week before travel. Quite
incredibly, these were administered before the FC Porto
match, even though any traveller knows about possible
reactions to injections. With the Greenhoffs and Pearson
laid low and the rest clearly struggling, United were anni-
hilated by the Portuguese 4-0. West Brom also took full
advantage by the same scoreline three days later. Steve
Coppell later suggested that this utter idiocy resulted from
some kind of back-stage deal between HMG and MUFC:
'We'll get your European ban lifted if you help us sell some
rockets to the ragheads' – yes, you can just hear some FCO
mandarin whispering that into Louis' ear, can't you?

Despite being betrayed by their club and government,
United gave an outstanding demonstration of playing for
pride two weeks later. With Coppell marauding and Porto
in terrified retreat, we won 5-2; there were moments, which
many will have recalled in December '94, when the 52,000
could actually dream that we might pull it around. By
throwing Sextonian caution to the wind and playing with
the nothing-to-lose cavalier brio Docherty taught, United
had proved we could have knocked out Porto. But we'd
also proved this was the way to play, for these players at
least. The lesson was soon forgotten.

Every grumbling Red on the Stretford End knew there
was more to our wintry decline than a few injuries. United's style and attitude were clearly changing. The all-
running, all-dancing panache demanded by Docherty had
begun to shrink into a more controlled, cautious, supposedly sophisticated manner. You could almost hear the
scraping and screaming of fixed wings being pulled back
into the body; if we were still nominally 4-2-4, it was
already evident that a successor-system was being infiltrated. Dark rumours circulated which suggested Cavanagh
and Sexton were not quite eye-to-eye on playing methods,
prompting Docherty to attempt a swoop for our coach
during September. By all accounts, it had been a close call.
Perhaps the sorely tempted Cavanagh recalled Doc's words

just in time: 'After leaving United, there's only one way to go – downtown.' And Derby County, already by 1977, was pretty low-rent downtown, too.

Throughout the winter, there was a schizophrenia about United, as if we were being pulled apart between Docherty past and Sexton future. Howlingly inept, over-cautious performances, such as the grisly double defeats by Coventry and Birmingham after Christmas, unfortunately seemed to signal the track ahead. But then you could go, say, to Loftus Road, watch an old-fashioned thriller finish 2-2 and believe the dream lived on.

Actually, that QPR match was of significant portent. Gordon Hill was outstanding – it did appear that when he was allowed to play his way, United flowed as of old. A superb far-post header and a last-minute equalizer gave him another double. But bear in mind two images for later: it was Hill who hared back 60 yards to prevent a QPR third with a brilliant tackle. And for his equalizer, he went in with a bravery and foolhardiness that would impress a Bryan Robson, getting crocked in the process. His teammates seemed very pleased with his all-round efforts; he went on to be man of the match in four of the next six fixtures and was en route to being top scorer yet again. Yet Sexton was already courting Denis Tueart – a man who played in Hill's position – and within three months had labelled Hill a work-shy, unpopular luxury. Was this the black-hearted truth? That the cancer destroying our season from within was our terrace hero himself?

Tueart wasn't the only Christmas present Sexton had on his list. December was as target-rich an environment as an Iraqi retreat. Gerry Francis, David O'Leary and John Deehan cropped up on back pages the most, the former virtually shoved into our embrace by a desperate QPR board. But Sexton would have a rather more dramatic *coup de théâtre* in mind, a mind which United's team made up for him on 17 December. On that day the classic Mark II line-up had its last chance to impress, against League leaders Forest. The intense embarrassment of the 4-0 defeat Clough's assassins inflicted has never been forgotten. Whenever United are humiliated at home, now thankfully so rare an occasion, two precedents always spring to mind: the 0-3 against Liverpool the following Christmas and this

25.10.75: Battle of Upton Park.

Paddy Roche: you just *know* where that ball's heading, don't you?

Gordon in 'hilarious' Norman Wisdom mode.

Arthur – Real Men *do* cry, after all.

21.5.77: Scousebusters.

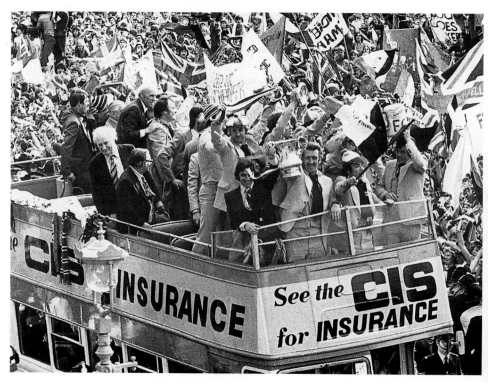

22.5.77: Manchester city centre.

(Syndication International)

Fatal Attraction, 1977 version.

(Popperfoto)

14.9.77: Clouseau clones run riot.

Love-struck in the honeymoon period: duration, six weeks?

25.2.78: Brookesy's sharp exit from Anfield.

4.4.79: Scousebusting classic.

12.5.79: Supersam brings a Red generation to orgasm . . .

(Syndication International)

. . . but, sadly, Captain Martin couldn't get this close to Sunderland on 89 minutes.

Incumbent and successor: from the sublime to the ridiculous?

. . . Or, rather, '*Out*'.

first, merciless execution. However bad any subsequent failures – York, QPR, Everton – there is always the consolation that we've seen worse.

Which reminds me – Paddy Roche kept goal that day, in the loosest sense of the word 'keep'. A month earlier he'd saved a John Robertson penalty at the City Ground on his comeback game and consequently racked up an 18-game run in goal. Memories endure of his blunders that day, not to mention one at Newcastle, two at Anfield, one in the Cup, one at QPR . . . need I continue? If not as abject as he once had been – and there were a few decent saves intermingled – Gary Bailey's swift rise through the subordinate ranks this season was still to be welcomed.

Before Sexton began to wield his scalpel, we would enjoy two last hurrahs, two final afternoons which had Docherty's legacy written all over them. On Boxing Day, United travelled to Goodison on the back of the Forest disaster to face a side unbeaten in 22 games – and won 6-2. *Grandstand*'s teleprinter needed to spell out the word 'SIX'; few would otherwise have believed it, just as few could contain their ejaculatory response to Macari's sensational goal. But then Boxing Day football has always been about stupid miracle results that have absolutely no aftereffects. Sexton's intention was already fixed; by the time of the last vintage display on 21 January, Joe Jordan was already on his way across the Pennines from Leeds.

His arrival surely acted as a spur to the players that day – but not as much as the identity of the visiting manager, Tommy Docherty of Derby. When he stepped on to the pitch to applaud each section of the crowd and receive their acclamation, he looked as self-conscious and even embarrassed as Sexton, though each had wildly different reasons, of course. United trounced an admittedly weakened County 4-0; even Martin Buchan got in on the piss-taking act with a finely taken fourth. Afterwards, Macari roared: 'We beat both Derby and the Doc. It was a different United today and you know why. We went out to win for Dave Sexton.' This was replete with ironies. For the efforts of those who'd once crossed the Doc now to do him down startled every observer. Why couldn't they play like this just for Dave every week? Clearly, the Doc's grip on the imagination endured. And they won playing like a

Docherty team, not Sexton's; there was a move which led to Greenhoff hitting the bar that was so fast, one-touch and exciting it virtually screamed 'Made By Tommy'. That the man of the match, scoring twice, creating two, should be Gordon Hill carried its own bitter-sweetness. If he'd been trying to prove his point to Sexton, it was to no avail; indeed, in reminding Docherty of his brilliance, he'd simply succeeded in bringing the day of his departure to Derby ever nearer. United didn't win again at home until April; by then, 'Merlin' was dead.

Jordan's home and away debuts came in the space of four days, against West Brom in the Cup. Any hopes that his signing would prove to be a key to the defence of our trophy were short-lived. It wasn't his notorious headed power that gave us a lifeline, but the unwitting Tony Godden's in the Baggies goal. Coppell and Hill blasted amusing one-twos off his bonce and post for a goal in each match, Stevie's being a last-minute saver at Old Trafford. Unfortunately, the emerging brilliance of Cyrille Regis ended our season, to the intense annoyance of the tiny but vocal NF United contingent. Regis would repeat this Jesse Owens-style payback the following Christmas. Grievously disappointing though knock-out was, at least it dealt the Hitlerite scum their just desserts.

Sexton now had three full months of nothing to play for, which would at least grant him the opportunity to continue his reshaping; Gordon McQueen, after four weeks of protracted negotiation, would be the next arrival (again from Leeds) at a cost of £495,000. You might imagine that ripping out the aerial strength of hated rivals by whipping out a big-boy wedge equivalent to nearly £10 million at '95 prices would have been a cause for delight. Yet the grumbling continued. The McQueen record fee was seen as a ransom, almost as if we were being blackmailed; moreover, established terrace heroes like the Greenhoff brothers and Pancho were clearly having their cards marked. We all realized we needed a bigger playing squad – but no one had the heart to select the victims for a selectorial firing squad.

Jordan failed to score for his first seven matches – this, fortunately, in pre-Birtles days – and in particular was out-monstered by the ogrish Mickey Droy at the Bridge, which didn't bode well. What was the point of a Tartan Terror if he couldn't scare anyone but dental cosmeticians? McQueen's nightmare debut in the 3-1 hammering at Anfield scarcely helped, as we saw at first hand his fatal tendency to be drawn out of position. Luckily for the players, fans' attention on those two afternoons was distracted by the raging terrace and tube battling. Sexton, however, had certainly noticed the pinpoint passing and stunning goal by a young, hairy Ray Wilkins at Chelsea. The mental image of his ideal term was taking shape, though the mystery remains as to how Mickey Thomas was to wheedle his way into Dave's vision . . .

United headed groggily for spring, a team in search of a *façon de vivre.* Jordan, Jimmy G and Pancho all had spells of injury, so few could predict confidently what Sexton's ideal attack was going to look like; similarly, Macari and Buchan's lay-offs kept Brian Greenhoff in the eleven, leaving the future of defence and midfield uncertain. Gordon Hill continued to score, but mainly from the spot, the cheeky grin now a much rarer sight; only Stevie Coppell, ever present and player of the year, seemed to be at the top of his game. United won just once from February to March, at relegated Leicester. Of the last nine home gates, only three broke 50,000, and that trio included the derby and farewell end-game. When only 49,000 come to see Leeds at OT – and a 0-1 defeat, natch – you know that the flame is barely flickering.

Thankfully, Jordan broke his duck at Newcastle, ensuring there'd be no Iranian hostage jokes about him at least. But a relegation side was allowed to snatch a point: McQueen gave away a penalty while Roche buggered up twice to bring Stepney back into the fold, ever the post-Paddy fireman. Typical '78 wretchedness – so too the derby, when City and Kiddo pulled back from 0-2 with the munificent help of Clive Thomas's temporary blindness. ('Temporary' in the sense of 'every other week', some used to say.) After a 1-2 home defeat to Everton, especially dismal given that 55,000 had made the leap of faith to attend, fingers were being pointed in every direction. But the digit that counted, Sexton's, arrowed towards just one man's head – Gordon Hill's.

Ignominiously dropped for the visit of Villa, Hill admittedly blew his last first-team chance a week later at Highbury. When QPR came to Old Trafford on 8 April, Hill was nowhere to be seen; his last appearance in a Red shirt came at Preston reserves, alongside such luminaries as Paterson, McDermott and Clark. The hideous, heart-breaking but sadly inevitable truth emerged – Gordon was to be sold to Tommy Doc's Derby for £180,000. Merlin had cast his last spell and Old Trafford was a seventies Camelot no more.

With Hill out of the way, the rest of the team appeared to set out to prove a point, much as they had against Derby County: they won four matches on the trot to help United finish an almost respectable tenth. Sexton formally switched to the 4-3-3 (and often a hard-line 4-4-2) he'd surely wanted all along and, for the time being, filled Hill's shirt with the gangly, hard-running frame of Ashley Grimes. So Hill's postertastic good looks and classic centre-parting were replaced by spotty ugliness and horrendous curly mop, mercurial flair by matey hard work. There is your symbol for the transformation that had taken place over ten months. Manager and players alike revelled in the post-Hill euphoria, in the supposed proof that Gordon had indeed been the problem. Just to rub it in, Grimes scored a brilliant goal against QPR at the very moment Hill was unhappily shuffling around in Preston, and scored coolly from the spot two weeks later. See? – anything Gordon could do, Ashley can do. Against West Ham McQueen, now settling in enough at centre-half to risk some trade-mark Gogo outbreaks, danced down the left and into the box to set up McIlroy in almost conscious parody of Hill. Who needs Merlin's wizardry when even our 'donkey defenders' can pull the same tricks? To Hill-worshippers like me – and that still included the majority of the Stretford End, no matter what the players said about him – such claims were specious and nauseating. This post-Hill run, cited in Sexton's defence by the Establishment over the summer as the rumblings endured, had been achieved against four of the bottom six teams. As Sexton himself would learn three years later – with delicious irony, from my point of view – late-season runs in dead rubbers are no guarantors of future triumph. Nor, in Sexton's case, adequate defence against incoming P45 missiles . . .

So United's one-hundredth birthday passed with an empty trophy cabinet which we'd never looked likely to fill after the most futile campaign since 1960–61. We were facing the second hundred years of our existence with a new, hard-faced system under a manager who'd disposed of the most Unitedesque player of his generation. (A fairly dismal 'celebration', then, if not quite as depressing as Liverpool's and City's centenaries. At least we hadn't witness a Souness wrecking twenty years of development or a calamitous Blue-style relegation.) And the players seemed happy; few offered any criticism of Sexton for the one, era-defining decision to sell Hill.

An itchy Hornbyist rash needs scratching. At about the same time, I experienced something very similar to what I childishly imagined United's players were feeling. We had an absolute bastard of a teacher at school. I now realize he was a bit of a child-molester, in a non-criminal way; any excuse to apply a Vulcan grip to your neck or a horny-handed slap on your arse. A disciplinarian of the nineteenth-century school – and that school being Dotheboys Hall – his wit was as merciless as his aim with the chalk, which he would throw at you in carton form. One cruel aside from him could keep you embarrassed for a fortnight. He was more unpopular with the Reds in class than Paddy Roche and Mike Doyle combined.

The trouble was, he was a fucking brilliant teacher and the parents loved him. Virtually everyone was getting straight A's; even the glue-sniffers at the back threatened to pass. No matter how much we wanted him dead, we all had to admit he got us performing like no other teacher. Anyway, one day we came into class and he wasn't there. The old sod was in hospital with cancer, or something happily life-threatening like that; you couldn't have made thirty kids any more joyous bar presenting us with tickets for a disco on his grave. For a couple of weeks, the buzzing relief took us even higher and we all sailed through the mock exams. But by the time the real thing arrived, we'd slumped; the glue-sniffers all failed and only four of the rest got A's. We missed out on the prizes we'd have won, which were worth hard cash; so no *Man U Annual '79* (£2.45) for me and no shiny cans of Evostick Red for the bootboys.

That bloody parental cod philosophy may be right: sometimes it's better in the long run to put up with unpleasant annoyances, even if it makes you unhappy, for a greater general good. Of course you can understand the United players' discontent; perhaps the majority of the players did loathe playing behind Hill as much as I used to dread our tormentor. But in deposing Hill, the team and the club lost more than a mere troublesome knave. Because, ironically, Hill was jettisoned for allegedly weakening the overall team – yet without his inspiration and unpredictability, the collective was actually grievously damaged. Whatever gains were made in United's 'class spirit' did not translate into Grade A achievements; without Hill's flair, goals and crosses, a second-place B-plus was all we would attain.

⚽ ⚽ ⚽

It's impossible to be cool and objective about Gordon Hill so I won't bother trying. To me, he was the most exhilarating talent I ever saw in a Red shirt, at least until Eric arrived. Few who were teenagers during the 1975–78 period will disagree: in a sense, he was our George Best. I could rhapsodize for hours about the sublimity of his touch, shot, speed and vision, recount in detail most of his brilliant goals and outstanding runs and recall precisely every minute variation in hairstyle and moustache cultivation (yes, he too fell victim to that infestation). Above all, he was the most unpredictable forward I'd ever seen; this was his greatest weapon yet also, in making him so hard to play *with* as well as against, his Achilles' heel. That and the fact that he was, in his own words, 'the world's worst defender'. For most of his two and a half years at Old Trafford, colleagues reacted to his on-field presence with a helpless schizophrenia – amazed admiration and gratitude for his goal-scoring and goal-making combined with anger and resentment at his lack of work-rate and team-play when we didn't have the ball. But as long as Docherty was in charge of a flair-driven 4-2-4, he was oxymoronically both a luxury and a necessity. Only when Sexton arrived to impose a system which required more workmanlike predictability from every cog in a new, 'efficient' machine did Hill supposedly become a liability. But for those first eighteen months, he was surely the incarnation of the extra ingredient which made that Manchester United team so special and so celebrated.

United should have known what they were getting. At Millwall, his behaviour on and off the pitch was legendary enough to secure him star billing in Eamon Dunphy's book *Only A Game*, published within months of Hill's transfer. His maddeningly mercurial performances, the outrageous exhibitionism, his unusual character riddled with contradictions – every page seems to be haunted by Hill. Coach Barry Fenton simply declared Hill to be a genius who couldn't be saddled with instructions or inhibitions; you had to take him as he was for he would never change. And he didn't: Steve Coppell bluntly states that Gordon was useless in training, baffled by any attempts to place him within advanced tactical frameworks, often unable to carry out the simplest order. Dunphy remembers telling Hill to 'watch that full-back – and he did: watched him running off as Gordon stood still'.

Hill was just all instinct and sorcery; but when it produced twenty goals a season and made another dozen, most colleagues and managers could learn to live with it. As long as they got to relieve their frustrations on him from time to time: Hill received more dressing-room bollockings, Pearson lectures and Buchan broadsides than the rest of the squad combined.

Hill didn't lack self-awareness, however. He'd simply turn round, admit his failings and ask: 'Do you want my goals or do you want me to defend? You can't have your cake and eat it.' His deficiencies weren't his problem but the manager's – if he was selected, it was to play *his* game to the best of his abilities. And the best of his abilities didn't include tracking back, marking up and tackling. So what was the point of expecting him to do it? If a team required their goal-scoring wingers to do all that too, get someone else in who could do it – he couldn't. The logic was infallible. He knew this wasn't going to endear him to his team-mates, leaving aside the effects his character had on them off the field, but he could live with that. 'We may not have got on with each other off the pitch but the minute we went on the park, we performed like the best of mates.' Bar the odd cuff round the lughole, he was right.

Ah, the infamous 'Hill personality'. There is a caricature Hill, the public face on display in the dressing room,
which led some to dub him a prat. He was bouncy,
bubbly, brash and all those other annoying characteristics
beginning with 'b', including, according to Louis
Edwards, 'a bastard' ('flash, Cockney' subdivision, to be
exact). Louis applied this charming epithet to his face
within three minutes of meeting Gordon, which tells you
something about the Hill effect. Coppell noted: 'Gordon
had the habit of blunt speaking and of rubbing people up
the wrong way,' although he did add diplomatically that
'you still couldn't help liking him'. Perhaps it was the
jokery and buffoonery which mitigated his abrasiveness.
When the United team assembled, Light Entertainment
Hell resulted. Cavanagh banged his 'lucky' Max Bygraves
cassettes into the deck, crooning along being mandatory;
Hill flew into 'hilarious' impressions of Norman Wisdom,
Michael Crawford and Bruce Forsyth. Some players actually claim this was good for morale; personally, this is not
the sort of thing I want to learn about my heroes. Alex
Stepney, not a Hill fan and never likely to offer any
Cockney solidarity, cruelly remarked to Jim White: 'He
thought we were laughing with him. We were laughing *at*
him.' As Gordon fancied himself to be a bit of a joker, he
also drew the attention of chief persecutor Lou Macari,
who began a two-year campaign of jovial Hill-baiting in
order to prove that he was still the puckish Pisstaker-
General. At least Gordon took it all like a man and turned
the tables once or twice, unlike his cowering, Lou-phobic
successor Mickey Thomas.

Perhaps there is a certain, um, charmlessness about this
vision of Hill. But you can argue that this was merely his
ego on display, in the psychological sense: as my diction-
ary defines it, the part of him that 'reacts to reality and
defines individuality . . . by awareness of social standards'.
The true Hill, as reflected in the *id*, could only be seen
away from Old Trafford altogether. The way Hill acted in
the dressing room could be seen as an understandable
defence mechanism. Here's a guy who's barely 22 but with
a great deal of insight into his nature and his capabilities.
He's thrown on to the biggest stage in Britain where only
the development of an exaggerated sense of confidence and

self-assertion can preserve him. He's battling all the time to defend his very existence against older, more experienced and hostile heads; moreover, he's got to find a way to coexist with and connect to a gang of lads whose social network is already well entrenched. The persona and *modus operandi* of Hill 'on duty' were what he required; the brash buffoonery can be seen as a protective shield, whether consciously devised or not.

For away from United, Hill comes across as a far more intriguing and likeable personality. If anything, he's reminiscent of Cantona, another player once lambasted for unpredictability and a difficult character. He immediately took himself off to Whaley Bridge to live, so he could be close to nature, eschewing the normal practice of sticking close to the lads and urban life. At 5 a.m. he would go out into the countryside, shoot a couple of rabbits – he loved *la chasse* as much as Eric – and just walk, think and enjoy the dawn. Those who learned to look beyond the joker found a loner, someone who could be shy and easily wounded; instead of a 'flash cockney bastard' ripping around town, they discovered a self-confessed 'country boy', actually happier with his own thoughts than being the centre of laddish japery.

And, ironically for someone criticized for laziness, he shared with Eric an absolute dedication to his art. He rarely drank or 'lived it up' like some young urbanite wingers we could mention, preferring quiet Cokes in his local; indeed, he appeared to share the Cantona view that a professional should do no other. In some ways he was never off duty, practising ball techniques wherever possible; if it meant a couple of hours volleying crumpled up paper across hotel rooms, so be it. He had the same Cantona drive – to be the best, whatever it took.

What clinches this interpretation of Hill for me is the way he talks about what it meant to play for United. He doesn't come out with the normal players' platitudes and tributes but speaks like someone who's truly taken in the spirit of United. He'll tell you about the feelings he experienced when walking on the Old Trafford turf, how he sensed past ghosts inspiring him, how the crowd produced some kind of metaphysical reaction in him. Or how he touched the shirt in the dressing room, remembering who had worn it, what it signified: 'It was a lovely shirt, richer, a purer red: I'd have to pinch myself into believing it was true, this is real, you're playing in George Best's shirt. If you've done that, it doesn't matter what you do after does it?'

I think Hill understood more than most how *we* feel about United. When he used to say, 'I thought I was a *Manchester United* player', he said it with such pride. He knew what we dreamt of seeing from our forwards; he knew that for two and a half years, he provided it. And so he wasn't ashamed to admit that when Sexton told him he had no future in his team, he cried his eyes out. Bollocks to going out 'looking hard', as if you haven't lost face: he wanted it known how much it hurt him to lose that pure Red shirt. He'd had three or four bad games in a row but was still top scorer, not that form and achievement mattered: this was a case, for Sexton, of eradicating systemic dysfunction. For the soulless engineer couldn't make an all-grafting, all-sweating 4-3-3 machine work with a loose flywheel like Hill spinning around. Team-mates who once could withstand the extra load Hill 'shirked' could no longer take the weight, not with Sexton's extra demands and tactical impositions.

Hill himself remembers leaving Old Trafford, tears in eyes, and seeing the graffiti 'HILL IN – SEXTON OUT' on a Warwick Road wall. It was a small consolation that the Stretford End thought the sale a crime. In later years it would stand as an emblem for Sexton's era: he sold Hill and bought Thomas – 'nuff said. There were a few days of tabloid nastiness, during which Hill suggested player-power as the accessory to murder, lampooned Sexton's tactics as requiring O-levels to understand and was labelled a Cup Final failure by the charming Louis Edwards. Docherty took him to sanctuary at Derby but the Baseball Ground, for both, was only a staging post on the way to decline and disappointment. Injuries ruined what remained of Hill's career. He'll tell you today that he won't complain about how things turned out; those two and a half years were 'paradise', ample compensation for later set-backs. All he will suggest is that we didn't see the best of him at United – yes, we saw the best he actually produced, but he knows he could have been *even better* had he stayed at Old Trafford, injury-free. Blimey: the mind boggles. And some people ask me why I've still got it in for Sexton . . .

⚽ ⚽ ⚽

If there was one feature of Docherty's classic team which was less than ideal, it was surely that they weren't very hard. No wonder they always preferred a battle of artistry and won the Fair Play League every year: this was not a bunch of lads you'd expect to do well in a car park bundle. Pearson looked hard but seemed to get injured every time he tried to mix it; most of the rest were too small, weedy or girlish. Lou Macari, bless him, would take on anyone – but fair-fight featherweights were few and far between. So if there was a strategy in Sexton's purchasing policy, it appeared to consist of building a classic spine of steel: big Bailey at the back, McQueen in front of him, an attempt to get Robson in the middle – and Joe Jordan at centre-forward. The double signing of Gogo and Joe in early '78 was nothing less than the transportation of Scottish granite cliffs across the Pennines, pure imported hardness fresh from the monster-factory that was Elland Road.

There was no symbolic declaration of intent quite like Jordan removing his front teeth before a game. (At least, not until the legendary old bird who used to whip out her falsies on the way to matches before giving all the coach lads free noshes.) Off the field, he remained the archetypal gentle giant, the family man with a serious and cultivated interest in life outside football. On the field he became the Tartan Terror, the gap in his dental formation all the better for spitting out opponents' blood. Leeds had done the hard work for us, creating a ready-made offensive weapon. When he arrived there from Morton, he stood at five foot ten and weighed ten and a half stone; he roared on to Old Trafford a six-foot, twelve-stone ogre. They'd given him a nervelessness and big game temperament to match: here was a guy who'd scored at a full Nou Camp, who'd already bagged a title medal. Unlike many Old Trafford striking imports to come, he would have no fears here. Typical had been the response in his first-ever reserve match for Leeds to the boot in the mouth which wrecked his dental insurance no-claims bonus – straight back into the saddle for full-on commitment and a rapid first-team call-up. As Bob McNab noted, 'The only fear around Joe was of the poor defenders chosen to mark him.'

If not the most prolific scorer – 47 in 220 games at Leeds – he was indisputably the classic barging centre-forward of aerial majesty many had said we needed. The surprise was his skill. Admittedly, this took more than a season to register fully, but by mid-1979–80 he had won over the last doubters to finish player of the year. His lay-offs were Hughes-class, his turn remarkably fast for such a titan and his first-touch much less clumsy than we'd feared. And of course, he excelled in precisely those areas we'd expected him to prosper – dominating in the air, terrifying defenders and taking the batterings so that others more lithe might infiltrate the gaps he'd created. Naturally, one shouldn't revel in the physical pain of opponents but there was a satisfaction to be had from waving the succession of Jordan victims off the pitch over the years: he was never a dirty assassin but if you messed with him, you paid the price. In an era when we missed some of the skill and panache of the Docherty years, he could be seen as a symbol of what had gone wrong. But he wasn't: instead, we were grateful to see his fight and passion as a substitute. Old Trafford has always loved its battlers and hardmen: it's a myth that we only lionize the fancy-dan artistes. Jordan would be followed by Norm, Hughes and Robson – that's a proud lineage to which to belong.

Joe should have been a mainstay of the early eighties, a rock around which to construct more artistic patterns; instead, he only lasted a year beyond the domain of this book. Not for the first or last time, we would lose a star over money, a grotesquery for a club of United's self-proclaimed status but in keeping with our tradition of blundering over strikers. AC Milan at least showed their appreciation of him in hard financial terms, which United failed to do; it was the start of an unpleasant continental connection for Reds in the eighties.

If Bobby Collins's discovery from Cleland hadn't quite exceeded the exploits of local hero Jimmy Delaney, he'd come a good second: Scots in particular will never forget the way he led the final charges into two World Cup Finals with typical ruthlessness. And if he'd left Leeds a good striker, he departed Old Trafford an even better one as we reaped his best contributions – a trick whose repetition we'd enjoy fifteen years on . . .

⚽ ⚽ ⚽

Red Army Despatches

By the summer of 1977, with United labelled the pariahs of English football after their spring outings to Norwich and Southampton, there was only one club who could match United's hooligan reputation – Chelsea. The two most notorious firms in the country had amazingly not met in competition since March 1974 when a 3-1 win had given Reds a glimmer of false hope in the relegation run-in. When United were promoted a year later, they had passed Chelsea on their way down. So whilst United had spent two seasons terrorizing the First Division, Chelsea had been building a reputation in the Second Division much as United had in 1974–75. Figures published in the *Evening Standard* in April '77 showed Chelsea to have the highest arrest rate in London, with West Ham and Millwall trailing some distance behind. Like United, all Chelsea away games were now all-ticket with tickets only on sale to selected supporters. Everything was set for the clash at Old Trafford on 17 September 1977, a mere three days after the St Etienne 'riot', of which more later.

In the lead up to the game, the press were in no doubt that this was a clash of the titans, and they didn't mean on the field. Two badges on sale to United fans gripped the hacks in a frenzy of righteous indignation. For 30 pence swag sellers were peddling badges reading 'MUFC I Hate Chelsea' and a second badge with the image of a gravestone featuring the legend 'Chelsea FC RIP September 17th 1977'. Chelsea had already played at West Bromwich and Ipswich that season and as their club secretary explained to the *Daily Mail* on the morning of the fixture, 'We have been congratulated by the police on the behaviour of our fans after both those matches, so we feel it is unfair to brand Chelsea fans in the same bracket as those of Manchester United.' The majority of Chelsea's fifteen hundred fans would travel to the game on two special trains, stewarded by club officials. After the 1-0 defeat, a mob of United gathered on the railway bridge intent on sending Chelsea back to West London with a flea in their ear, as recalled by Stretford Rick and Chris from Droylesden:

'Chelsea was the first time I can ever remember United being really organized for trouble at Old Trafford. At first the police wouldn't let Chelsea out because too many United were waiting on Warwick Road to have a pop at them. We hid down the two alleys that run from Partridge Street to Warwick Road, behind all the shops and the alleyway parallel to Warwick Road. As Chelsea came past the houses, we all came out of the alleyways armed with empty bottles and the like from the shops. It was a right do, to say the least . . .' – *Stretford Rick*

'This was my first game. I just couldn't believe the scenes on Warwick Road. Twenty years later the only memory I have of the game is Brian Greenhoff heading over an advancing Alex Stepney and a Chelsea played nipping in to score from two yards. But outside afterwards! There seemed to be thousands of United fans just waiting to get the Chelsea supporters. To an impressionable thirteen year old the atmosphere was intoxicating. I couldn't believe that so many blokes wearing butcher's coats and the like were intent on aggro. I'd read about it in the papers, of course; my father, who'd been a season ticket holder for twenty years, had tried to stop me going. The game had been terrible but watching all those United fans baying for Chelsea blood got me hooked. – *Chris, Droylesden*

In Wythenshawe, five miles from the ground, the Royal Crown was turned into a bloodbath. For the *Daily Mirror*, this was a continuation of the events at Old Trafford.

'Staff and regular customers fled in terror as 100 rampaging thugs laid into each other with bottles, glasses and pieces of furniture. Damage totalled more than £1,000. Fifty people were taken to hospital and one Manchester man suffered a fractured skull. The vicious brawl erupted late on Saturday night as Chelsea fans celebrated their 1-0 win over United. "They had been lively all evening," said pub landlord Alan Panter. "Suddenly I heard a shout of 'Come on you bastards' and all hell broke loose." Thirteen windows, twelve chairs and six stools were smashed as fighting spilled out into the car park. Police held forty-nine fans overnight.' – *Daily Mirror*

The Old Trafford meeting was, however, only a forerunner to Act Two in the clash of the titans. Rob from North Manchester takes up the tale for the game at Stamford Bridge on 11 February.

'*Everyone* went to the game at Stamford Bridge. We went early to Piccadilly Station where there was meant to be a coach to pick us up to take us straight to West London. After we'd been waiting for over an hour we realized that it wasn't going to show and we ended up having to take the service train down to Euston. We arrived late at the game and paid into the Chelsea end. Even though United were banned from this game, there was a definite mob of United in the ground.

'After the game the police kept the United fans in as they tried to clear the street outside of the waiting Chelsea fans. By the time we left the ground, Fulham Broadway was clear but as we got on the tube, United only had one carriage, Chelsea the other five. There was one copper at the end of each carriage to "stop trouble". We had to change trains at Kensington High Street. As we pulled into the station we could see that it was packed with Chelsea, five or six deep – we knew there'd be trouble. The doors didn't open straight away and Chelsea were trying to prise them apart. At the front of the Chelsea mob was one incognito United fan, biding his time; as the doors opened he hit two Chelsea fans either side of him and dived inside.

'Everything went crazy. They started smashing the windows. I thought they were going to kill us. Other passengers were cowering on the floor. We took the seats and held them up against the windows as protection from the sand buckets and fire extinguishers that were coming in at us. It seemed like ages but it must have gone on for a couple of minutes at least. If they'd got in the

carriage, God knows what would have happened. Underneath those seats were huge acid batteries – someone picked one up and said: "Come on, let's do 'em." I don't think Chelsea could believe we were having a go back at them, as all at once we piled out of the carriages to attack them. There were no more than a hundred United at most, maybe as many as five hundred Chelsea. By this stage the police had just abandoned the station and locked the exit doors. We battered them all over the place, running them down the electrified tube lines, surging up the stairs and ran them out into the street. All this took place over a period of twenty minutes. It was some of the worst football violence I've ever seen.'
– Rob, North Manchester

Outside, the battle was fought along some of the poshest streets in London, with cars overturned and Saturday afternoon shoppers scattering, terrified by the rampaging hordes.

The Sunday papers were in no doubt that this was top quality aggro. 'RIOT – Red Army Takes On Shed' screamed the *News Of The World*, describing the incidents at Kensington High Street as well as fights at Sloane Square and Monument. In all there were only 38 arrests, though this was typical; throughout the seventies, arrest figures were ridiculously disproportionate to the amount of bedlam caused by fans, a sure sign of the general lack of police control. Attendance at the match was only 32,000, a massive 20,000 below expectations. The threat of violence had yet again adversely affected the gate; and for once, the blood-curdling predictions had been appropriate.

Little did we realize that 1977–78 would be our last chance during the Red Army years to mount an invasion of Europe. Outrageously experienced Euro traveller Blackpool Phil recalls the four cross-Channel ventures of the decade, trips that, in some ways, set the patterns of behaviour that we still follow today.

'As a teenager there were several pre-season tours of Ireland, Scandinavia, Belgium etc. But I needed to save my pennies from the hot dog stand to get me through the domestic season. By 1976 when we qualified for our first proper Euro sortie for seven years, I was well up for it and two of us quickly booked a full week in Amsterdam – hence a rather nervous approach to my boss.

'Ajax away had a magical ring to it and by going for a week, we made sure we did it in style. Flights were booked for the day after Newcastle away; unfortunately we chose the cheapest departure airport, which was Lydd in Kent. This involved travelling the length of the country. Anyway, fly we did and by lunchtime on the Sunday we were happily settled into our home for the next six days. We had tried to get match tickets from Old Trafford but in a pattern to be repeated many times in the following years, we were told they were only being issued to those on the club trip. This was a real blow as within an hour of our arrival our first taxi driver had taken us to a nearby newsagent, where we were able to purchase two tickets for the away end at half the price for which they were being sold to club travellers! Why do they never learn?

'Our primary objective, as two teenagers let loose in Amsterdam for the first time, was obviously to find the red-light area – and how we struggled. As we all now know it is the biggest and most easy to find red-light district in the world. But we were too shy to ask and spent the whole night in a fruitless search. As the end of the night approached, we purchased a sex guide from a street vendor, but unfortunately we were so drunk by then we couldn't follow the directions on the map! We had been ridiculously close all night but had never quite made it.

'Our final bar of the night offered the chance to play darts against a topless old tart for ten guilders, and we convinced ourselves that this was as good as it got – the centre of the infamous red-light area! It was certainly a very disillusioned and sexually uninspired couple who wearily returned to their beds that night.

'The next day saw the first Red arrivals. I started off with high fives for each new party that we met, but as the day wore on it became clear that this was to be a major gathering and I was rapidly going to be wearing my palms out. The red-light area was unmissable now as every English person proceeded to gather in the surrounding streets and alleyways. This was a whole new world acting as a shining beacon for every Mancunian to hit the city. I lived in the area's bars for the next few days, leaving my bar stool solely for regular trips round the narrow walkways, taking in untold delights on offer to anyone willing to part with fifty guilders. At this time, the area had a certain charm that has since been replaced by seediness, and we loved every minute of it. The girls all spoke to you as you patrolled their streets and we got braver as the drinks flowed. I spent two nights thinking that a request for a light was simply that, before realizing that the girls were after more than a spare match! I bought a cigarette lighter, even though I didn't smoke and was very impressed every time I had to use it!

'My courage grew, but this was all to change by the day of the game. The ranks of the Red Army had gathered *en masse*, and it was becoming increasingly difficult to retain my bar stool in the Old Sailor. By early afternoon the curtains were closed in all the windows as the girls enjoyed the equivalent of the navy landing in port. Within hours, however, the curtains were closed for different reasons as their English guests availed themselves of free pleasure and robbed the takings. Drink bills were left unpaid – oh, that delightful continental fashion of only charging you when you offered to pay – and sex shops were raided with lots of unwelcome stocktaking.

'The Red Army was definitely in town and the locals were not happy. Several Hell's Angels armed with heavy bike chains soon encouraged people to leave the area and skirmishes occurred at regular intervals. The girls refused to entertain English clients and the bars refused to serve them beer. Time to move on, we realized, and we adjourned to Dam Square where one of the biggest ever gatherings of Reds had assembled. This was a magnificent sight, with thousands of feather-cut, Sammy McIlroy lookalikes massed together, singing in unison.

'I spoke to an American couple in a bar and will never forget the bloke asking if all these English guys were here to see the Queen on a royal visit . . .

'The journey to the ground was equally eventful with the United fans living up to their reputation of the time. Locals were robbed and beaten up, tram drivers were relieved of their takings and girls were touched in intimate places. The trams rocked with singing fans and it was hard to believe that they stayed on their tracks. It was unsavoury behaviour, from a largely unsavoury bunch, but there was a reputation to be lived up to in a time before the more sophisticated casual era.

'We were met at the ground by hundreds of police with dustbin lids and giant poodles on leads! This presented a ridiculous scenario, but these poodles were nasty pieces of work and very effective at keeping everybody under control. There were between eight and ten thousand United fans there that night – a magnificent turnout and I'm sure the onlooking Dutch fans took this as the role model for their own development over the years to come, when they adopted the hooligan pose just as it went out of fashion in England. The game was uneventful in itself, but the fans were memorable and presented an exhibition I shall never forget. We lost on the night, but won a brilliant return at Old Trafford to move on to a second round tie against Juventus three weeks later.

'Leading one-nil from the home leg we journeyed to Turin with the general feeling that we would probably lose, to end our European adventure. Prophetic indeed as a weak display saw us go out in insipid fashion, with a three-nil defeat.

'I had opted for a one-day trip organized by David Dryer (yes, he was going all that time ago) and hoped to save my leave for the next round. I left work at six in the Tuesday evening, drank all night at Manchester airport and went straight to work on the Thursday morning without telling anyone why I had taken a day off. I turned up having had no sleep and having drunk constantly since last leaving work. A great experience, despite our defeat and probably more enjoyable than subsequent visits to Turin with either England or United.

'We caught a six a.m. flight and were strolling

around the city centre before most Turinese were up for breakfast. There was a smaller turnout than Amsterdam due to distance and cost, but it was still a healthy gathering of Reds, who reacquainted themselves with their fellow European travellers. We drank in every bar we came across and amazed the startled Italians with an incredible capacity to consume vast amounts of alcohol. It seemed that everyone was there for only a short time and intended to make the most of it.

'Bar after bar literally ran out of beer and I have an abiding memory of panicking bar owners desperately carrying crates along the streets, in an effort to restock before everyone moved on to the next bar. They were clearly making massive profits. My drinking colleague, Johnny K, spotted the keys left in a motorbike beside us and, fancying himself as a surrogate Eddie Kidd, decided to take it for a quick spin round the square. The owner was not best pleased as Johnny raced round on the wrong side of the road, too drunk to realize that he was abroad.

'The police were called and chased "Eddie", whose response was to crash into a parked car and abandon the bike. He ran into our bar, straight past the bike owner, but despite the fact that he was bleeding and had torn his jeans, the police refused to believe that their prey was stupid enough to return to the scene of the crime and proceeded to arrest the owner instead for gesticulating at them in a violent fashion! This was too much for me and I decided to take a rest in a quiet spot – apparently I slept for hours before being woken up in a drunken stupor, in the gutter of Turin's busiest street!

'The game approached and the locals were unhappy that so many Reds had taken residence in the bars surrounding the ground. It was impossible to buy a beer as it had all been drunk and tempers frayed as Juve fans marched along the centre of roads thronged by drunken English fans. The large flags, so common in Italy, provided an ideal target for grabbing hands and I lost count of how many I saw change hands – and I don't mean as a result of the traditional scarf-swopping exercises.

'Nightfall heralded the build-up of a tremendous atmosphere, but unfortunately the team didn't perform and we were well beaten. There was a torrential downpour throughout the game, and placed in the front section, we bore the brunt of the full deluge – those flags certainly came in handy.

'We were pelted with fruit during the proceedings and the consequence of all this was a very unhappy Red Army, found departing from the stadium at full-time. A token police presence did little to deter the boys from running amok as they left. Trams packed with laughing Italians provided the perfect target for a venomous attack. Windows went through all over the place and locals, terrified of their English assailants, scattered in all directions. Another victory for diplomacy and international relations.

'So that was that – only two games, but enough to whet our appetites and leave us craving more from next season. The team did their bit with a glorious Cup Final win against Liverpool, and we were off to St Etienne for several days of "Allez Les Verts" – the only words the inhabitants of St E are apparently capable of uttering. We went down by train with a couple of days in Paris thrown in. The night before we spent in Lyons along with several other Reds and travelled the short journey into St Etienne on the morning of the match. I normally like to be in our venues before the actual day, but it was a good decision on this occasion as St E turned out to be quaint and quiet with few bars, with several of those that did exist electing not to open.

'St Etienne were by far the biggest side in France at the time, and this was apparent as fans from all over the country arrived throughout the day, completely decked out in green. Our French counterparts seemed determined to spend the day outside the ground in chanting mode, but we had other ideas – to find bars and beer! We were, as ever, successful and embarked upon a mega drinking session which ended with predictable consequences.

'The few bars that did open acted like a magnet for the wine connoisseurs from Manchester. When informed that there was little beer to be found, we openly welcomed the proffered petrol cans full of claret that seemed to be the only thing available. This had to be the alkie's dream – drinking wine from petrol containers sold over the counter in all the bars at ridiculously cheap prices! The paucity of bars led to inevitable overcrowding, so much so that in the two bars closest to the ground, hundreds of people spent the whole day taking in the rays whilst drinking on the roof! Fortunately, the roofs were flat, but it certainly presented a bizarre sight to the bemused locals.

'We drank solidly throughout the day from these bloody petrol cans, and I obviously blame the vino for my lunchtime purchase of a £16 St Etienne shirt for a friend back home, followed by two further purchases of the same type of shirt at different times of the day – having completely forgotten my earlier purchases. I was seriously bewildered (and poor!) when I discovered my pillow for my afternoon nap was not one, but three shirts.

'We were well bladdered by the time the game approached and, despite having this time managed to obtain tickets from Old Trafford, entry into the ground revealed that there was no segregation and we took up our places in the midst of the French crowd. There was a lot of surging (or was this the wine?) and my mate Paul briefly lost his sense of decorum as he grabbed a particularly attractive left breast during one strong push. This amused me greatly, as she reacted with a magnificent right hook, catching him full in the face and knocking him out! Great stuff.

'As kick-off approached, more and more Reds were pushing their way into the centre, much to the annoyance of the St E fans who had taken their places many hours previously. In some sort of strange pre-arranged ritual, the French threw bread at the English (there was a bread strike in the UK and the stuff was hard to get!), causing severely negative reactions. This may have originally been intended as a humorous gesture to take the mickey out of the visitors. But it was not treated as such and all hell broke out. The French cowered, the police waded in, and the United fans attacked. We were drunk and right in the middle, unsure of what to do. As the police regrouped and used batons indiscriminately, we decided we were better off with the French fans and shyly edged over to our left – a good move as many innocent Reds made unwelcome head contact with the police batons.

'The players were bemused as this went on, but it didn't stop them turning in a superb performance and returning to OT with a very creditable one-one draw. However, back in England, we were branded as having been responsible for causing the "riot" and were ordered to play the return game at least 200 miles from Manchester. Plymouth it was and another great victory saw us earn a trip to Portugal to play FC Porto in the next round.

'This was a hard one to get to, with very little time to make arrangements and I reluctantly decided to go for my first club trip. It wasn't that bad really, it's just that it ultimately comes over as a glorified school trip. We got there early and had several hours to ourselves, but they still ensured that you didn't get your match ticket until two hours before the match, when you had to walk down the centre of a coach to prove you were sober! Full of confidence that we could manage this simple task, we still drank to excess during the day. However, the people on the trip were definitely more reserved than our normal drinking partners, and there was a high level of nervousness prevalent.

'Oporto is an old city with an attractive riverside area, full of bars. We camped out there for the day and worked hard at warding off any curious locals. The game was a late kick-off, and we enjoyed lots of beers in the warm climate as we discussed our chances.

'The club had arranged a sight-seeing tour for the afternoon, but I think only three people actually went on it from our group. We drifted round all the various bars we could find, and generally had a pleasant time – unusually for me on a Euro trip, I can actually remember most of the build-up and I looked forward to the game with some hope.

'We made it through the coach ticket ordeal without too much trouble, and even managed a last vodka attack in a bar next to the ground, before being

rounded up and encouraged (i.e. forced) to go straight
in an hour before kick-off. This was sacrilege to a
dedicated bar person like myself and instilled in me a
dislike of organized travel that has remained to this
day. I then had to endure a four-nil defeat, which
effectively ended our interest for the season and
denied us any further travelling opportunities, despite
a highly spirited attempt at putting the situation to
rights in the second leg.

'It turned out that under Dave Sexton's management
we were denied any further European involvement for
the rest of the seventies. As soon as Sexton came, I
could tell he was the type more suited to a one-day
club trip than five days of wild abandon. Thanks,
Dave, for denying me more opportunities of shortening
my lifespan . . .' – *Phil, Blackpool*

⚽ ⚽ ⚽

It was one of the most eye-catching photographs of the
seventies. A picture that summed up what football had
become in that decade. One scarf-bedecked football fan
being led away by a St John Ambulance man and police
officer, with a dart buried to the hilt in the bridge of his
nose. It was the photograph that propelled United fan Peter
Brookes on to the front page of every Sunday newspaper in
the land on 26 February 1978.

'I'd gone on the Dave Smith coach to the match. It was
my first visit to Anfield, although I'd been going to
away games since the Second Division so I was fully
aware of what went on. Anyway, we were stood about
three-quarters of the way back from the pitch, in the
Anfield Road End. In those days it was all standing
with United occupying just a bit less than half the end.
I was stood about six people away from the Liverpool
section to my right. Early in the first half various
objects started flying over – the usual sort of thing,
stones, coins, even the odd egg. About half way
through the first half, the score was still nil-nil; I felt
something hit my nose. At first I just thought it was a
stone or coin, but as I put my hand up to my face I

could feel the dart sticking into the bridge of my nose. It was one of the plastic barrel types you get in the pubs and was buried so deep that the tip had just come through my nose on the other side. I tried to pull it out but it wouldn't budge. I made my way down a gangway to the front. I wasn't in that much pain, but as I was being led around the pitch, a photographer ran up to me and asked what had happened. I stretched my arms out in a "don't know" fashion and that was the picture that made most of the Sundays the next day. Me with a dart in my nose and my arms outstretched.

'I was put in an ambulance with a Scouser and taken to Walton Hospital. The irony was that the Scouser was in much worse condition than I was; he'd been hit full in the face by a brick and looked a right mess. All the time there was a CID guy with me: I think it looked a lot worse than it was and maybe he thought I was going to die or something.

'At Walton Hospital they tried to pull it out, but every time they pulled on the dart, my head went with it. In the end it took four people to get it out: three pulling my head one way, the fourth pulling on the dart. My parents picked me up from Liverpool and took me back to Manchester and that was the last I thought about it really.

'However, the next day I got up to go to the newsagents and as I walked there, people were staring at me in the street. I had no idea why until I got there and saw my photograph on the front page of nearly every paper in the shop. That day an avalanche of newsmen seemed to descend on our house. They all wanted a picture of me looking fairly innocent; I suppose it suited their story to say that it was my first game and that I'd never be going again. I think they treated me pretty fairly, with one exception. The journalist from the *Sun* wanted to make out that it was United fans who'd thrown the dart. No doubt it would have made better copy; we were just outcasts in those days and he kept on insisting that it could have been United fans who threw the dart, even though it entered my nose through the right-hand side and there couldn't have been more than half a dozen Reds to my right before the Liverpool section began. In the end I just told him to piss off.

'The next day my story was on page four or five of most of the papers and the broadcast media started getting interested. I did *Radio Newsbeat* with Richard Skinner, an interview on GMR and more lucratively one for the Radio 4 *Today* programme, which I got paid for. I was still getting paid royalty cheques for that interview three years later. Every now and then they'd play it and send me a cheque for £12! By the end of the Monday, however, I was pissed off having to do all those interviews; the novelty had worn off and my father ended up talking to the Granada *Tonight* local news show because I couldn't be arsed.

'The most surprising thing about the whole episode was the letters I got from all over the country. In the week that followed I must have received fifty letters a day. I got fan mail from girls who said they'd seen my picture and liked what they saw and wanted to go out with me. Unfortunately I never took any of those offers up. The vast majority of letters were from fellow football supporters sympathizing with me, including a few from Scousers saying how disgusted they were. Remarkably there was one letter from a woman in Oldham who was a big United fan and she sent me twenty quid. We sent each other Xmas cards although we never met; then a couple of years ago I got a letter from her daughter, telling me that she was dying and could I go and see her in hospital. I was quite nervous meeting this woman who seemed to hero-worship me for no apparent reason.

'In the end the whole thing blew over and though I missed the next game at home to City to placate my mother, I was going to away games again by the end of the season.'

There's a lot of Reds about nowadays involved in 'unofficial' United – running fanzines, coaches, supporters groups – who entered into the Old Trafford Brotherhood during the late seventies. Like the early seventies kids raised on elders' tales about the sixties lads, our twenty- and early-thirty-something generation have been shaped by what

they saw of Doc's Red Army. We could hardly claim to have
been amongst its soldiers but the touch and taste of cordite
remain indelible memories. *Red News* editor Barney looks
back on the seventies and, in particular, a visit from Leeds.

'Despite seeing the great United success that has come
in my adulthood during the nineties, there is still a
part of me that wishes I had been born two decades
earlier. There are no perverse emotional reasons. Just a
solitary wish that my one real true love – to others, my
bizarre obsession – Manchester United, had been able
to cultivate me during a period over which all Red
old-timers reminisce with longing and adulation. To
them, despite only one trophy, it was the best period of
supporting United that they have ever had.
   'Admittedly, I don't envy some of the seventies'
more "afflicted" trends – the unbelievably distressing
fashion items (flares, flowered clothing of all sorts)
worn with confidence and described as "new style";
nor the denim jackets carrying hundreds and hundreds
of ridiculously bad football slogans, such as "Sexton's
soldiers", and especially not the bovver boots and long
white coats worn by some of the younger element of
United support in an attempt to look particularly cool
on the Stretford End. But it was the sheer madness of it
all which made the period so grand, the "anything
goes" mentality which dominated Old Trafford and the
away grounds across the country playing host to Manchester's finest. And this was the period when violence
took over – when United went to places like Norwich
and, as you do, decided to take the ground home with
them after the match.
   'Those who were there know the score of the seventies at United. Those – like me – who only played a bit
part have since been regaled with the tales of Norwich
and St Etienne; the mad trips to Merseyside and
Newcastle (where United fans used to meet at 6 a.m. to
play football with Geordies by the ground and then go
ballistic later on in the afternoon); and the ground-
taking excursions into the North Bank, the Shed and
all other possible away locations. Even the home
games provided mad moments . . . How Our Martin

would have crapped himself if he'd been in charge in those days.

'For all these and many other reasons, a part of me yearns to have been a real part of it; of following the Reds all over, seeing them in new grounds during the promotion year, getting pissed when only a few hundred travelled – all unofficially – to the European matches. And this at a time when we didn't have those in authority suppressing the atmosphere at matches by creating a semi-fearful Old Trafford, in which United fans are worried about showing any kind of emotion for fear of being permanently ejected. In the seventies not only did things like that never happen, you would never have *imagined* them happening.

'I was fortunate enough to come from a family that supported United, lucky to see the Reds for the first time at the age of four, even more fortunate to see them at Old Trafford at five and then go irregularly thereafter until I started to see the team as much as possible. But even at an early age, my recollections of matches are inter-linked with the travels to them and the occurrences off the pitch. Thus Martin Buchan's great goal against Everton is recalled alongside a memory of a few hundred Everton fans jumping literally through the carriage windows – the door handle must have been a bit too much for them to cope with – on the little train from Manchester Piccadilly and attacking any Reds they could. Realizing that this Red Army basically consisted of a few old men and their sons, they proceeded to smash up the carriage, until arrival at Warwick Road saw them change colour dramatically as a platform full of Reds waited to show them round the stadium . . .

'Other recollections from the decade sprinkle across my memory such as a game at White Hart Lane providing the sight of three female Spurs fans attacking a lone female Red by Seven Sisters and using her as a football until the police arrived on horseback. Or the dreadful period at Highbury where we didn't win once during the seventies, when the only United spirit came from the Red Army who treated the taking of the North Bank as one of the "must-do" operations of the year.

(One such campaign manoeuvre saw nearly as many Reds in the North Bank as Arse fans!)

'But my most striking memory seems to epitomize what the decade was all about. Leeds United were the opponents at Old Trafford on 1 March 1978. It was my first game against the bitter Yorkshire rivals, and the initial feelings inspired in me by the Yorkshiremen that day are with me nearly twenty years later. The journey to the ground was a fairly tense affair; the people who travelled with me obviously realized what the game meant – the War of the Roses, the only battle to have been played out for the whole of the twentieth century – and the police were out in phenomenally large numbers. As I was a youngster, these were the days when you excitedly went through the turnstiles as soon as they opened, read and reread the programme and then paid full, rapt attention to all the acts being played out in front of you.

'We were perfectly positioned by K-Stand's penalty box and, as these were the days of large early escorts, it was the away fans (or those not sufficiently clued up to avoid capture by the police at the train and coach arrival points) who arrived en masse early to watch the home fans arrive. And thus the goading began. Due to the traditional hatred, the Stretford End was fuller than usual at that early time. Both home and away standing ends were filled with 20–30-year-old men (the standard seventies football supporter) and I must say, admittedly with bias, that there was a hatred apparent on the faces of the Leeds crowd that is unmistakable to this day.

'As kick-off arrived, the Leeds fans were taking more sections than they'd been allocated, spilling over from one into the next. Despite the attendance being far below capacity, the same was happening to the United Road and the two factions edged closer and closer to each other. The police (Smiley included) tried defiantly to hold back the crowd as they came no more than 150 feet from each other. Every bodily fluid was being thrown between the two, and despite a constant tug of war taking place between the Reds and the police, and between the

211

police and Leeds, the two lines held firm. This was now enthralling all the Red crowd – the Stretford End began cheering on the Reds from afar and as the Leeds fans were pushed back by an increasing number of police, a big roar went up. A very small number of people got on the pitch, quickly pushed back in and only once did the end break – and only for a matter of seconds – with just a few direct scuffles but a lot of missile-hurling violence. If the lines had broken that day, there would simply have been the greatest football stadium riot imaginable – those in the United Road in the seventies would not have let anyone take liberties on their patch.

'I'd never seen anything like it, and as the game progressed mounted police arrived – on the pitch – to add their presence in an attempt to quell the tug of war still taking place. By mid-way through the first half, riot police (in full helmet and yellow uniforms) arrived – it had to be explained to me what they actually were – to replace the knackered Old Trafford beat regulars. With riot police and police horses in formation (every once in a while encroaching on to the pitch, and every once in a while pissing on the pitch – the horses that is, not the police!), the 150 tiny short feet separating the two sets of fans remained unbreached. The atmosphere – unlike anything you could ever see today – was like the proverbial cauldron; the team tried their hardest, backed by total support, but the hobbit Bryan Flynn stole a goal in the dying minutes. After some final attempts by both fans to get at each other, and the arrival of even more police and horses, it was the final whistle. As I left the ground, chaos ensued.

'So it was another game I had seen to chalk up, but really it was so much more than that; the passion shown was incomparable to anything I'd seen before. I'd already been hooked, but this transported me from merely loving United to being completely bowled over and *in love with* United. I'm fortunate enough to be able to see United every week in the nineties, follow them to new dizzy heights, and travel all over Europe to those top *craic* European away trips but from everything I saw during those fifty-odd games in the seventies, I still wonder what great times I would have had if I'd been born in 1951 and not 1971. Then I might even have seen that great match at Wembley – but that's another completely different regret . . .' – *Barney*

1978–79

I write this under the baleful influence of a sharp reminder that grisly post-hammering Monday mornings, so common a currency during the Sexton years, can strike during the best of times. Five-nil at St James' Park '96; enough of an embarrassment to conjure up memories of Roche, Sloan and Connell. IMUSA's Andy Walsh is being quoted on the radio, sounding a Manc Attitude battle cry: 'We're not worried – Newcastle have had more new dawns than the Zulus.' Tee-hee! A hundred apoplectic Geordies jam the switchboards.

We know what we're on about, of course. The last twenty years have presented Reds with many a shimmering horizon, soon stolen from us by gathering dark clouds. August 1978, however, was not one such tantalizing moment. A black-hearted cumulo-nimbus was towering over us virtually straight from kick-off. On the opening day twelve months before, a 4-1 splattering of Birmingham had sent hopes soaring; this time, few emerged from the tediously strained 1-0 defeat of the Brummies with any such illusions. Within months, United's spirits would sink to a level of angry, bitter discontent not equalled until the winter of 1989–90. On both occasions, it seemed only a miracle could save the helmsmen from being swept away by the ferocious Stretford End tide. Such as the kind of miracle only the magic of the FA Cup can produce . . .

One of the keys to eventual salvation would be provided by Jimmy Greenhoff – ironically, Sexton spent much of the summer trying to lose this key down the back of the sofa, permanently. Tommy Docherty would later accuse Sexton of trying to dump all 'his boys' before their sell-by date;

already Hill had gone, Forsyth was on his way back to Scotland and Jimmy appeared Bridge-bound for £75,000. But Jimmy resisted staunchly, however much sources within Old Trafford suggested to the press that Greenhoff had 'only been a short-term buy' and 'hadn't really produced the goods yet'. Jimmy survived only because Pearson had to undergo a knee operation, the happiest consequence of an injury ever until Dublin's fracture opened the road from Leeds. Imagine Sexton's six-month record if Jimmy'd gone: sold Hill, sold Greenhoff, bought Thomas – and he wondered why fans questioned his judgement, and Docherty his objectivity?

If Jordan & Greenhoff were the answer to the questions up front, at least until Ritchie came up with a poser or two, other queries went begging. The bleeding left-wing stump left after the severance of Hill continued to spurt for another three months as McCreery, McIlroy, Grimes and McGrath were all tried and discarded. Of course, under Sexton's new system, we were no longer looking for an orthodox left-winger as such, but some amorphous left-sided central-yet-a-bit-wide guy who could cross, tackle, run, make the tea and pretend to understand A-level tactics. In short, a left-leaning Coppell. But, as the song said, There's Only One Stevie Coppell.

By November, Sexton had decided no solution lay within the club's current personnel. Yet when McIlroy took Hill's shirt and allowed Brian Greenhoff in at Number 4, we looked close to Sexton's ideal. Unfortunately, they were only given four chances as an ensemble. Not that fans approved of this Sextonian ideal: of course they didn't. But if this was the system we had to live with, then Brian and Sam together in the middle was surely a superior version to the Welsh remix Sexton was about to spin. After all, three of our four better early performances came courtesy of this Bri & Sam engine-room, against City, Ipswich and Arsenal. But once the new Number 11 arrived, Brian had to make do with whatever games he could get when Macari was injured, or take his chances in United's ever-changing kaleidoscopic defence. Within the year, he'd left Old Trafford, another favourite son and Docherty boy lost.

The defence remained the most serious unsolved conundrum, as suggested by the grotesque fact that we were to concede more than we'd score for the first time since relegation. And this under a manager who'd reshaped and/or wrecked a classic line-up in order to shore up these very defences: had Buchan not stayed injury-free, both Wembley and mid-table safety would have been an impossibility. Injuries, attacks of bad form and apparent managerial indecision resulted in seven different full-back combinations taking the field this season as if by rota – this in front of a goal that contained Paddy Roche for the first three months. A recipe for Pot Noodle Instant Disaster or what? Just add one over-heated centre-half in a slump and stir. (That ingredient being McQueen, who started inconsistently and went downhill over the New Year). Leave to stand for three months, taste, and pour away in disgust.

So: an attack constituted by default, with Jordan still a year from his best; a misfiring, disjointed midfield; a defence of shifting quicksands, Paddy Roche in goal; and don't forget our so-called back-up, which consisted of a pissed-off McCreery, a half-decent Grimes and the (then) wholly useless McGrath and Paterson. However shocking Jim Callaghan's announcement in October that he wouldn't be going to the country – the worst piece of timing since Abe Lincoln suggested a night out at the theatre – it was nothing compares to the incredulity which greeted Sexton's contemporary protestations that United could still challenge for the title. What title would that be, then? Manchester's most boring side in fifty years? Britain's most booed manager? The fastest fall from grace since Chappaquidick? For United's component problems were compounded by Sexton's imposition of a playing style and system entirely alien to our traditions. Even when we won this way, it could be as joyless as a dry fuck. In any event, we were hardly winning at all. The system which was supposed to increase efficiency, control and success, at the price of losing flair and excitement, was producing precisely the opposite effect and leaving fans with the worst of both worlds. Sexton's System, like Callaghan's pay pact with the unions, was fundamentally unsuited to – and unloved by – those upon whom it had been imposed. A Winter of Discontent was just reward for both.

Flash-forward to January. A bemused Jim Callaghan returns

from a foreign junket as strike-bound Britain sinks into the mire. Rubbish on the streets, the dead unburied – the full Tory PPB catalogue of horrors. 'Crisis? What Crisis?' cruelly paraphrase the tabloids. Uncanny how Sexton's befuddlement would be echoed by Callaghan so precisely when, in November, Dave faced his own Red rebellion from within the movement. In United's case, the mountain of rubbish was what we were watching, the grave-less dead the men in Red shirts – but the villain was Sexton, not our unhappy heroes. Fans travelling to struggling Birmingham were festooned with 'Sexton Out!' badges; a week before at Old Trafford, they had booed United off the pitch after a 1-1 draw with Ball-inspired Southampton, disgusted by the lethargic, arhythmic long-ball shite United had offered them.

Let us skip briefly over the antecedents, for the memories are dismal. Thrashed at Ipswich, then unjustly through in the League Cup against Stockport's minnows thanks to last-minute miracles. Four one-one draws of unparalleled awfulness, mostly saved by last-gasp equalizers, punctuated by slow hand-clapping and calls for Pearson's return whilst we were outplayed. Shattering humiliation at home to Bristol City, a performance not much bettered against Middlesbrough – booed off again despite a 3-2 win. The very worst? Beaten at home in the League Cup by Watford, Third Division trundlers whose one decent player, Luther Blissett, ran us ragged. I can still remember every minute of the aftermath, frozen in my Main Stand seat. We were next to the box and could see Elton John leaping around like he'd been pokered up the arse (well, you never know . . .). In every other direction were completely shamed faces, a sight I'd never witnessed before. Angry, disappointed, sad – but never ashamed. My Dad hurried me away home, almost apologetic that he'd allowed his child to see such a pornographic display. I was too young fully to understand the reasoning or express it in such a way but I knew this: we'd been buggered royally on the pitch that night, but the guy who was really shafting us was supposedly one of ours. His sticker came out of the Panini album: Sexton had made his umpteen-thousandth enemy.

All right, there had been the odd shaft of light. In any other seasonal summary, the 3-2 win at Leeds would warrant a half-page celebration but not in this context. (It was fantastic, though, to hear Leeds singing 'McQueen and Jordan are homosexuals', see them chucking rocks at Gogo and then to delight in his reply, an 11th-minute goal.) The final minute of the derby, filled with exaltation over Jordan's winner, made up for the preceding 89 minutes of brainlessness; there'd also been an admirable fight-back to get a 2-2 draw at Villa Park and a 4-2 win at Molineux. But of the fifteen opening matches, ten had been criminally treacherous – a betrayal of a legend. United were slow, over-cautious, too methodical and deliberate, without imagination, as penetrative as an 80-year-old's stiffy – in short, as Allison and Docherty categorized both Manchester clubs before the derby, boring. Reds can forgive lack of success but they will never accept lack of style.

Sexton didn't understand, not at that moment anyway. 'But we're fifth in the League', he mused, entirely missing the point. An infamous article in the *Daily Express*, headlined 'Cold Trafford', explained the 'Real Voice' of the Stretford End to Sexton in a cutting prose he could comprehend, since he was clearly deaf to the language of the terraces:

> 'It does not matter where United are [in the League] but what they are . . . Old Trafford demands performance, entertainment, skill, pedigree . . . at the moment it is bleeding to death with boredom. United do not want to be fifth in any League if the football that got them there is restricted, inhibited, lacking in vision and the unorthodox. Sexton has given fans a team in the puritan image of himself – a puritan side that unfortunately responds to frustrations with a profligacy that would not have pleased Oliver Cromwell one bit.'

In contrast, David Meek called United's fans 'spoiled, arrogant and unfair'. I may be subjective, but I think I know which of these two opinions reflected historical truth.

United lost 5-1 at St Andrews, an ignominious nadir yet one which we would equal in depth over Christmas. Tarantini, a Cantona of his day at least in temperament and crowd-thumping prowess, got away with an incident which resulted in Brian Greenhoff being knocked out cold. Frozen out forever henceforth was Paddy Roche: not too ill a wind, then. The introduction of Gary Bailey would not be the only change to the team but he'd be just about the only truly good one. For Messrs Sloan and Connell were about to emerge from the Central League, 'bolstered' by the signing of Mickey Thomas from Wrexham as the answer to the Number 11 problem. An answer that merely prompted further questions such as 'Who the fuck is he?', 'How's he got in the team?' and 'When is this bastard going to score?' (Answers: 'A hard-working failure', 'Mad Sexton thinks he's better than Hill' and 'March, if you're lucky.')

Bailey's immediate task was to convince Sexton he didn't need to spend £440,000 on Coventry's Jim Blyth. Few fans needed any convincing whatsoever, the ludicrously overpriced Blyth eventually failing a medical to save Sexton the embarrassment of another transfer disaster. A blinder against dad's Ipswich, a blunder against Everton, then another stormer at the Bridge: by December, he was secure. Poor Paddy Roche really did look the class geek next to this Aryan god. Bailey was immeasurably bigger, better-looking, cockier and generally a testament to good genetics. His positioning could be off at times and his cross-work dodgy but as a hunky, dominating shot-stopper, he was everything that a quivering defender wants to feel behind him. A young Peter Schmeichel, watching on telly back home in Denmark, had a new hero.

Sloan contrived to be completely anonymous during the defeat of Ipswich, so much so that few realized he'd played; a positive liability at Everton, he was scarcely heard of again, except in facetious *Red Issue* headlines. By the time we visited Chelsea, Thomas was ready to take his place. 'He won't be overawed,' boasted Sexton. 'He's come here hungry to prove himself.' Months later, Sexton was still claiming 'his purchase has been my most important decision' – by which time an entirely overawed Thomas had taken to getting pissed up before matches and had proved only that he was no Gordon Hill. Twenty years later, proper grown-up scribes like Jim White – *homme sérieux* enough to appear on *Late Review* and write only for the best qualities – can still get worked up sufficiently to devote an entire back-page column to the travesty that was

Sexton's *de facto* replacement of Hill with Thomas. The teenage rage he once felt came roaring out at the mere sight of Thomas's name in a book; never let it be said that Thomas wasn't inspirational.

To be fair, Mickey started well in the win at Chelsea: but it had been a terrible match against a terrible side in front of a terrible crowd. At Derby, those carrying a torch for Hill had to grit their teeth. Despite Hill and Daly combining to put Docherty's side one-up for a triptych of vengeance, United romped to a 3-1 win with Thomas clearly out-rating his predecessor. But the true joy that day had been the performance of Andy Ritchie, stepping in for the injured Jordan. Here was a Manc lad who looked the part in every way; only eighteen for a fortnight, a natural goalscorer whipped from under City's noses in Giggsian fashion. The record books don't say so but he really scored twice that day, striking up an instant pupil–teacher relationship with Greenhoff. When he scored again in the defeat of Spurs a week later, the buzz was sensational. This was a player on a fast-track to idol status, already virtually a complete cult-hero in seven days. Surely Jordan and Pearson would have more claims to contend with on their return than just each other's? But Ritchie was stirring, unpredictable and thrilling: one for Deadly Dave's execution list, then.

Whatever lift Thomas and Ritchie's entrances gave the team didn't even last out the year. Over eight excruciating 'festive' (arf!) days, Bolton, Liverpool and West Brom gave us a triple-whammy of Christmas hidings which our arses still remember. You could, at a push, blame the 0-3 at Burnden on the pitch; add that extra *alma mater* bite from Gowling, Morgan and Dunne plus Connell's atrocious debut and you've got a viable explanation. To lose 0-3 and 3-5 at home to Liverpool and West Brom brooked no flip excuses. Each in their own way thrust our existential crisis back down our throats. If Sexton still didn't think we had serious problems, the superior players and teamwork of our opponents held up every flaw for his examination like the dripping entrails ripped from a hunted animal.

(You may recall I mentioned my co-scribe's Strettie induction against Liverpool the previous season, hooked for life by that 2-0 riot. My cousin was taken for his first ever match to this Liverpool game. When he got home, he simply said, 'Never take me there again' and – possibly in trauma – refused to discuss anything he'd witnessed. These days, he actively loathes footie, makes dance music and has got married. It's all gone horribly wrong and it's all Dave Sexton's fault.)

Yes, Liverpool were at a peak of sorts, on their way to a record points total; nevertheless the appalling ease of their win, at an arrogant stroll on our ground for Christ's sake, was surely the greatest humiliation we've suffered against any Scousers in thirty years – and I include the four and five-nils of later years. The particular lesson of the day? That our supposed drive for efficiency, control and sophistication was a sick joke.

West Brom is at least to be recalled with some pleasure. After all, this is the game to quote at those who tell you a one-nil win is always better than any defeat, no matter how entertaining. Moreover we should have been grateful for small mercies. Here we were, at 30 December already, and this was the first match Old Trafford had seen this season in which we saw attacking football as it was meant to be played at its spiritual home. For once, we'd thrown off Sextonian inhibition and take someone on in a contest of art rather than attrition. Despite the snow, the temperature and the defeat, any genuine lover of the game emerged flushed hot with the thrill of it all. And yet the lesson was, in some ways, as severe as the one dealt by the Dirties. We were so obviously no longer the supreme entertainers, capable of beating anyone with gusto and flair on our day. For this *was* our day: we played at an attacking peak. The reality was West Brom were even better at 'being United' than we were. No one in Red could match the inventive brilliance of Cunningham and Regis; no one had the outstanding drive of Tony Brown and fight of Robson. When Regis scored that outrageous Scoreboard Ender to silence the black-taunting scum, I almost felt pleased for him; not just on political grounds but because West Brom had so clearly responded to Docherty's old challenge and built a side to entertain and win. They had shown us where we'd gone wrong – they'd almost done us a service. In four days, two great sides had told Sexton the truth, that his eighteen months had produced a side that could not win a championship of either Efficiency or Entertainment. And if he did at least know that we demanded one or the other, one must suspect he never got to grips with the fact that we'd probably prefer the latter.

What a cold, miserable, doom-laden winter that was, for the country and United. Both had reached a crossroads, a knock-out to decide the future. I suppose Callaghan's match with the unions was the more crucial and immediate; defeat against the giant-killers of TUC United would mean at least five years of Thatcherism, a prospect even more fearsome than another season of Sextonia. And if Dave's side lost their Cup match against Chelsea, the sack would not follow quite so fast as it could have in January 1990 for Alex Ferguson. But surely an early Cup exit would spell termination for Sexton come the summer – certainly, only United's continuing presence in the Cup seemed to be preventing Dave's lynching come late February. If there were those secretly praying for such a Cup defeat in order to get Sexton eradicated, just as there were similar prayers in 1990, then their imprecations were at a very low murmur; the support for United's Cup campaign was at its vocal best.

The weather wiped all but the Cup from January, for which every Red was grateful after months of League horrors. Yet in some ways, the Chelsea home tie had Nightmare on Warwick Road written all over it too. Macari and Thomas injured, rusty Pearson playing his first match of the season, Jimmy Nicholl forced into emergency midfield . . . but somehow the players found the left-over festive spirit, despite those Christmas kickings, to romp home 3-0. Ashley Grimes belted a thirty-yarder, Jimmy swooped in for a superb header – it was the Charlton & Law Revival show. And there could be no greater trouper on stage than Pearson, combining with Jimmy for old time's sake as if he'd never been away. Any hopes that this 1977 double-act would be the one to take us all the way were dashed a fortnight later in the fourth round at Craven Cottage. Amidst an absolute barnstormer which brought the very best from Bailey, Pearson created our goal before becoming the dead meat filling in a Fulham sandwich. Tragically, he never played for us again. United, at least, lived to fight another day by escaping the onslaught with a 1-1 draw.

A nationwide thaw meant that League football would be

back to await us in February, keen as ever to embarrass and disappoint – Arsenal duly obliged with a 2-0 win at Old Trafford. Thank God we had derbies and Cup ties to take us out of ourselves. League fixtures were becoming the equivalent of Monday mornings back at work, a soul-destroying and never-ending futile routine. We made the most of what felt like a ten-day holiday. Obliterating City 3-0 at Maine Road constituted the outstanding awayday of the season, fittingly only four days after Denis Howell had lifted the ticket restrictions on travelling Reds. Two-goal Coppell ran the Blues into the ground; McIlroy and a returning Macari completely controlled the frozen midfield; and Andy Ritchie scored against those who'd given him footballing life in the first place. Lovely. Significantly, Albiston had returned to full-back and would not miss another game, instantly helping us to keep four clean sheets in five games. Our Derby Double ensured City would finish below us for only the second time in ten seasons; whatever our problems, there could be no smug crowing from that lot at least. Especially not after their trip to Gay Meadow.

Two days later, Fulham finally submitted after struggling and wriggling on the hook like these awkward-bastard minnows always do. Tony Gale's arse played the killer ball for the only goal, Jimmy's third in the Cup already. At Colchester in the fifth, infamous graveyard of Leeds in '71, Jimmy struck again for the winner whilst Arthur Albiston cleared brilliantly off the line with ten to go. These two heroes of Wembley '77 were undoubtedly on a roll; that old Brent bog stench had the nostrils a-twitching already . . .

Back to work, back to Old Trafford, back to bollocks. Any first flushes of Wembley Fever disappeared with a few splashes of icy cold reality. Two abominable displays against Villa and QPR brought forth the most cacophonous catcalling anyone could remember at OT. The Stretford End's point was all the more telling in light of the results: a 1-1 draw and a 2-0 win. How blatantly did it have to be expressed? – a win without style is like an ejaculation without an orgasm. For the players, this must have been a disconcerting time. Jimmy Greenhoff's angry gesture to the fans after the QPR match suggested some players didn't understand that we saw most of them as innocent victims, soldiers who were only obeying orders, some perhaps in full knowledge of their commander's

223

stupidity. For the board, the attendance figures were rather more than merely disconcerting: 44,000 for Villa, 36,000 for QPR, both technically overestimates too; these were not viable income generators for a club of United's ambition. Any workplace management knows that the first sign something is critically wrong with an enterprise is a high absentee rate. United now had 20,000 missing, more lost legions than at any time since the darkest pre-relegation days. Unless it was FA Cup time, who'd want to clock in at Sexton's factory for hours upon hours of mind-numbing meaningless shite?

Sexton's response to the low attendances would have been classically comical if not so indicative of having one's head in one's colon: 'Attendances are low because of all the postponed games recently – people have got out of the habit of going.' Those who'd always argued that Dave could've solved many problems if he'd communicated more with the public were rapidly realizing how wrong they'd been. Total silence would've been preferable. Another Sexton excuse for the team: 'There are lots of young players who need time to learn and are still finding their way.' Eh?? This was the oldest United team for years, all well-blooded in football's trials of character. No, the only education that was still needed was Sexton's – a lesson or two in the philosophy of Manchester United, for a start.

In the wake of the QPR débâcle, David Meek sparked a local navel-gazing epidemic with one of his 'shut-up-you-scum' pieces. He wrote: 'United's magic bubble has burst – concede that the halcyon days are over. United no longer have the gift to win and entertain by divine right.' He went on, as usual, to defend the status quo, scold the fans for their impatience and to blame the Stretford End for the team's condition. To my eyes, and those of many fans, this represented both a craven surrender and a gross distortion. Only twenty months before, Meek like everyone else had heralded the return of the glory days, rightly stating that with a tweak or two United would be title material. Now, instead of declaring Sexton had taken the wrong fork and that it was time to get back on the road Docherty discovered, he was simply advocating continued blind support and an abandonment of hope. Why should fans have accepted that the halcyon days were over, that they no longer had the right to expect more of what we'd enjoyed from '75 to '77?

Meek's psychology was that of the collaborationist; most Stretford Enders preferred the Resistance. Because United do have a right to expect entertainment and success. Not, perhaps, by divine right, but certainly by virtue of the fact that we are the biggest, best-supported and most well-resourced club in England. And by the fact that any entertaining United side will draw capacity crowds and maximum revenue, trophies or not; and by the fact that virtually every pro in Britain would eat his own excrement if it got him a transfer to United. With fundamentals like that in place, Sextonian failure is intolerable. Being boss of United is not the hardest job in England at all but the easiest. It's the equivalent of being President of the USA: everyone wants a Green Card, you've got half of every resource in the world plus more money and weaponry than anyone else. If you can't keep that outfit at Number One, you should be shot.

The response from the public in the *Evening News* postbag summarized the Stretford End view quite succinctly:

'There are no excuses for the decline of United to mediocrity. Under Sexton, we have been a disgrace . . . our League position belies the drivel which has been served up. The Red Army has remained faithful beyond the call of duty . . . but has realized blind faith is not enough.'

'Sexton has turned an exciting team into a kick-and-hope outfit at a cost of one million pounds. The present team is the most boring ever seen on our pitch . . . if they do play to a pattern, I wish someone would explain it to us.'

'This is not about trophies. It is the style of play and class of player that we criticize. We have woken up and become more critical and stopped being kidded by fatuous remarks from management and press but we are told to shut up. Well, we now know it is no use to the club just to be blindly faithful.'

Whether they voted with their feet or their pens, the fans' view was largely unmistakable. As Peter Finch yelled in the contemporary Oscar-winner *Network*: 'We're mad as hell and we're not gonna take it anymore!' And at least

Finch got to cop a handful of Faye Dunaway's melons. The only titting about we got to see was on the pitch . . .

Only the players remained silent, as they always do unfortunately. But in later years, as each left or wrote memoirs, the truth emerged. The Greenhoff Brothers, Steve Coppell, Alex Stepney and Sammy McIlroy all voiced similar concerns about Sexton with varying degrees of vehemence. He wasn't as good a motivator or communicator as they required, certainly compared to Docherty; they felt they were over-coached and over-tacticianed, and that his systems didn't suit their mentalities and skills; his minimal media presence left them feeling exposed to public scrutiny and undefended; and his personal tension, such a contrast to the Doc's breezy insouciance, infected all with the dressing-room screaming ab-dabs. The post-Hill euphoria had long disappeared.

And yet, and yet . . . within five weeks of this renewed civil war, United's supposedly roundhead puritans had emulated their cavalier predecessors and reached Wembley. That old black magic which the FA Cup weaves so well, to adapt Sinatra. Of course, there were good footballing reasons for this extraordinary resurrection. McQueen proved to be a Cup battler *par excellence*, Joe Jordan came good and – most miraculously – Mickey Thomas looked like scoring occasionally. Admittedly, just as in 1990, skill and artistry were not the telling attributes but simple gutsy determination and fight. And in that, the team benefited from the most important factor of all: the wholehearted and relentless support of the Red Army. For in a life-or-death Cup battle, when glory rather than useless points is at stake, all divisions are healed. Like a nation going to fight, political differences and class war must be put aside for the sake of unity: a Manchester United once again.

White Hart Lane, 10 March, in an era when that stadium was still a temple of passion and not a modern mausoleum. Fifty-three thousand inside, including a full battalion of travelling Reds, some enjoying the renewed opportunity for a mass aggro and full-tilt footie combination as much as at any time in Doc's days. Ossie Ardiles leads a newly promoted but sharply improving Spurs side

with gorgeous skill and vision, completely dictating the
first half. They're the favourites, we're the underdogs and
we're a goal down. Perfect. At such moments, careers and
futures hang in the balance – then Mickey Thomas forces
the ball home to get us a replay and repay Sexton for his
faith. A full-time pitch-invader deals Ardiles a slap, as if
to warn him of the vocal and footballing pummelling that
awaits at Old Trafford.

Macari didn't understand that he needn't have made any
public appeals for the Stretford End's support: this was the
Cup, this was Old Trafford, this was war with the Cockney
twats. Here were 56,000 ready to fight, the first fifty-plus
gate since Boxing Day. Jordan destroys Spurs' defence
while McIlroy wipes out Ardiles before scoring the clinching second. After eight months of rubbish, United are
through to a semi-final against the Dirties at the dustbin,
which has a nice kind of logic to it.

There were still fourteen mainly rearranged League fixtures left but who could give a fuck? Need us to play ten
matches in twenty-six April days, mate? No problem. Bang
on the autopilot and dream of Wembley. Few could be
bothered to jeer: it was all so pointless. And almost literally
so too – in one nine-game stretch, we scored just five goals
and lost badly to both Bolton and Liverpool. Ordinarily,
cause for revolution. But life feels rather different when
you've got a semi or final ticket burning a hole in your
obsolescent flares' pocket.

Just one League match stayed in the memory: the incredible 4-1 thrashing of Leeds a week before the semi-final.
Leeds hadn't lost away in six months yet Andy Ritchie, a
raw kid with more attitude than experience, smashed a
hat-trick which threatened to deny the sheep their place in
Europe. Two of those goals were jaw-droppingly brilliant,
finishing of a savagery we weren't used to any more. We
had seen the future, or so we thought; actually, many
thought they'd seen the present and were stunned to see
Sexton drop him at Boro three days later. Now there's a pub
quiz question for you: how many players have been booted
out of a team after scoring a treble? (Er, just Andy, as a
matter of fact.) Welcome to the world inside Dave Sexton's
skull: it's a cold and lonely landscape indeed. But he was
right to pick Jordan for the semi. Against such monsters as

Case, Souness and McDermott, we'd need every ogre we could get.

There is a gut-churning deadliness about a Cup semi-final that cannot be surpassed. True thrill-seekers, those who really get off on football's equivalent of flatlining, love them more than the finals themselves. That old truism happens to be true: no one remembers a beaten semi-finalist and there is nought but bitterness to remember in defeat. Glory, to some extent, is shared at Wembley: the dead get a sort of afterlife, as we were soon to discover. Death in a semi is final. It's the existentialist's choice of footballing event.

Gut-churning too was the opposition team-sheet. This Liverpool side had a grim perfection about it, as loathsome, smooth and deadly as the KGB of the fifties. Later Dirties sides would be far more entertaining and rack up massive unbeaten records of dizzying consistency; the 1984 incarnation may have been the best all-rounders. But this particular eleven had the greatest impact on me and my mates. For they were the first Liverpool side that frightened us, that made us watching feel we were going to be beaten before they'd even kicked off. The '76 and '77 sides were flawed, beatable, plainly still mortals within reach who'd only just scraped their titles. In '78, they were even second best to the infallible Forest. But despite the fact that Forest knocked Liverpool out of the '79 European Cup and went on to win it, we all knew Liverpool were the best. Dalglish had fully flowered — come on, let's admit it — into the best British player since Best. They were about to finish with a record 68 points and conceded only 16 League goals all season. More to the point, the memory of our 1977 triumphs against them had faded. All I could think about in the run-up to Maine Road were the twin wellyings they'd given us since and all I wanted was to see my heroes spared any such humiliation. Who would have thought United had the ability to pull off the smart one-two that would amaze a nation?

Fifty-three thousand at Maine Road on a Saturday — obviously not City playing, then. For 18 minutes, Liverpool strut, then score. There is no time to articulate any notion that the ghost of Christmas past has returned because Jordan heads home within 60 seconds. Thirty thousand Reds mentally take back everything they said about Ritchie and Joe. And then go mental.

That goal lifted some sort of curse. Today's game suddenly tilted away from the seemingly predestined one-sided romp and became a counter-thrusting battle of near-equals. When McDermott put his penalty against the post. Liverpool began to crumble at the edges. Brian Greenhoff, in an unusual Number 10 position, wheedled through such a crack to hook in our second on 56 minutes. So all we had to do was defend against European champions for over half-an-hour . . . So we panicked a tad and missed good chances and our arses were going a bit and Liverpool were all over us like acne on Fowler and, and . . .

I suppose they were always going to score. But with only eight minutes to go too, with Wembley almost tangible – and it had to be Hansen, didn't it, whose smug arrogance offended even then. Defeatism was rampant during those intervening days. Buchan, Sexton, Coppell: in interviews, they all sounded like men who'd given their all and feared they couldn't summon anymore. Going into enemy territory to Goodison, to face a subtly reshaped Liverpool whose new 4-3-3 line-up spoke of hunters hungry for the kill . . . if only McQueen's header had crept in, if only Stevie hadn't screwed wide. But after Ray Kennedy's header cracked against the bar in the replay, our defenders seemed to grow before us. And despite ceding second-half midfield command, we took everything they threw at us. The irony of it all: we resembled Liverpool on a tricky Euro awayday, soaking up and breaking fast. Still, few could believe we wouldn't crack first. But Martin Buchan overcame Dalglish in one of his greatest personal triumphs, inspiring every defender around him. With twelve to go, Jordan flicked to Thomas: his smart cross found Jimmy Greenhoff ten yards out who stooped gracefully to head past Clemence. Image of the year, no question: United's coolest player in the classic three-stripe away kit, roaring to the heavens on his way to Wembley. To think that if Sexton had had his way, Jimmy could've been down at the Bridge getting relegated . . .

And so to the Final, our third in four years – at the time, a phenomenal achievement in itself. Not an experience that is easy to discuss and I wasn't even there, which proved to be very handy when the bedroom was at close proximity for a good sob at the end. So I leave this to the words of those who witnessed a double miracle at first hand, starting with Jim White, author of the magisterial *Are You Watching Liverpool?*

'There was no prospect of a ticket. It was 1979, my second year at college away from Manchester and, unlike 1977, I hadn't been to enough games to accumulate the tokens. Being eighteen and a student, I was not exactly Gerry Anderson in the string-pulling department; I was resigned to watching United against Arsenal in the common room bar, dodging the sneers of the rugby followers. Then, on the Friday morning, with less than 29 hours to kick off, I was in a lecture at the end of which a lad stood at the front of the hall and asked if anyone liked football. Thinking he was proposing a kickaround on the Downs or something, I stuck my hand up. I was the only one to do so (well, it was a Middle English lecture).

' "You don't", he said, flourishing a bank-note-sized piece of thick paper in his hand, "fancy going to the Cup Final do you?"

'Did I? I nearly wet myself. It turned out his dad was a director at Middlesbrough and had sent him a ticket. The lad himself, going through a difficult phase, didn't much care for football and wondered if anyone could give the thing a good home. The home I could give it was in the Buckingham Palace class. He didn't even charge me.

'The next morning I got the early train to London and travelled north on the tube to Stanmore, to meet two mates I knew were coming down from Manchester. One of them had secured a brace of tickets from a bloke who lived down their road (it was Martin Buchan). So there we were, the luckiest three gits in red, winners of the lottery that is Cup Final ticket allocation, joining the joyful hordes down the Jubilee Line. When it turned out we had belting seats, opposite the royal box and we were only two rows apart, we thought nothing could go wrong.

'But for 80 minutes, everything did. It was the most miserable 4,800 seconds of football in our football-watching careers. "Sod this for a lark," said the man next to me as events dragged towards their inevitable conclusion; and off he went, assuming Arsenal were going to take the thing 2-0. Immediately into his place sat a big fat man, a pie-eater of some pedigree. I don't know where he came from but we were soon to be introduced.

'The man had barely squeezed into his new position, when suddenly, unexpectedly and totally against the run of play, McQueen stuck out a telescopic leg in the Arsenal area and made it 1-2. We leapt up, the fat man and I, and slapped each other on the back. We were still on our feet, roaring more in hope than expectation, as two minutes later, McIlroy, stumbling, stuttering, never quite in control, picked his way through the Arsenal defence as if through a minefield. And, we scarcely believed it, with two minutes to go, he equalized.

'The fat man and I, we became intimate. We wrapped our arms around each other (mine didn't quite make it round his midriff) and bawled meaningless monosyllables of triumph and relief into each other's faces. We bounced forward in our emotion, tottering over the seat in front of us, tumbling as one and sending the representatives of the Rutland FA, or whoever else it was deemed worthy of a prime spot at the Cup Final, running in spluttering indignation.

'Meanwhile, as we tottered, down on the pitch, straight from their kick-off, Brady had started to weave towards the United area. Nicholl, though, had fallen asleep; McQueen was still celebrating his goal; and Buchan was still wondering why he had wasted two tickets on the half-wit who lived down the road: Brady galloped past them all. He made it to the by-line, crossed and Bailey, practising his victory interview with South African television, let the ball run to Sunderland at the far post.

'No haircut has less deserved the prominence Sunderland's fright frizz was about to attain. As he tucked the ball away, his hair, his fancypants grin, his stupid blue collars flapping like a bird's wings as he

231

ran off in his victory dash, were all about to become etched on a thousand Red nightmares. The final whistle went almost before he had returned from some sort of sexual congress with Rix by the corner flag.

'The fat man and I stood silent, open-mouthed, three rows in front of where we should have been, our wedding plans abandoned. Next to us was a new neighbour. He was an Arsenal fan, a spotty youth, who in his moment of victory did what any self-respecting supporter would do. He stood over us, stricken in our desolation, and waved his hands in a double V-sign at us. He yelled at us, with foam flecking the corners of his mouth, in a screaming fury.

' "Why don' you two," he said, "just fack orf ap norf?" 'I think it was Nick Hornby.' – *Jim White*

'When Alan Sunderland scored their third goal, it was the worst moment of my football life. I never want to live through anything like that again. I nearly collapsed with excitement when I scored. To lose after that was like winning the pools only to find you'd forgotten to post the coupon.' – *Sammy McIlroy*

'When United pulled level, I was dreading extra-time. We were shattered and our sub was on. To concede another goal must have been such a sickener for them. You really do have to feel sorry for them.' – *Liam Brady*

'It's easy to say the players should have played out the last minute with cool care. But they're only human and if they had been so unemotional that they could have turned their backs on Sammy's goal, then they would never have found the spirit to battle back in the first place.' – *Dave Sexton*

'At 2-2 my imagination ran riot. I was so convinced we were going to win I could even see the headlines in the Sunday newspapers. The score would be 4-2. It was inevitable; we were tall and strong, full of running and they were shattered.' – *Steve Coppell*

'True, it wouldn't have been so heartbreaking if we'd

simply lost 0-2. But this way, at least we showed people we could fight.' – *Gary Bailey*

'United began the season as a bunch of lads in search of an identity. At Wembley, they found that identity and ceased to be lads. They became men – brave men. United proved the old British qualities of fighting to the bitter end are not dead. They proved that the word defeat need not be a dirty one – not if it comes the way it did for the magnificent Manchester United.' – Daily Express *editorial*

'In defeat, Manchester United's honour and pride is still intact.' – *Dave Sexton*

'Arsenal bastards – that was our Cup, ours . . .'
– *United fan, quoted in the* Daily Mail

Once again, the nation would marvel at the turnout in Manchester for the returning beaten heroes; once again, promises from the rostrum to go back and win next year were said and momentarily meant. We'd been here before, all too recently. Reaching Wembley saved Sexton: it probably brought the club and fans closer together than they'd been since late '77. This season had provided success of a sort, however bitter-sweet the taste. We may still have lacked flair, but perhaps we were going somewhere after all. At least Sexton had rebuilt team spirit – that much was obvious. And in McIlroy's brilliant run and shot for the equalizer, 1978–79 provided the single most exhilarating United goal-frenzy of modern times. Bettered anywhere, perhaps, only by the one that followed seconds later. Bastarding Arsenal bastards.

(PS: Thatcher won the election too. Worst week of the decade contender or what?)

⚽ ⚽ ⚽

You could convincingly argue, from a nineties viewpoint, that nothing on the pitch during 1978–79 matched in importance the financial upheavals off it. November 1978 can be seen as the moment, in Michael Crick's words, when United ceased to be a football club and became a business:

the genesis of the plc behemoth.

When Roland Smith became chairman of the plc in the nineties, some were surprised, given that he had hardly covered himself in glory at British Aerospace. But in many ways, what United has become over the last thirty years is at least partially the child of Smith's parentage. Certainly, the rights issue was his idea and the later general flotation a logical if delayed consequence. Few realized that by the mid-seventies, the Edwards family firm was in trouble. Years of being known as 'suppliers of second-class meat at first-class prices' were catching up with them. When the Edwards clan bailed out, within days of the United rights issue approval, it cost tycoon James Gulliver only £100,000 to take control and the firm's true worth stood at a mere half-million. (Ironically, Gulliver transformed the outfit into Argyll Foods and made it a £2 billion outfit by the mid-eighties, which might illustrate the gulf in financial acumen between him and the Edwardses – perhaps precisely that between an acknowledged genius and guys with no A-levels.) If the Edwards family wanted to make serious money, it would now have to be through United alone. Smith's suggestion provided the route.

Nevertheless, it was always argued that the primary purpose of the issue was to raise cash for the manager to spend – £1 million to be exact. But it wasn't just the cynics who realized that the Edwardses would certainly benefit themselves. Both Sir Matt and Les Olive opposed the issue, correctly pointing out that United's cash reserves, supporter-base and healthy Development Association accounts were ample reservoirs should further transfer funds be required. And when rebel activist John Fletcher proposed a less unusual scheme (for those days) which would've raised £2 million, the board oddly argued that such a sum was more than required!

An indication of the wider motivation was provided by Louis Edwards in 1977 when he asked a colleague: 'How much do you think a United fan would pay to have a share certificate on his wall?' He and his advisers had been considering a 'free share' issue, giving, say, ten new free shares for each one already held. Big shareholders could then sell off thousands to sentimental loyal fans without seriously threatening their own control of the club. It wouldn't just have been a licence to print share certificates but a licence to print money. Fortunately, FA rules were discovered to prohibit such a scheme.

The rights issue as finally constituted was the next best thing. For every share already held, each holder could buy 208 new ones at £1 each. As the figure of £1 was an undervaluation, holders could then sell off as much as they liked at a good profit. Sure, you had to find the money to buy your allocation first – but when you know you're bound to cash in later, you lay such a risk-free bet without hesitation. As far as the Edwardses were concerned, there was only one problem: by 1977 they only held just under half the shares. Since keeping control of the club was almost as important as making money, they would need a much greater holding to maximize the benefits of the scheme, and to ensure it would be passed in the first place. Ideally, they'd want to acquire enough shares – say three-quarters – so they could sell off some, make a profit, yet still retain at least 50 per cent control. And at one point there was talk that these £1 shares might eventually hit £8 each; the potential profits were enormous.

It would be a mighty fine deal to pull off, to increase control *and* make a fortune without any fundamental change in the underlying business; indeed, a rare near-impossibility. For how could they hope to acquire more shares cheaply enough before the issue? Surely everyone else would be seeing pound signs before the eyes too? Not if they didn't know what was planned. Beryl Norman and Elizabeth Hardman, neither of whom were privy to the issue project, were both persuaded to sell their small stakes to the Edwardses. Director Alan Gibson parted with a huge stake of nearly a quarter of the club's shares only after being told the rights issue had been dropped.

The Edwardses now had 74 per cent of the shares and could proceed to drive through the rights issue plan before capitalizing on the aftermath. But they had done so only by breaking the club's own articles, which stated shares had to be offered for sale to the board as a whole first. Far more seriously, the crucial holdings had been acquired through, essentially, insider trading. In 1977–78, this was not illegal, merely unethical; the law was changed to make it a crime in the eighties when the government realized there were

fewer and fewer proper gentlemen in the City. Before
Thatcherism perverted the nation, insider dealing was
simply seen as a sin, as something no self-respecting man
of honour would stoop to; for, in order to benefit from an
insider's prescience, some poor genuine investor outside
the loop had to get stiffed – which is what happened in this
instance. If Beryl Norman and Elizabeth Hardman, who
received £22,000 for their holdings, had held on to them
and instead invested £25,000 to take up their rights issue
allocation, they would now be worth about £6 million.
Alan Gibson's stake, sold for £200,000, would if maintained now command well over £50 million for his surviving family.

In the end, the £1 million proceeds were not immediately spent on players at the time. The purchase of Butch
Wilkins was easily offset by the summer sales of Pancho,
Greenhoff and McCreery. The new goalkeeper Martin
Edwards had suggested financing did materialize, but at a
cost of five, not five hundred, thousand – Gary Bailey. Nor,
admittedly, did the share price rocket quite as much as the
Edwardses had hoped. Martin sold some immediately to
repay a third of the loan he'd taken out but chose to keep
the rest. Publicly, he became a martyr to his overdraft, often
describing how he'd had to struggle along with his debt.
But in fact, he was soon sitting on a realizable profit of
millions, not to mention his shareholding in other compa-
nies; the overdraft was maintained out of choice, not
absolute necessity. Within just five years of the issue, his
stake had sensationally exploded in value to £10 million.
Only then did the ironies become apparent, as Edwards
twice in the eighties came within inches of cashing in and
selling out. For back in '78, those arguing for general
flotation had been beaten down by protestations that the
Edwardses must maintain their control, allowing them to
continue to nurture the club without having to fend off
predators. Those persuaded into selling their shares to the
Edwardses were fed the same line: we're just trying to
ensure our control. However, in the eighties when Maxwell
and Knighton offered to buy the club, it was a rather
different story.

Once the warfare had ceased and the issue passed, many
were prepared to rally around the Establishment flag where

it felt comfortable and warm. David Meek, naturally, predicted we would soon be applauding the deal, and that Louis had a good record of stewardship and could be trusted. As he spoke, *World In Action* had already begun their year-long investigation into Louis Edwards, their interest ironically sparked by the very rights issue that was supposed to have saved his career. When Granada broadcast *The Man Who Bought United* in early 1980, it tended to be the revelations about bribing schoolboy players' parents, the dodgy meat business and the odd spot of tax avoidance which created the greatest furore. Looking back, such 'sordidness' seems so very tame and even inconsequential. The shenanigans with his crappy pies never mattered: to find one company which dealt honestly with sixties and seventies councils would be a miracle. Compared to the Poulson scandal, this was very small beer, or sausage rolls, indeed. Moreover, now we know many clubs did use under-the-counter methods in dealing with both the Revenue and stars of the future. Secretly, many fans might approve: if the end result is more money and success for United, who cares? Were we really so naive then?

Perhaps not: maybe it was just the shock, coming so soon after the Docherty affair, of having Sir Matt's own club, supposed paragons of virtue, being exposed as being less than saintly in such a blockbusting fashion. Some thought it also exposed a hypocrisy, the chairman who'd fired a man for alleged dishonesty and infidelity revealed to be a bit of a crook himself. Such portrayals of black and white simplicities and contrasts were always idiotic. Sir Matt's United were never untouched by the grisly realities of surviving at the top. There had always been the necessary compromises at the margins, ever since the war – a bit of Cup Final touting here, deal-swinging payments there, blind eyes turned somewhere else. Had people already forgotten the hefty fine United had to pay for irregularities in 1969? It is not the fact of an impropriety which matters but its scale. How could Sir Matt and others have kept United surviving in the jungle if they'd decided to draw the line of acceptability just below complete purity? The skill and judgement, the exercise of real morality, comes in defining where compromises with life's dirty but necessary demands must cease. Turning a deaf ear to players touting

Cup Final tickets was one thing; dealing with a manager shagging a colleague's wife another. Similarly, Louis' brown-bag tinkering and minor fiddling could be put down to well-intended roguishness. But insider dealing and breaking promises to Sir Matt was another.

Martin Edwards, rather inelegantly, appeared to blame Sir Matt for Louis' death, remarking in 1990 that had Matt backed the rights issue from the start, no controversy would have arisen and no *World In Action* investigation instigated. That's some combination of sophistry and charmlessness in just one sentence. Sir Matt, of course, had objectively been correct to oppose the deal in any event. But Louis had hardly helped keep Matt onside. The gents' agreement between the two that Matt would eventually be chairman was seemingly never going to come to pass, as Matt had begun to realize. However, when Louis went back on a solemn promise to elevate Sandy Busby to the board and instead promoted the claims of his own kid Roger, he forfeited any right to expect Matt's support. Somehow, that breach of promise seems to me to be more regrettable than most of what *World In Action* alleged. It came as little surprise when Martin eagerly clambered upon the platform his father had built for him to beat Sir Matt to the vacant chairmanship in 1980. Matt didn't want to fight and accepted the presidency with typical grace, a grace some felt Martin hadn't deserved and which he himself failed to match; it is said Matt was only looking for a couple of years at the top to complete a career in the best possible way but Martin wasn't offering.

The result of 1978's shadiness? Well, Martin Edwards has pulled in hundreds of thousands of pounds in salaries and bonuses, millions in sales of share parcels and seen his £600,000 holding grow to £80 million. Perhaps to take issue with that is to succumb to personal jealousy and class envy. We have, after all, just won three championships: there's not much time left for quibbling about remuneration when you're celebrating glorious trophies all the time. But we're heading into uncertain times as a club. Les Olive's warnings in a letter sent to Louis in 1978 come to mind: that the rights issue paved the way to excessive dividend payments – and by implication a slavery to market senti-ment – and to the threat that the club might one day fall into unwelcome hands as a result of the opening up of United's shares to a wider dealership. United have paid out £14 million in dividends alone since 1992, during a period when our net balance of transfer expenditure has only amounted to a couple of million. Predators circle the club, both friendly and hostile, threatening to take us God knows where. The share price and earnings-per-share ratio have become as important as our League position: never forget Robin Launders' suggestion that a club now need not be winning trophies to maximize market potential.

I could go on with a full-scale rant about the deficiencies of United's modern plc status but you'll have heard it all before. There is an impressionistic irony here though. Louis was the 'crook', the dodgy dealer, the midwife to all this at its rather hole-in-the-corner birth. Martin has subsequently benefited and is now shiny and clean, a paradigm of good behaviour and fiscal rectitude: his office will never see a brown paper bag or bundle of well-thumbed readies. Yet the tackiness of the modern United, with its consultancy fees, share options, executive incentive schemes and directors' service agreements – the paraphernalia of the nineties fat-cat corporate trough – somehow seems more unsavoury than any of Louis' antics. There was an earthy honesty about his dishonesty, if you see what I mean: today, the fact that self-enrichment is so antiseptically legitimized, then rubbed in our faces via glossy annual reports and accounts brochures, nauseates me. Capitalism: don't you just love being in control.

⚽ ⚽ ⚽

They do say revenge is a dish best served cold but in the case of Docherty versus his Legion of Enemies, this was surely a platter almost frozen solid. By November 1978, when court proceedings finally began, all the main participants had already left Old Trafford. Deep in the misery of the Sexton years, fans could be forgiven for regarding the revelations as an ancient history lesson rather than hot current affairs. Such is the dilatory nature of English justice, seen so recently in the cases of the Scott Report, Wallace affair and Maxwell scandal. Resolution is so delayed that victims never have the satisfaction of seeing perpetrators skewered when their blood-lust is at boiling point and public outrage at its height. It's an obvious conspiracy in the Establishment's interest and consequently a state of affairs which will never be tackled.

Willie Morgan, as the recipient of the libel writ, did at least have two years to prepare his battle plan. The result was an overwhelming arsenal of offensive weaponry which succeeded in making plaintiff Docherty look like the defendant: 29 counts of alleged impropriety and an array of celebrated star defence witnesses including Stepney, Macari, Ted MacDougall, Paddy Crerand and Denis Law. (Oh, and Barry Fry was there too.) Court-reporting legislation meant that every allegation could be aired and repeated in print without fear of action. Tommy now admits that 'suing Morgan was the biggest mistake of my life', a statement of the bleedin' obvious, of course. You wonder how smart Docherty ever was. Knowing that every man he'd ever crossed would emerge in court, that every questionable act would be disinterred for examination and that the whole caboodle would be repeated verbatim across the front pages, how did he ever hope to emerge with any credit even if he had won?

Looking back, it appears the question of the case was never 'was Tommy the worst manager ever?' as Morgan had alleged. Instead, it rapidly descended into a dissection of Docherty's character, probity and wholesomeness. Anyone who's ever seen Docherty's facial language when questioned on controversial matters would have known he'd be a witness-box disaster. The intense rapid blinking, the visible shrinking, the tremble in the lips, the involuntary twitching . . . if any observer could see this, why couldn't he?

At the end of the third painful day, during which Docherty admitted lying to the court about the Law Affair, he withdrew the action and turned to face costs which reached nearly £60,000, plus a consequent perjury trial. If *The Doc vs Morgan* had been catastrophic for his reputation and bank balance, then *The Doc vs The Queen* threatened his very liberty. But few tears were shed for him amongst the defence witnesses. Denis Law had been reluctant to enter the box – never a problem for him as a player – but Paddy Crerand was actually disappointed to miss out:

'I had a thing or two to say,' he grinned. Indeed he had: the Doc Treatment Paddy endured was less well known and deserved the airing already granted to Law and Morgan's tales of woe. How Docherty appointed Crerand assistant manager and seemed to undermine him within weeks. How he froze him out, occasionally asking Pat to leave dressing rooms before games. And, most contentiously, how Docherty told the board Crerand was supposedly drinking too much to get himself organized and do the job. Docherty eventually got his wish, as he always did with black artistry – Paddy left the club via Northampton, his invaluable services lost to United for a decade. Fortunately, we supporters got him back eventually; now, to us, he's a general of sorts once more.

Add to that the rehashing of Docherty's Cup Final ticket touting, used as a partial excuse for his 1977 sacking, and the football world had a portrait of Docherty's personal and financial dealings which was hardly going to strengthen a job-hunting CV. And so Tommy would claim that the case ruined him professionally. But then who had brought it in the first place? Nemesis had followed hubris, as always. Like Kasparov fatefully taking on Deep Thought and losing, Docherty had appeared to believe his end-game winning streak had made him invulnerable. He would escape a prison term in 1981 only after a court decided his courtroom lies were 'not deliberate'. We're back where we started with the Scott Report, aren't we?

Since 1981, Docherty has responded in a variety of ways to these events. At times, with some justification, he has defended certain naughtiness by citing precedent: everyone dealt in Cup Final tickets, he was just more honestly brazen about it. In other matters, he will continue hotly to deny what every other witness will aver is the truth. Sometimes, he simply refuses to refer to the crux of an issue; elsewhere, he has changed his tune to suit the harmony of the times. Willie Morgan told Jim White that, in court, Morgan's barrister asked Willie to tug on his gown every time Doc lied in the box: after half an hour, he abandoned the tactic. So frequent was the tugging from below that the gown was losing its tailored shape.

Recently, on Piccadilly Radio, I listened as Docherty, in the space of two minutes, claimed to have been at The Dell,

241

then said he'd missed the match, then said he'd seen it after all – without breaking stride. Suddenly, I understood the concept of 'undeliberate lies' and a lot else about the Doc's career too. To be a true and effective Machiavellian requires so much more cunning, intelligence and thoroughness than Tommy ever possessed. Lies must go undetected, back-stabbings left without dabs, badmouthing confined to the most trusted. The truly evil black art practitioners can meet all these requirements. Tommy was never evil; he was just a bit of a naughty lad burdened with a credibility gap. But he hurt people and did them harm none the less – I guess that is what he still had to pay for in the end.

⚽ ⚽ ⚽

Brian Greenhoff had been sub for the 1979 Cup Final but never got on the pitch; it had been that kind of season for him. By August, he was back in his native Yorkshire, unfortunately at Leeds rather than Barnsley, a £350,000 fee befitting his England international status. And come May, he'd be in the Leeds side, helping snatch the title from Sexton's admittedly distant grasp. Not that he looked particularly delighted to do so. All right, he'd left Sexton, fuming: 'I couldn't work with that man. I just didn't like him. You could say we had a minor tiff.' But though born a sheepshagger, he became a true Red: and as many before and after have discovered, no other club can inspire quite the same magic from a player.

Brian needed the inspiration too. Big brother got a first-born's share of the natural skill and touch; Brian made do with courage, determination and effort. Yet he ended up with the caps and a burgeoning reputation as an 'advanced' player – a centre-back who could also bring the ball out and pass a bit. Actually, you'd expect no less from a converted midfielder but most outsiders had forgotten that was where he'd started out as a kid and Busby favourite.

Brian, undoubtedly, was our Mr Versatility – some might say the seventies version of Clayton Blackmore, if they want to be rude. Memorable games as emergency centre-forward – none more so than in the notorious Rangers 'friendly' – proved the point, as did a sterling stint between the sticks once or twice. They used to call them 'bits 'n' pieces players' and they went out of fashion for most of the eighties; now they're all the rage once more in these days of multi-system campaigns and new positional labels. At one point it looked as though he might slip through the cracks or even, God forbid, become a Tommy Jackson, but he fought through a succession of early seventies injuries and patches of bad form to become the one success of relegation year. He found it within himself somehow to fill Jim Holton's giant shoes in the centre of defence for the best part of three years – two five foot ten backs withstood the onslaught of many a marauding twin attack, to the amazement of most observers. And when McQueen was signed, it appeared Greenhoff had been offered a return to his first love, the bustle of midfield battle. But Wilkins' arrival finally scotched that hope.

So Docherty's prediction that Brian would one day succeed Martin as permanent captain never came to realization, although he did eventually manage to overcome his alleged habit of throwing up with nervous excitement before a match. I always thought that a nice touch: it shows passion, a sense of commitment to the shirt and one's performance. The Cup of Tears in '76? They were famously Brian's tears above all, a defeat taken as hard by a gritty Yorkie as by any Mancunian Red. If United didn't quite give Brian everything he'd hoped for in his career, Wembley '77 must have come close – winners' medals for him and Jimmy, the brother he'd hero-worshipped as a lad and whose Barnsley Boys Number 4 shirt he'd once worn with such familial pride.

After United, injuries and bad luck blighted his four years at Leeds; there was a reunion with Jimmy at Rochdale but glory was in short supply. Perhaps this was a glimpse of the workmanlike career he might have had if Sir Matt hadn't taken him aboard back in '68. Brian won't make any all-time United sides but, as the lampooned cliché goes, he always gave 110 per cent – and for a few mid-decade years at least, he truly did perform better than nature had perhaps intended.

On the day of the Cup Final, brother Jimmy was only a week from his 33rd birthday. There were many, back in autumn '76, who'd said we'd been mad to buy an apparently over-the-hill thirty-something in the first place. Here was a player who'd won all his good medals early at Leeds; the seventies had taken him to the Midlands, treading backwater. Sure, they still trotted out the old line for him – 'best uncapped player in England' – but not many thought he would be adding much to his claims as he passed 30. Once again, that old United magic was all that was needed. If Brian's tragedy was that he left Old Trafford too early, then Jimmy's was that he joined too late. But what an Indian summer: by the time we took the field against Arsenal, Jimmy was already a Cup-winner scorer, a fans' player of the year and the man credited with steering United to Wembley once more. Not bad for an old-timer, so recently as the summer of '77 being spoken of as a sellable stop-gap.

It was typical of him that he should start life at Old Trafford with a cool understatement. Instant explosions were for Flash Harrys; Jimmy was a class act. Intelligent, artistic, visionary, self-effacing – he always struck me as the gentleman's player, as a guy who would glide rather than bustle. The nearest we had to Cantona, perhaps; one for the connoisseur. Yet he was as popular on the Stretford End as any of the more 'in yer face' types, seemingly with his own song and fan club within weeks of arrival. If anything, our appreciation of him was even in advance of the management's. He made Pearson and others around him play more subtly than ever before. Stevie Coppell simply declared: 'Jimmy was the best I ever played with. Whenever you needed him, he was there.' His ability to see the whole picture, to make it move as he wanted and to think ahead of every opponent made him special; so, naturally, he excelled at snooker too. The Greenhoffs were good cricketers as kids – I can easily imagine Jimmy coming in at Number 4, knocking elegant off-drives and cuts all over the shop and still having time to calculate the perfect declaration.

Years later, you often discover that your heroes are arseholes. I can think of three or four players whom I absolutely worshipped but, having learned what they were like off the pitch, would cross the road to avoid. How reassuring, then, that no one ever had a bad word about Jimmy. Modest, genuine, respected and, well, 'nice' are all you'll ever hear of him. Just for once, the images of a player and man dovetail sweetly. If you know any different, I don't want to hear it. The picture of his '79 semi-final winner is staying on my wall no matter what.

⚽ ⚽ ⚽

Red Army Despatches

Most media attention in the seventies to do with travelling Reds focused on trains and club coaches, with the odd ferry thrown in; but then, as now, many still preferred to join the armoured columns of cars and little vans whose natural habitats were motorways and service stations. Swinton Dave recalls a typical away day, going to Villa in October 1978:

'Our intrepid band never cared for trains and their stringent timetables; no, we used the ultimate moochin' machine, the Salford Van Hire. Its uses knew no bounds. There was a kid used to travel with us called Norman who was always skint. However, if we procured a ticket for him and a few pints, he turned into a regular stunt man. I swear to God he used to skate down the motorway holding on to the van door. Many was the time we hauled good ol' Norm back into the van at 60 or 70 mph with his trainers on the verge of combustion.

'On this particular occasion we'd hired a furniture van which became rather pungent as we hurtled south down the M6. No problem: we hoisted the roller shutters, let in some air and drank and cavorted for all to see. The West Midlands Force – humourless bastards even then – took umbrage; we were forced to stop adjacent to a service station, got dragged out of the van, and the driver was told to carry on to Villa Park cargo-less. Big mistake!

'As we ambled on to the service station car park, on our side of the motorway, three coach loads of Spurs supporters were pulling in on the northbound side. We gave them the customary signs and abuse across six lanes of traffic and thought nothing of it. We were from the North, well hard; all Cockneys were soft as shite as everyone knew. The genetics of this mob, however, had obviously gone slightly awry. They were now charging across the motorway bridge to our side. Delusions of grandeur or what!

'Now in our midst that day was a young lad who would later go down in Red Army folklore. In those days he was affectionately known as, well, let's call him Mr Laker – after Sir Freddie, who also fancied himself as an entrepreneur on the travel front. He was no mug when it came to battling either and he seized the initiative straight away. We had to stop them pouring out of the door of the service station otherwise we were doomed. By the time we reached the door, only four or five had emerged; these were duly despatched with Mancunian aplomb. The problem now was to keep the rest at bay.

'This band of North London zealots were having none of it, however; they'd now become totally unhinged and had seized every piece of cutlery from the restaurant and were brandishing it at the windows with a fervour not seen since Bannockburn. The inevitable happened: the door was breached and we back-pedalled at speed. I wasn't averse to being punched, but the thought of being skewered with a piece of Charles Forte's dinner service filled me with wind. During the ensuing mêlée, families scattered, women screamed and a poor bloke changing his tyre was stampeded into the tarmac. Meanwhile, in an act of abject cowardice, I steamed on to a coach full of old ladies, on a day trip somewhere and crouched unashamedly in the aisle as they drank their tea.

'Eventually peace was restored by the police. (I take everything back – don't you just love 'em?) I rejoined my bloodied and beleaguered army on the forecourt as they reassembled. The next problem confronted us: how were we going to get to Villa Park? The police had given us an ultimatum – clear the service area or be lifted. Hilton Park had been wrecked, whole families had shat themselves in unison and the police understandably wanted us away.

'Enter our hero, Sir Freddie; he'd been bending the ear of a farmer who'd just sold his prize bull and was filling up his ox chariot with fuel. A deal was struck – Freddie secured a berth for 50 pence each. The faces of the Villa supporters outside the Witton Lane as we were disgorged through the small side door of a vehicle obviously meant for sheep or Leeds fans, was a picture. For once they must have thought the media weren't lying – these Man United supporters really were animals, as we stood there covered in straw and bull shit.' – *Swinton Dave*

Colin from Sale was another regular highwayman:

'There used to be an all-night transport caff, 'The Bear's Head,' where you'd get your first lift to Knutsford or any other motorway service stop. Then the battles with the Scousers would commence at every stop. These were open warfare and you could really come unstuck if you and your partner got caught out trying to sort a lift when a van load of Scousers would spring on you. That's what happened to me and Maca near Brum once. After a mad chase over the motorway, we ended up about a mile down the M with a van full of Scousers driving up and down the hard shoulder in hot pursuit. So after spending half-an-hour in a ditch, we crossed back over and started to walk – it was 4 or 5 in the morning. We ended up hitching in some rich pisshead's Jag and getting his £180 wedge off him. Those motorways were a bit of a jungle in those days, really.' – *Colin, Sale*

Of course many observers might have commented that, judging by the clothes United's lads were wearing, they all belonged in the jungle anyway. *United We Stand*'s House Of Style sniffs the denim:

' *"Bury the past. Empty the shelf. Decide it's time to re-invent yourself"* sang Pet Shop Boys in "DJ Culture" and what a nice thought that is. House Of Style would dearly like all and sundry to believe that he has spent his entire life in stylish garb, from Gucci nappies to today's Stone Island ensemble, but lurking in my mum's photo collection is scandalous proof that this is definitely not the case. The snap is dated

21 May 1977 and shows a smiling seven-year-old boy in full kit, complete with bar scarf and clutching a pennant and a four-foot-high poster of Martin Buchan. The haircut is very Grange Hill and if you look closely you might catch a glimpse of a "Gordon Hill Is Magic" badge. Yeah, okay, so now you're all sniggering, but I can justify the get-up, 'cos United had just battered the Scousers to take the first trophy of my lifetime, thereby wiping away the painful memories of Bobby Stokes. And, besides, everybody dressed sad in those days.

'The seventies has often been heralded as "The decade that fashion forgot" and you're not wrong pal. The sharpness of the sixties seemed to taper out and what developed was truly sad indeed. In clobber the rule seemed to be "the bigger the better", so ties, lapels, shirt collars and trousers went west and hair became big and brash. The youth movements of the day never set the fashions seen at the match in the seventies; it was never going to be the done thing to go to the game dressed as a hippie/punk/disco dancer – and looking like a glam rocker was probably going to get you ballroom blitzed. Instead the seventies fans donned an eclectic mixture of the everyday fashion of the time and quirky garbs just for matchday. So on the one hand you had lads in Oxford bags (pinstriped wool pants, four-button waistband, side pockets, twenty-eight-inch bottoms) and tri star jumpers (check out the famous picture of Buchan parading the Second Division trophy and look at the kid on his left) and on the other you had butchers' coats and denim jackets covered in big badges and patches and satin scarves tied around the wrist. You can just imagine grown lads, sitting in their bedrooms, sewing patches of Churchillian "V" signs, coloured red, black and white and carrying the message "United Rule OK", onto their coats, thinking "I'll look the business on Saturday"!

'Of course earnest casuals really do have to doff their Ralph caps to the United fans of the seventies. Throughout the decade they had Euro-wide renown for their antics at home and away. So intimidated was everyone by Doc's Red Army that it wasn't unusual for towns to shut down when we came out to play. Tube and bus drivers would go on strike, so frightened were they of transporting the fourteen or fifteen thousand Reds who often travelled away. Famous liberties were taken against clubs who nowadays fancy themselves a bit, a particularly nice case in point being the 1977 FA Cup semi-final where we outnumbered Leeds by three to one and invaded their end to such a degree that one commentator was led to state that "Hillsborough looked like an egg with a whole bottle of tomato ketchup poured over it". After the match the despondent Leeds fans were chased all the way back to the train station, on foot, as South Yorkshire buses were on strike that day! On another special day the United contingent alleviated the boredom at Norwich by wrecking the stadium. One young Red obviously forgot how decrepit Carrow Road was and started jumping up and down on the roof of the stand. Within seconds he fell through and landed on the terraces thirty feet below. Rumour has it that he would have died had his Oxford bags not operated as a parachute.

'Seventies fans are a soft target when it comes to fashion analysis. To be fair, though, they were starved of style gurus. Nowadays, you can look at Giggs and Cantona out on the town in their Armani and Mugler and you want to look like them, but the players then all dressed like your uncles. Christ, Gordon Hill aside, most of them *looked* like your uncles! These days United may go to Wembley in Hugo Boss, but the whistles in 1977 look like they came fresh out of Greenwoods' window. It's interesting that the cool characters who sprang to life in the decade wanted nothing to do with the style of the time – Tommy Hilfiger, Giorgio Armani, Paul Weller and Johnny Rotten all said a big "Thanks, but no thanks" to the fashions of the day, but then they always knew that they were living in topsy turvy times. Times when City won trophies, United got relegated and Brutus Gold was *the* label to wear (its chief model is now Alan Shearer!). So when I look at that picture of me these days, I smile and convince myself that I didn't know any better then, and I breathe a huge sigh of relief that Fila and Lacoste were only a few years away.' – *House Of Style, 1997*

1979–80

There used to be a series on Radio Four called *What If? . . .*, devoted to historical hypotheses – what if JFK hadn't been shot, if Hitler had beaten the Soviets, if Callaghan had called an election in '78 and so forth. Sadly, they never got around to an equally pressing question: what if Jimmy Greenhoff hadn't missed virtually the entire 1977–80 season through injury? This should have been his peak season, up front with Jordan; Macari could've stayed in the middle, Thomas kept safely in the reserves where he could get pissed to his heart's content and United would have won the League. Sketch out any number of dizzying eighties possibilities after that. Plausible?

It was to be a summer of 'what ifs' all around. Pearson was sold to West Ham as punishment for having the cheek to ask for a decent pay rise, this in an era when some United players could earn more by opening supermarkets than playing. How limp the manager's fiscal machismo looked a few months later as United ran out of strikers. Brian Greenhoff stomped off to Leeds, muttering that he couldn't work with Sexton; McCreery had had his fill and left for London. Doc's boys were getting thin on the ground – half the team were now Sexton's creatures, and most of the rest fairly happy converts.

The three-quarters of a million quid raised went south to prop up ailing Chelsea and their ridiculously elephantine East Stand in exchange for 'midfield general' Ray Wilkins. Funny phrase that, 'midfield general': in these post-*Blackadder* days, we all recognize that 'general' signifies someone farting about well behind the lines, doing very little but with a great deal of style, whilst the poor bloody infantry gets a hammering. During 1979–80, some would claim to have seen that caricature brought to life long before Stephen Fry's version.

And that still left a million quid from the share issue to spend, didn't it? Or perhaps not: Sexton revealed that he wanted to spend that sum on West Brom's Bryan Robson but was told the money wasn't available. Two years and one managerial life later, we got Robbo at a 50 per cent premium and Big Ron reaped the rewards. Sometimes, you have to marvel at the fact that Sexton professes to be so unembittered by his OT experience.

Wilkins's fee was a record between English clubs, a fact even more remarkable today than then, perhaps. It had been a mad summer. Michael Robinson cost City little less and West Brom paid £600,000 (£5.5m) for Peter Barnes; City even spent a third of a million on Wrexham's Bobby Shinton which, in the wake of the Thomas deal, made the Welsh club the world's greatest tat salesman until Ratners' reign. And as the season kicked off, Allison was still trying to buy Steve Daley from Wolves, tee-hee . . . now there's a 'what if?' of truly Bitter poignancy for you.

Later in the season, Sexton would try for the South American class acts of Passarella and Roberto; he ended up with one-man Balkan disaster-zone Jovanovic. Such was the luck of the manager. Where else could we finish but second? However near we got to Liverpool – and, technically, it would be a damn close shave – Sexton never shook off that stench of honest, hard-working but cursed loserhood. In contemporary comparison, he was always football's Michael Foot.

The key to United's frankly unexpected title challenge was provided by that rarity, a settled defence. The previous season, we conceded more than one goal in 18 League matches; this team, that would only happen half-a-dozen times, leaving every other game ours to take if we had the attacking balls. Bailey and Buchan were ever-present; McQueen had the equally mountainous Moran to deputize when injured; Nicholl, the seventies prototype of David May, had finally adapted to his less-favoured right-back role and didn't miss a match. With Albiston established at left-back – and Houston taking up mid-season slack when Arthur got crocked – we conceded just 29 goals in 41 games (excepting Portman Road as a freak). This was championship defending. On the back of that, you could bore your way to a title. After all, isn't that what Liverpool did for most of their 18? And at many moments during the season, that's precisely what the lads grumbling their way home at the back of a 257 would suggest United were doing.

Poor Wilkins had a bewildering August; watching the ball pinging artlessly about, especially in tedious away draws, he looked like the vicar who'd stumbled upon an orgy. But by mid-September, we were still unbeaten – we'd put Spurs out of the League Cup and boasted a 100 per cent home record. Macari had discovered a second youth upfront, his clinching goal against Boro a swivelling, crashing top-corner delight. We'd even found joy at Villa Park, usually a scene of disappointment, winning 3-0 amidst gratitude that old nemesis Andy Gray had left. Unfortunately, he'd only gone as far as Molineux where he inspired our 3-1 defeat two weeks later. And by then, we were into the first mini-crisis of a gremlin-ridden season.

Jordan had come off injured at Villa and would be out for two months, allowing Grimes to rush on and seize the day with a goal. No Pancho, Jimmy or Joe – what better moment for Andy Ritchie finally to prove his worth? He got his 90 minutes against Derby but needn't have bothered, so embarrassingly starved of service was he. Hill's own goal gave us victory and top berth; here was a chance, with Forest and Liverpool out of sorts, to race away. Instead, Sexton selected a forward line of Grimes, Coppell, Macari and Thomas to take us through to November, leaving natural target-man Ritchie to kick his frustrated heels in the stiffs. They called it the Midget Line – and it produced a goal-tally of matching size. Macari did well but the others mustered just two goals between them in two months. Not only did we fail to win any of the next five away matches but our home victories were a woefully unconvincing thrill-free zone. Only when Ray Wilkins finally came to life in the 4-0 defeat of Stoke did we get our money's worth. A wretched sequence climaxed in a Maine Road mudbath as struggling City pasted us 2-0, an unknown Tony Henry grabbing the headlines. McIlroy admitted the team had been too complacent from the off that day, suggesting we'd done the team no favours by suppressing the instinct to boo the buggers off occasionally.

The sole beneficiary of Sexton's apparent vendetta against Ritchie was Joe Jordan. Not only could he waltz back into the team unchallenged, he had unwittingly made more of a point with his absence than previously by his presence. From this moment, he never looked back – by May, he was Player of the Season. Old Trafford clutched him to its collective bosom against Palace as he gave a vintage display of what we'd missed, namely marauding courage, dominant power and a forward focus of frightening intensity. The Stretford End crackled with bloodlust as he piled into both their keeper and star signing Francis before exploding with relief as he wrested a 92nd minute equalizer to maintain at least the image of Fortress Old Trafford. Liverpool, ominously, moved to the top of the table but what a psychological lift the return of Joe's toothless roar had given both crowd and team.

A week later came the full pay-off. For all its deficiencies of style, 1979–80 still managed to provide three or four afternoons of near perfection, games which included spells the equal of anything produced under Docherty. Sexton had recently remarked, with extraordinarily rare mouthiness, that 'someone's gonna catch it from us very soon'. John Bond's Norwich were those someones, destroyed by five goals of which Coppell's spectacular solo effort was the most stellar. A hack gushed that he'd 'never seen such sustained attacking fervour'. For this week at least, United's name back at the top didn't make the table look quite so much 'like a house without a roof', to quote Hornby. Remarkably, within four weeks United would twice match this level of lethality – yet paradoxically they would end that month clad only in the garb of no-hopers. United's trips to Anfield tended to have that effect.

Excellent December away wins at Spurs and Coventry provided further testimony of a United rejuvenation, a team full of vigour and fight if not artistry. McQueen, back from injury, scored at Highfield Road whilst his partner in tartan-hued terrorism Joe Jordan smashed so-called hardman Don McAllister all over White Hart Lane. Sandwiched in between, sadly, came the most unwelcome dose of foreign affairs since Tehran '77.

Sexton chose this very moment to haul the lads off to Marbella for a spot of mid-week R & R, surely a classic case of opening presents before Christmas. They came back sluggish and sangria'd, from the look of them, sand still in pants, to labour chronically against Leeds. The 2,000 locked out were fortunate to be spared Grimes's missed penalty and a display of keeping from Lukic which brought forth 'John for England' calls. Laughable, I know – as much as the claims being made for their 'teenage scoring sensation' Terry Connor. (*Who he? – Ed.*) But the little sod's goal was enough to deny us the second point and Liverpool went top – for the duration, at it happened. A critical advantage had been lost; the title would now be Liverpool's to lose. There is, I suggest, a case to be made which posits footballers should never be let out of the country during a season unless they've qualified for Europe. If they haven't earned their foreign beano with their footie, why should they get a bleedin' holiday? Foreign travel only mucks your system up anyway. (A refined version of this argument is that David May should simply have his passport cancelled, along with the entire population of Liverpool, but that's for later years.)

Christmas at Old Trafford would've been idyllic if it hadn't been spoiled by having to go to Liverpool, though I suppose that's a downer at any time for any reason. (How do those uncool enough to still want to go to Cream face it? What tingle of anticipation can survive the dread of having to traipse through Scouse-ridden streets?) On the 22nd, United blew away European Cup-holders Forest in a 23-minute typhoon of attacking verve, three goals virtually removing every trace of the stain left by Xmas '77. Afterwards, Cloughie was presumably punch-drunk (or maybe just . . .) and declared Forest could still catch the leaders. But their challenge effectively died at that instant and they were to finish a poor fifth. The other likely lads of Arsenal received an equally imperious 3-0 dismissal a week later and would come fourth. Two of the three main challengers had been effectively knocked out in seven days.

But not, alas, the third. Whipped up into festive frenzy by our Jordan-inspired rebirth, we went to Anfield on Boxing Day looking, at last, to prove a point: that we could live with those Scouse bastards, that 'we could roll up our sleeves and take them on' in Joe's words. Was it too much to ask, just one point to carry aloft back to Manchester as if it were the bloody title trophy itself? It soon transpired that even a semi-decent performance was too much to ask. Humiliated and outclassed, United's best shot had come direct from Gary Bailey's boot. Two-nil was a merciful scoreline. Though we may have regained our pride against Arsenal three days later, no one ever let us forget the lesson we'd learned at Anfield – that we were irrevocably second best. And that truth seemed to seep through the club's body like slow-release poison for the next three troubled, angry, morbid months.

'Happy New Year' my arse. Here's an indication of how God's cookies were crumbling for us. The FA Cup third round replay at Old Trafford – Spurs the visitors. As usual, we've done that hard bit, getting a result in London; now, at nil-nil with an hour gone, Joe has splendidly crippled their keeper to force playmaker Hoddle into goal. Clearly, this tight-shorted exemplar of naff was already a Chosen One long before he realized it, surviving a full 60 minutes without being beaten. As if to take the piss, Ardiles then curls an outstandingly brilliant winner past Bailey with a minute of extra time to go. Fortress Old Trafford breached: and none of that clichéd bollocks about 'concentrating on the League' was much consolation on a cold January night, I assure you.

Three days later, United fans in a crush at Ayresome Park involuntarily pushed over a wall, killing two poor sods who happened to be passing. The one-all draw promptly forgotten, the fact that the ground was a decrepit shit-heap and Boro cretins had been inciting Reds from outside didn't assuage the grisly feelings of guilt as national fingers pointed accusingly at Manchester. So Niki Jovanovic's signing was supposed to cheer us up: 'an investment for our future', boasted Sexton, hilariously. This revoltingly expensive unknown careered wildly and disastrously through a debut at Derby on 2 February, a level of performance above which he would rarely rise. In hindsight, he could be appreciated as a great comedy turn, though obviously at the time his cartoonish bewilderment and hideous misjudgements were scarcely side-splitting to us.

Late goals snatched a lucky win; the papers called United's team 'pretenders and robbers', which was a bit harsh. It's not like they were ripping us off or anything. Unlike some other Reds in the news that week . . .

Four days earlier, Granada's *World In Action* had screened the results of their in-depth investigation into the business practices of chairman Louis Edwards. Shit that had been circling the fan impatiently for over a year (cf. 1978–79) splattered home to sensational effect; for a fortnight, the media tried to out-trump each other with speculation as to the doom that awaited the club. The *Mail* won the prize: 'United could win the League – only to be thrown out of football altogether!' (Two one thousand-to-one chances multiplied together – literally, a one-in-a-million shot.) Against Bristol City, a couple of 'Edwards out!' banners were clearly visible: for the first time ever, terrace protesters had their demands met within days as Louis checked out permanently.

Martin Edwards blamed Granada for Louis' death, as though obesity, old age and a champers 'n' cigar lifestyle had nothing to do with it, but this was an understandable reaction. The hard-faced view was that his prompt death had done the club a perverse kind of service since most of the authorities' inquiries were immediately discontinued as the man was dead. United escaped relegation or expulsion and the Edwards family went on to make nearly £100 million from their shareholding. But Louis was just a lad, a rogue, a rascal, a 'Billy' – hardly a Robert Maxwell. Many at United genuinely grieved for him and were ready to forgive that penultimate ignominy. *Si monumentum requiris, circumspice* (if you seek his monument, look around you): a man who'd built the Theatre of Dreams could hope to have some marginal fiddling put into perspective, after all.

Given such 'noises off' to contend with, it was hardly surprising that the main stage actors were fluffing their lines and missing cues – nor that us plebs in the stalls responded with the vocal equivalents of eggs and tomatoes. Just one decent showing, a 4-0 defeat of grotty Bristol City, stood out like sweetcorn in a turd and provided Louis Edwards with his last afternoon of Old Trafford pleasure. Otherwise, we stank. Wolves, supposedly preoccupied with their forthcoming League Cup Final, beat us 1-0 at home, Liverpool making an obvious point with a 5-3 win at Carrow Road. Nil-nils at Brighton and at home to Everton plumbed new depths of toothless tedium, the 5,000 Reds at Goldstone bellowing 'What a load of rubbish' and other discontented favourites. And even though Bolton were beaten 2-0, Old Trafford responded with howls of derision; that evening was emblematic of the entire Sexton period. For there had been moments of utter sublimity, most notably when Coppell scored a classic, and we had won – yet the boredom, caution and witlessness surrounding those moments were all that remained in the memory. You could characterize the entire era using this microcosmic Wednesday. Some success and efficiency, a few afternoons of unforgettable brilliance but mostly dull despondency.

Even David Meek saw the simile, penning another infamous apologia for the status quo in the guise of a match report. Steve Coppell later emerged to back the Meek/Sexton view: that United had to learn to be successful first, then develop style and flair afterwards. The example used by Coppell? Leeds under Revie. 'Leeds were static and defensive on the way up . . . they were boring for a long time but became quite entertaining later on. I think United can develop in a similar way.' Aarghh! Just the comparison no Red wants to hear. Leeds were boring not just for a while, but for an entire decade from 1964–73; at best, they managed 18 months of proper entertainment. Gordon McQueen, whilst mounting a similar defence, couldn't help conceding: 'Frankly, I don't blame the fans who criticize. If I'd been watching some of our games, I would have been complaining as well.' And both he and Buchan admitted that being second best in such a mediocre year wasn't much to boast about, although both were right to suggest Jimmy Greenhoff could have restored the lost artistry to great effect.

The trouble with all these arguments was that United fans always believe we can do it differently, that we can get to the top precisely by being entertaining and full of panache. The Leeds/Sexton route is for everyone else, football's mortals. We are United – moreover, every Red had seen it done our way for themselves, whether by Busby or Docherty. So there was little point in telling them it couldn't be done. Had United burst out during 1980–81 with some brand of beautiful flowing footie and stormed all before them, then fair enough. But we didn't: furthermore, most critics of Sextonism always knew United wouldn't do so as long as Dave was the manager. A northern version of QPR '76, even if he could have achieved it, would still not have sufficed.

Nadir of nadirs: Portman Road, 1 March. 'What time is it, Rag?' asks a Bitter at school next day. 'Six past Bailey?' Title-challengers beaten six-nil and it could've been a record eight had Gary not made three saves from two penalties. Every hack and fan who'd been telling us for months we were the least credible pretenders to a crown since Lambert Simnel found complete justification that afternoon. This was no inexplicable miracle, such as St James' 96, but an entirely inevitable, almost comic, comeuppance.

We had, as we have seen elsewhere, a manager with a knack of making unlucky and/or stupid decisions at critical moments, right? Here's a good 'un: 'Martin Buchan, would you mind man-marking little Eric Gates, who'll no doubt pull you all over the park gleefully, just as he always does?' For 45 minutes, the hapless Buchan pursued the goblin Gates, who couldn't believe his luck: United had marked the unmarkable. Mariner and Co. piled into the gaping holes and helped themselves to goals. Two: United's squad was still too thin, yes? Here was the result of having to rely on Grimes, Jovanovic and – shriek! – Tom Sloan, who all played. You actually felt we'd missed the injured Mickey Thomas, which speaks volumes. Three: United were too easily cowed into nervous defensiveness by the tensed-up tactician on the bench. At Ipswich, quivering players trying to play it safe and cool as instructed instead provided a never-ending supply of aborted back-passes, skewered clearances and mind-melting mistakes – Danny Baker could have squeezed an entire video out of it. Poor Stewart Houston never played for us again. What a memory to take to the grave of your last United appearance. At the completely opposite end of the emotional spectrum cavorted the Liverpudlians, derby-day winners and now so much odds-on as to be unbackable. As Alex Ferguson would say, we were in a Devon Loch scenario. Unbelievably, by the end of March, it would be the unlikely figure of Mickey

Thomas who'd come galloping to the rescue.

He'd been out for six games, treating his injury under an assortment of UV and heat lamps which appeared to affect his genetic make-up – how else to explain his roaring form when he returned, banging home four goals in five games and creating most of the others? Perhaps this was what Clayton Blackmore was up to all those years on his sun-bed, looking to replicate the Thomas Effect upon his own Welsh mediocrity? Mickey's comeback goal beat City in the worst derby of modern times, rather pleasingly deflected off Tony Henry whose goal had slanted the November match in City's favour. He and Jordan combined to win at Palace, whilst Liverpool lost across the capital at Spurs. Suddenly, we were game on, just four points behind. A result at the City Ground could take us into Easter Monday's Scouse showdown with a title, rather than pride, for which to play.

Instead, another Welsh nightmare called Thomas chose to make his mark on our season. Clive of that ilk not only gave Forest an outrageously unjustifiable penalty but booked, then sent off, the saintly Sammy Mac, presumably for pointing out the presence of a fatherless masturbator on the pitch. Not until Gary Birtles' last minute dancing goal did we look beaten, but spirit had not been enough. The dozen variations of headlines all spelt out the same message – disaster.

Now Easter Monday represented our own Ardennes Offensive – a last-ditch, throw-every-tank-in attempt to forestall a lost war, for anything but victory in this battle would make Liverpool champs-elect. We had one battered, bruised and rusty weapon in the armoury, hastily repainted with a Number 4: Jimmy Greenhoff.

These metaphors of war are not out of place. The mutual loathing between the two sets of terraced Reds had taken the ancient Lancastrian rivalry well beyond the almost good-humoured needle of the '77 Cup Final. Vast racks of 'MUFC – I Hate Liverpool' aggro badges were rapidly denuded; Munich songs had become the common Kop refrains. Not for the first time, the Dog and Partridge's shattered window-panes would be evidence of a new world order up north.

The contemptuous arrogance of the Anfield Machine during the opening exchanges was instantly reminiscent of their early preening in 1979's semi-final; when Dalglish scored early, the comparison was unavoidable. Quite beautifully, the afternoon became an encapsulation of Essence of '79. Once again, we struck back so promptly that Liverpool were shaken from their complacency. Once again, Jimmy would ghost in to apply the *coup de grâce*. When Dalglish hilariously missed an open goal, the game swung much as it had when Kennedy hit woodwork in '79. Above all, the faithful responded just as they had last year. Internal disputes and troubles forgotten, the Stretford End never looked or sounded finer. Those final ten minutes before kick-off as the fans approached take-off decibel levels were as excitedly anticipatory as any I can remember. So what if Liverpool still only needed eight more points from six games to win the title? This afternoon had surely been more a matter of restoring honour than hope.

Pride and vigour flooding through the veins, United roared to the finishing line winning five games in nineteen days. There was always the chance that injury-hit Liverpool, stuck in the morass of an epic semi-final saga with Arsenal, would slip; bar one dropped point, they didn't. Andy Ritchie returned to thrash Spurs with another sensational hat-trick, providing us with another 'what if?' of the kind with which we began the chapter. Tommy Cavanagh had snottily remarked before kick-off that, 'Ritchie will have to score five to earn his place in the team', open testimony that Andy would never get the fair crack to which he was entitled. His treble constituted the perfect riposte but to no avail. The management decreed, to general incredulity, that 'he didn't have enough of an all-round game to be in the team'. Gee, how terrible it must've been to have a guy who was only any good for scoring brilliant hat-tricks.

A dodgy penalty and even shadier free-kick beat Coventry in the Old Trafford finale; we knew that the team circling OT at full-time were not going to win the League at Elland Road a week later but this was a true lap of honour, if not of triumph. Two months ago, we'd been booing this lot off the pitch, then watching East Anglian slaughter. They'd show some real United grit to bounce back and deserved the applause. Sexton, presciently, later remarked he felt he'd not warranted such a hearty send-off. Turned out he was right, of course: but under optimistic spring sunshine, you could believe in a tomorrow if you wanted.

How would Tony Blair have put it? 'New Beginning. New Decade. New Leader. Higher than we've been in a generation. Vote New United – Vote Sexton.' Seductive stuff. But if we'd known he was going to replace Ritchie with Birtles, he'd have lost his bloody deposit . . .

We lost 0-2 at Leeds whilst Liverpool put four past Villa. Losing the title at Elland Road to Liverpool would be neatly inverted twelve years later but there was never a scintilla of 1992's anguish here: the Scousers still had an ace of a fixture up the sleeve had the improbable occurred. The impulse that drove 17,000 Reds to mount the biggest invasion of Leeds ever seen was one of near-religious zeal, an expression of irrational belief in the possibility of miracles. All right: and the prospect of a decent punch-up too, for some.

In some ways, it had been a fitting end to the Red Army Years, for they had been something akin to the Crusades. Troops imbued by a particular inspiring doctrine, led sometimes by lions, sometimes by donkeys, hopes raised on every new seasonal expedition only to be dashed more often than fulfilled. A similar paradox too: our crusaders believed in the purest, noblest and most artistic values on the pitch yet would fight like wild animals off it to defend those very colours. We didn't capture our particular Jerusalem either but then Reds have always found the means to be more important than the ends. If the fans of the seventies, and often the players, left one great legacy for the more 'successful' decades to come, it was surely this: it ain't what you do, it's the way that you do it. (I'm sure this is what top Red Terry Hall had in mind when he chose to cover that song.) Singing, playing, swaggering, fighting, winning, losing – there's a Red way of doing them all. And for my generation at least, those Ideals For Living were established by the Red Army Years. Though we can do without the clothes and haircuts, ta very much . . .

Red Army Despatches

The Coming of the Casuals
As the seventies drew to a close on the terraces, the colour was slipping away from the fans. The sea of red and white to which we had become accustomed was being gradually diluted; scarves, hats and the like were going out of fashion

as fast as 'Top Trumps'. Not that we should over-emphasize this development; we're only concerned here with the cutting edge in the Strettie, not the acrylic slacks and zip-up bomber jacket brigade in the main stands. But certainly the scarf-twirling banks of red at the End were soon to be a thing of the past and given the tactically hamstrung crap often served up as football in front of us, it seemed appropriate. The reason, however, for this change was that the Perries were coming.

When you start generalizing in the area of football fashion, you're on dangerous ground of course. How can you apply blanket labels to areas of the ground that can hold up to 15,000 Reds? In the eighties not *every* lad in the United Road Paddock was a total nutter; not every person in G Stand is clinically brain dead. But surely it's safe to observe that the 'casual movement' which began to sweep British terraces at the turn of the decade found its greatest support in the North West; and that in Manchester, the most infamous subset were the Perry Boys, who soon made their sharply cut presence felt in the Strettie. No colours as such; excellent Martin Fry haircuts; a plethora of designer labels; above all, an intense, almost Mod-like attention to image, detail and smartness. The contrast with the flared denim/tight T-shirt/excesses above-neck hair of the mid-seventies norm couldn't be greater – and at least looking back on pix of yourself from the period doesn't make you cringe in horror.

As for the reputation of this new breed, Wellington's phrase about his own troops springs to mind: 'I don't know what effect these men will have upon the enemy, but, by God, they terrify me.' The casual image was one of classic post-modern confusion; clothes speaking of money, style and status in society but probably concealing the heart – and the bloodied Stanley knife – of the warrior. In fact, a fighter intent on camouflaging his nature from public and police could scarcely have come up with a better disguise. In retrospect, it seems remarkable that the rest of the world took so long in catching up to what had happened.

Rival fans, of course, were totally *au fait* with every nuance of ever-changing terrace fashion; soon, the footie/fashion cross-over had become yet another arena for tribal dispute. The most celebrated manifestation of this new culture would be *The End* zine, a more talked-about-than-read publication from Merseyside run by the lumbering plumbers who later became The Farm. The letters pages provided the forum for gangs of fashion-victim footie fans to air their increasingly pathetic rantings about who was wearing the hippest trainers and coolest labels as well as the more predictable 'who duffed up whom' arguments. Rereading back issues only induces tedium so save yourself the bother. The only 'historically significant' issue in it was 'Who started Casual?', an honour usually claimed by Scousers simply by virtue of repeating 'We wuz first, like' to as many sociologists as possible. As we all know, there's been no new trend out of Liverpool since Merseybeat, unless you count manslaughtering Italians of course.

The casual era lasted, if we're generous, from about '79 till '84/85 whereupon Manchester took a lead in killing it stone dead, north of London anyway. Each club had their own well-defined looks which changed as rapidly as the season according to the dictates of *The Face*, *I-D et al.*, often resulting in a confusing congruence of style – Mickeys were complaining in '83 that you couldn't tell the Mancs from the Scousers until they 'asked you the time'. If it had any significance as an era beyond establishing style as an important permanent feature of the tribal rivalries, it was that it confounded all those journos and academics who were trying to make sense of football violence. It is also probably fair to say that the casual extended the life of football hooliganism well into the eighties; by changing the methodology and image of the fighter, it set back the authorities' attempts to counter aggro by years just at the point when they'd seemed to have designed an effective strategy.

Whether you view the casual era as a golden age of football culture or a disgraceful aberration, it was certainly richly symbolic; it marked the end of the seventies, the decade that style forgot, and heralded the designer label-dominated eighties. And at the home of United, somehow the casual seemed to be the perfect inhabitant of what was becoming 'Cold Trafford'.

So the end of the decade – and the end of this book – is signalled by more than a merely calendrial change. The sort of mass, disorganized aggro which characterized the mid-seventies had been struggling to stay alive since mid-1977, when the police, government and clubs began to get their act together in the wake of the Carrow Road riot. The disappearance of colours and the coming of the casuals meant more than simply changed appearances; a complete behavioural and ideological shift occurred at the end of the seventies which, in particular, dictated a very different kind of aggro. We hope to produce a paperback book before 1998–99 kicks off about this 1980–86 period, entitled *The Casual Years*, to complete a modern trilogy which we began with *United We Stood* in 1994. If you were an eighties boy, we want to hear from you; please write to us c/o Headline or *Red Issue* and help us get it right.

Appendices

- Summary of United's first-class playing record 1972–80
- United's first-class results tabulated by opponents, December 1972–May 1980
- United personnel 1972–80 – Old Trafford career records
- Players' appearances and goals season by season 1972–80
- United in the transfer market: complete record of dealings 1972–80
- Reds On Duty: United's internationals 1972–80
- United's attendance record home and away 1972–80
- Invading Division Two: the Red Army 1974–75

United's Playing Record 1972–80 Summary

SEASON	HOME					AWAY					TOTAL				%	GOAL AV. FOR v AG.	POS.	FA CUP	LGE CUP	EURO COMP	BIGGEST WIN/LOSS	
	P	W	D	L	F-A	P	W	D	L	F-A	P	W	D	L	F-A							
1972–73	23	10	07	06	28-22	24	03	08	13	23-45	47	13	15	19	51-67	43.6	1.09 v 1.43	18th	R3	R3	–	3-0	0-5
1973–74	24	08	07	09	24-22	21	03	05	13	15-28	45	11	12	22	39-50	37.8	0.87 v 1.11	21st	R4	R2	–	3-0	0-3
1974–75	27	21	05	01	59-17	24	09	07	08	23-22	51	30	12	09	82-39	70.6	1.61 v 0.76	1st	R3	SF	–	5-1	0-2
1975–76	25	20	04	01	48-17	27	11	06	10	35-37	52	31	10	11	83-54	69.2	1.60 v 1.04	3rd	RU	R4	–	5-1	0-4
1976–77	32	21	07	04	65-31	27	08	07	12	38-50	59	29	14	16	103-81	61.0	1.75 v 1.37	6th	W	R5	R2	7-2	0-4
1977–78	24	11	07	06	42-28	27	08	06	13	43-52	51	19	13	19	85-80	50.0	1.67 v 1.57	10th	R4	R2	R2	6-2	0-4
1978–79	26	13	07	06	39-29	27	08	11	08	39-45	53	21	18	14	78-74	56.6	1.47 v 1.40	9th	RU	R2	–	4-1	1-5
1979–80	23	18	03	02	46-10	24	07	08	09	25-34	47	25	11	11	71-44	64.9	1.52 v 0.94	2nd	R3	R3	–	5-0	0-6

Biggest Win: 7-2 v Newcastle, League Cup, 1976–77
Biggest Defeat: 0-6 at Ipswich, League, 1979–80
Biggest Away Win: 6-2 at Everton, League, 1977–78
Biggest Home Defeat: 0-4 v Forest, League, 1977–78
NB: West Brom in 1978–79 were the first to score five at Old Trafford since Burnley in 1962.

Fortress Old Trafford – United's best post-war home League success-rates:
1955/56: 92.86% 1966/67: 90.48% 1995/96: 89.47% 1946/47: 88.1% 1964/65, **1975/76,**
1974/75, 1979/80: *88.1% 1964/65,* **1975/76,**
1994/95: 85.71%
NB: United were unbeaten at Old Trafford in all competitions between 1 Feb 1975 and 21 April 1976 – 63½ weeks.
United's seven straight wins in the New Year of '77 was their best streak since 1965.

United's Results December 1972–May 1980

For a different perspective, we have broken down the results by opponent so you can see how United did against each of the good, bad and downright ugly teams of the seventies. Results are listed horizontally in the order they were played; Old Trafford games are in bold type, non-League matches in italics. Percentage success-rates over the 1972–80 period are given in brackets.

Season (Opponents)	1972–73	1973–74	1974–75	1975–76	1976–77	1977–78	1978–79	1979–80
AJAX (50)	—	—	—	—	*0-1;2-0*	—	—	—
ARSENAL (30)	1-3	0-3;1-1	—	3-1;1-3	1-3;3-2	2-3;1-2;1-3	1-1;0-2;2-3	0-0;3-0
ASTON VILLA (61)	—	—	2-1;0-2	2-1;2-0;1-2	2-3;2-0;2-1	1-2;1-1	2-2;1-1	3-0;2-1
BIRMINGHAM (59)	1-3	1-0;0-1	—	2-0;3-1	2-2;3-2	4-1;1-2	1-0;1-5	—
BLACKPOOL (100)	—	—	3-0;4-0	—	—	—	—	—
BOLTON (67)	—	—	3-0;1-0	—	—	—	0-3;1-2	2-0;3-1
BRENTFORD (100)	—	—	—	2-1	—	—	—	—
BRIGHTON (75)	—	—	—	—	—	—	—	2-0;0-0
BRISTOL C (55)	—	—	—	—	2-1;1-1	1-1;1-0	1-3;2-1	1-1;4-0
BURNLEY (80)	—	0-0;3-3	—	2-1;1-0	—	—	—	—
CARDIFF (100)	—	—	1-0;4-0	—	—	—	—	—
CARLISLE (75)	—	—	5-1	—	—	1-1;4-2	—	—
CHARLTON (100)	—	—	—	—	—	—	1-0;3-0;1-1	—
CHELSEA (56)	0-1	2-2;3-1	—	—	—	0-1;2-2	—	—
COLCHESTER (100)	—	—	—	—	—	—	*1-0*	—
COVENTRY (54)	1-1	2-3;0-1	—	1-1;1-1	2-0;2-0	2-1;0-3	3-4;0-0	2-1;2-1
C. PALACE (83)	2-0	—	—	—	—	—	—	1-1;2-0
DERBY (64)	1-3	0-1;2-2	—	1-2;1-1;2-0	0-0;3-1	1-0;4-0	3-1;0-0	1-0;3-1
EVERTON (61)	0-0	3-0;0-1	—	1-1;2-1	0-3;4-0;2-1	6-2;1-2	1-1;3-0	0-0;0-0
FULHAM (88)	—	—	2-1;1-0	—	—	—	*1-1;1-0*	—
HULL CITY (50)	—	—	0-2;2-0	—	—	—	—	—
IPSWICH (39)	1-4	1-2;2-0;0-1	—	1-0;0-3	0-1;1-2	0-0;2-1	0-3;2-0	1-0;0-6
JUVENTUS (50)	—	—	—	—	*1-0;0-3*	—	—	—
LEEDS (67)	1-1;1-0	0-0;0-2	—	2-1;3-2	2-0;1-0;2-1	1-1;0-1	3-2;4-1	1-1;0-2

LEICESTER (50)	—	0-1;1-2	—	0-0;2-1;1-2	1-1;1-1	3-1;3-2	—	0-2;2-1
LIVERPOOL (41)	0-0	0-0;0-2	—	1-3;0-0	0-0;0-1;2-1	0-0;2-0-1-3	0-3;0-2;2-2;2-1-0	0-2;1-0
MAN C (60)	—	0-0;0-1	1-0	2-2;0-4;2-0	3-1;3-1	1-3;2-2	1-0;3-0	2-1;1-1
M'BORO (58)	0-1	0-1	0-0;3-0	0-0;3-0	2-0;0-3	1-2;0-0	3-2;2-2	—
MILLWALL (100)	—	—	4-0;1-0	—	—	—	—	—
NEWCASTLE (80)	2-1	2-3;1-0	—	1-0;4-3	2-2;7-2;3-1	3-2;2-2	2-2;1-0	—
NORWICH (59)	1-0	—	0-2;2-2;0-1;1-1	1-0;1-1	2-2;1-2	1-0;3-1	2-2;1-0	1-4;5-0;2-0
NOTT'M FOR (44)	—	—	2-2;1-0	—	—	1-2;0-4	1-1;1-1	3-0;0-2
NOTTS CO (75)	—	—	1-0;2-2	—	—	—	—	—
OLDHAM (50)	—	—	0-1;3-2	—	—	—	—	—
ORIENT (75)	—	—	2-0;0-0	2-1	—	—	—	—
OXFORD (67)	—	—	4-0;0-1	3-1	—	—	—	—
PETERBORO (100)	—	—	—	—	—	—	—	—
PLYMOUTH (100)	1-0	—	—	—	—	—	—	—
PORTO (50)	—	—	—	—	0-4;5-2	—	—	—
PORTSMOUTH (75)	—	2-1;0-0	—	0-1;2-1	1-0;0-4;1-0	2-2;3-1	1-1;2-0	—
QPR (44)	2-1;0-3	—	2-1;0-0	0-1;2-1	1-0;0-4;1-0	2-2;3-1	1-1;2-0	—
SHEFF UTD (60)	1-2;1-0	—	4-4;2-0	5-1;4-1	—	—	—	—
SHEFF WED (75)	2-0	—	1-0;1-0	0-1	2-2;2-1	—	1-1;1-1	—
S'TON (67)	—	0-0;1-1	—	—	1-1;2-0	1-1;2-0	—	—
ST ETIENNE (75)	—	—	—	—	—	—	3-2	—
STOCKPORT (100)	2-2	1-0;0-1	—	1-0;0-1	3-0;3-3	3-2	—	4-0;1-1
STOKE (61)	—	1-2;0-1	3-2;0-0	—	2-2;2-2;2-1-0;3-3;1-2	—	—	—
SUNDERLAND (57)	1-1	—	—	3-2;1-1	2-3;3-1	2-0;1-1;2-0;1-1	1-2;3-1;2-1;1-1;0-1;4-1	
TOT'HAM (56)	—	—	—	—	5-0	—	—	—
TRANMERE (100)	—	—	0-0;2-3	—	1-0	1-2	—	—
WALSALL (50)	—	—	—	—	—	—	—	—
WATFORD (0)	2-1	1-1;2-1	1-1;2-1	0-4;2-2	0-4;1-2;3-1;1	3-5;0-1	2-0;0-2	
WBA (38)	2-2	3-1;1-2	—	1-2;4-0	1-2;3-0	1-2	1-3;0-1	
WEST HAM (39)	0-1;2-1	1-2;0-0	2-0;1-0;1-1;3-2	0-2;2-4	3-1;1-2	4-2;3-2		
WOLVES (57)	—	—	1-0;2-1	2-0;1-0;1-3-2	—	—	—	—
YORK CITY (100)	—	—	—	—	—	—	—	—

Of the clubs we played at least half-a-dozen times, the 'bogeyest' were Arsenal (30%), West Brom (38), West Ham and Ipswich (39); our whipping boys were Newcastle and Burnley (80), Leeds and Bolton (67).

United Personnel 1972–80

PLAYER	JOINED	DEBUT	(appearances/goals)				TOTALS	DATE LEFT/TO
			LGE	FA CUP	LGE CUP	EURO COMPS		
ALBISTON	Jul 72	09.10.74 v City	379/6	36	40/1	27	482/7	Aug 88 to WBA
ANDERSON	Oct 72	14.04.73 at Stoke	19/2	–	–	–	19/2	Nov 74 to Swindon
BAILEY	Jan 78	18.11.78 v Iwich	294	31	28	20	373	Sep 87 to Sth Africa
BALDWIN*	Jan 75	18.1.75 at S'land	2	–	–	–	2	Feb 75 to Millwall
BEST	Aug 61	14.9.63 v WBA	361/137	46/21	25/9	34/11	466/178	Jul 74**
BIELBY	May 70	13.3.74 at City	4	–	–	–	4	Dec 75 to Hartlepool
BUCHAN G.	May 73	15.9.73 v Wham	3	–	1	–	4	Aug 74 to Bury
BUCHAN M.	Mar 72	4.3.72 at Spurs	376/4	39	30	10	455/4	Aug 83 to Oldham
CHARLTON	Jan 53	6.10.56 v Ch.Ath	606/199	79/19	24/7	45/22	754/247	May 73 retired***
CLARK	Nov 73	10.11.76 v S'land	1	–	–	–	1	Sep 78 to Derby
CONNELL	Aug 78	22.12.78 at Bolton	2	–	–	–	2	Aug 82 to Glentoran
COPPELL	Feb 75	8.3.75 at Bolton	322/54	36/4	25/9	12/3	395/70	Oct 83 retired
COYNE	Oct 73	24.4.76 at Leicester	2/1	–	–	–	2/1	Mar 77 to Ashton
DALY	Apr 73	25.8.73 at Arsenal	111/23	10/5	17/4	4	142/32	Mar 77 to Derby
DAVIES R.	Nov 74	30.11.74 v S'land	8	2	–	–	10	Mar 75 to Sth Africa
DAVIES W.	Sep 72	23.9.72 v Derby	16/4	1	–	–	17/4	Jun 73 to Blackpool
DONALD	May 78	7.10.70 v P'mouth	4	–	2	–	6	Jan 73 to Partick
DUNNE	Apr 60	15.10.60 at Burnley	414/2	55	21	40	530/2	Aug 73 to Bolton
EDWARDS	Dec 63	19.8.69 at Everton	54	10	4/1	–	68/1	Mar 73 to Oldham
FITZPATRICK	Sep 61	24.2.65 at Sun'land	117/8	11/1	12/1	7	147/10	Jul 73 retired
FLETCHER	Aug 69	16.2.74 at Derby	7	–	–	–	7	May 74 to Hull
FOGGON	Jul 76	21.8.76 v Brum	3	–	–	–	3	Sep 76 to S'land
FORSYTH	Dec 72	6.1.73 at Arsenal	101/4	10/1	7	1	119/5	Aug 78 to Rangers
GRAHAM	Dec 72	6.1.73 at Arsenal	43/2	2	1	–	46/2	Nov 74 to P'mouth
GREENHOFF B.	Aug 68	8.9.73 at Ipswich	221/13	24/2	19/2	6	270/17	Aug 79 to Leeds
GREENHOFF J.	Nov 76	20.11.76 at Leicr.	97/26	19/9	4/1	2	122/36	Dec 80 to Crewe
GRIFFITHS	Jun 70	27.10.73 at Burnley	7	–	–	–	7	Apr 76 to USA
GRIMES	Mar 77	30.8.77 at Arseal	90/10	5/1	6	6	107/11	Aug 83 to Coventry
GRIMSHAW	Dec 72	10.9.75 v Brentford	1	–	1	–	2	Aug 79 to part-time
HILL	Nov 75	15.11.75 v Villa	101/39	17/6	7/4	8/2	133/51	Apr 78 to Derby
HOLTON	Jan 73	20.1.73 v W Ham	63/5	2	4	–	69/5	Oct 76 to S'land

HOUSTON	Dec 73	1.1.74 at QPR	205/13	22/1	16/2	7	250/16	Jul 80 to Sheff U
JACKSON	Jul 75	16.8.75 at Wolves	19	4	18	2	23	Jun 78 to Waterford
JAMES	Jul 65	12.10.68 at L'pool	129/4	12	12/2	1	161/4	Jan 76 to York
JORDAN	Jan 78	28.1.77 v WBA	109/37	12/2	4/2	1	126/41	Jul 81 to Milan
JOVANOVIC	Jan 80	2.2.80 at Derby	21/4	1	2	2	26/4	Nov 82 to Yugos.
KELLY	Apr 72	20.12.75 v Wolves	1	–	–	–	1	Apr 77 to USA
KIDD	Dec 63	19.8.67 at E'ton	203/52	25/8	20/7	16/3	264/70	Aug 74 to Arsenal
LAW	Aug 62	18.8.62 v WBA	309/171	46/34	11/3	33/28	399/236	Jul 73 to City
MacDOUGALL	Sep 72	7.10.72 at WBA	18/5	–	–	–	18/5	Mar 73 to West Ham
McCALLIOG	Mar 74	16.3.74 at Brum	31/7	1	6	–	38/7	Feb 75 to South'ton
McCREERY	Sep 72	19.8.75 at Brum	87/7	7	8/1	7	109/8	Aug 79 to QPR
McGRATH	Oct 76	9.11.76 at Villa	28/1	–	2	4	34/1	Feb 81 to USA
McILROY	Aug 69	6.11.71 at City	342/57	38/5	28/6	10/2	418/70	Feb 82 to Stoke
McQUEEN	Feb 78	25.2.78 at L'pool	184/20	21/2	16/4	7	228/26	Aug 85 to HKong
MACARI	Jan 73	20.1.73 v W'Ham	329/78	34/8	27/10	10/1	400/97	Jul 84 to Swindon
MARTIN	Jan 73	24.1.73 v Everton	40/2	2	1	–	43/2	Dec 75 to WBA
MORAN	Feb 78	30.4.79 at S'ton	231/21	18/1	25/2	14	288/24	Aug 88 to Gijon
MORGAN	Aug 68	28.8.68 v Spurs	238/25	27/4	25/3	4/1	294/33	Jun 75 to Burnley
NICHOLL	Nov 71	6.9.75 v Spurs	197/3	26/1	14/1	10/1	247/6	Apr 82 to Toronto
O'NEILL	Aug 68	5.5.71 at City	54	7	7	–	68	Aug 73 to Southport
PATERSON	Jul 74	10.11.76 v S'land	6	7	2	2	10	Jul 80 to HKong
PEARSON	May 74	17.8.74 at Orient	139/55	22/5	12/5	6/1	179/66	Aug 79 to W Ham
RIMMER	May 63	15.4.68 v Fulham	34	3	6	3	46	Apr 74 to Arsenal
RITCHIE	Oct 75	26.12.77 at E'ton	33/13	4	5	–	42/13	Oct 80 to Brighton
ROCHE	Oct 73	8.2.75 at Oxford	46	4	3	–	53	Aug 82 to Brentford
ROGERS	Aug 75	22.10.77 at WBA	1	–	–	–	1	Jul 79 to QPR
SADLER	Nov 62	24.8.63 at Sh.W.	272/22	23/1	22/1	16/3	333/27	Nov 73 to Preston
SIDEBOTTOM	Jan 71	23.4.73 v Sh.Utd	16	2	2	–	20	Jan 76 to Hud'field
SLOAN	Aug 78	18.11.78 v Iwich	11	1	1	–	12	Aug 82 to Chester
STEPNEY	Sep 66	17.9.66 v City	433/2	44	35	23	535/2	Feb 79 to USA
STOREY-MOORE	Mar 72	11.3.72 v Hdfld	39/11	–	4/1	–	43/12	Dec 73 retired***
THOMAS	Nov 78	25.11.78 at Chelsea	90/11	13/2	5/2	2	110/15	Aug 81 to Everton
WALDRON	May 76	4.10.76 at S'land	3	1	1	–	4	Apr 78 to USA
WILKINS	Aug 79	18.8.79 at S'ton	160/7	10/1	15/1	8/1	193/10	Jun 84 to Milan
YOUNG	May 68	4.4.72 at Sh.Utd	73/1	5	9	–	97/1	Jan 76 to Charlton

*signed on loan only **registration held whilst on loan to various clubs ***made temporary comebacks

Players' Appearances and Goals Season by Season 1972–80

PLAYER	1972–73	1973–74	1974–75	1975–76	1976–77	1977–78	1978–79	1979–80	
ALBISTON			2	3	21	37	42	28	
ANDERSON	7/1	12/1							
BAILEY							37	47	Ever-present 79–80
BALDWIN			2						
BEST	23/6	12/2							
BIELBY		4							
BUCHAN G.		4							
BUCHAN M.	47	45	50	52	46	37/1	48/2	47	Ever-present 73–4,75–6,79–80
CHARLTON	41/7								Top-scorer 72–3
CLARK					1				
CONNELL							2		
COPPELL			10/1	49/5	56/8	51/9	53/12	46/9	Ever-present 77–8,78–9 Player of Year 77–8
COYNE				2/1					
DALY		16/1	46/13	51/11	28/7				
DAVIES R.	17/4		10						
DAVIES W.	5								
DONALD	28								
DUNNE	1								
EDWARDS	6								
FITZPATRICK	2								
FLETCHER		6							
FOGGON					3				
FORSYTH	9	21/1	45/1	35/3	5	4			
GRAHAM	19/1	26/1	1						
GREENHOFF B.		39/2	49/4	50/1	57/5	35/1	40/3		Player of Year 76–7
GREENHOFF J.					34/12	27/6	44/17		Top-scorer & Player of Year 78–9
GRIFFITHS		7						4/1	
GRIMES						17/2	21/1	27/2	
GRIMSHAW				2					
HILL				33/10	56/22	41/19			Top-scorer 76–7,77–8
HOLTON	15/3	37/2	17						

The following table lists player appearances/goals by season (figures shown as appearances/goals; a single figure indicates appearances only).

Player									Notes
HOUSTON								17	Ever-present 75–6
JACKSON	26					37	25		
JAMES	20/2	48/7	52/2 · 20	51/5 · 3	37				
JORDAN	23/2					16/3	37/10	36/13 · 2	Top-scorer & Player of Year 79–80
JOVANOVIC									
KELLY	24/2			1					
KIDD	25/4								
LAW	14/2								
MacDOUGALL	18/5								
McCALLIOG	11/4	27/3 · 2							
McCREERY			31/4	37/2 · 7	22/2	16		1	
McGRATH	30/6				23/1	2		45/8	
McILROY	14	51/10	51/13	57/3	47/9	51/9		37/9	Top-scorer 73–4 / Ever-present 74–5
McQUEEN	16/5				14/1	47/7		44/9	
MACARI	36/6	47/18	45/16	53/14	37/11	38/6			Top-scorer 73–4,74–5,75–6 / Player of Year 74–5,75–6
MARTIN	16/2	19	9			1		9/1	
MORAN	42/3	44/2	42/4 · 1		46/3	29		47	
MORGAN	17		25	55/1				2	Player of Year 72–3
NICHOLL						3			
O'NEILL	17		5	5	38/15	2			
PATERSON		37/18	49/14	53/19					
PEARSON			2	2	4 · 23 · 1				
RIMMER	4				4	21/9 · 16		11/3	
RITCHIE		2							
ROCHE	3	2	5		23	16			
ROGERS	2				1				
SADLER	22 · 2	16							
SIDEBOTTOM									
SLOAN		49	47	57	28	4		5	
STEPNEY	43	45/2				33/2			Ever-present 1973–4
STOREY-MOORE	31/6	2/1		4				40/10	Top-scorer 74–5
THOMAS								42/2	
WALDRON									
WILKINS	33	32/1	22	1					
YOUNG	32/1								

United in the Transfer Market 1972–80

(As explained in the note at the front of the book, the figures in brackets are 1996 equivalent values.)

INCOMING

Dec. 1972–1973

George Graham (Arsenal)	£120,000 (£2.85m)
Alex Forsyth (Partick)	£100,000 (£2.4m)
Lou Macari (Celtic)	£190,000 (£4.5m)
Jim Holton (Shrewsbury)	£91,000 (£2.2m)
Mick Martin (Bohemians)	£25,000 (£600,000)
Ray O'Brien (Shelbourne)	£20,000 (£500,000)
Gerry Daly (Bohemians)	£22,000 (£550,000)
TOTAL IN	**£568,000 (£13.6m)**

1973–74

Paddy Roche (Shelbourne)	£15,000 (£350,000)
Stewart Houston (Brentford)	£45,000 (£1m)
Jim McCalliog (Wolves)	£60,000 (£1.4m)
Stuart Pearson (Hull)	£200,000 (£4.8m)
TOTAL IN	**£320,000 (£7.55m)**

1974–75

Ron Davies (Portsmouth)	£43,000 (£950,000)
Steve Coppell (Tranmere)	£60,000 (£1.3m)
TOTAL IN	**£103,000 (£2.25m)**

OUTGOING

Ted MacDougall (West Ham)	£170,000 (£4m)
P. Edwards (Oldham)	£13,000 (£300,000)
Carlo Sartori (Bologna)	£45,000 (£1m)
Wyn Davies (Blackpool)	£14,000 (£300,000)
TOTAL OUT	**£242,000 (£5.6m)**

David Sadler (Preston)	£20,000 (£480,000)
Jimmy Rimmer (Arsenal)	£36,750 (£880,000)
Ray O'Brien (Notts Co)	£40,000 (£960,000)
P. Fletcher (Hull)	£33,000 (£800,000)
TOTAL OUT	**£129,750 (£3.12m)**

George Buchan (Bury)	£10,000 (£220,000)
Brian Kidd (Arsenal)	£85,000 (£1.88m)
George Graham (P'mouth)	£35,000 (£770,000)
Trevor Anderson (Swindon)	£25,000 (£550,000)
Jim McCalliog (South'ton)	£40,000 (£880,000)
Willie Morgan (Burnley)	£30,000 (£660,000)
TOTAL OUT	**£225,000 (£4.96m)**

1975–76

Gordon Hill (Millwall) £85,000 (£1.5m)	Mick Martin (WBA) £20,000 (£340,000)

1976–77

Alan Foggon (Boro) £25,000 (£375,000)	Alan Foggon (S'land) £30,000 (£450,000)
Chris McGrath (Spurs) £30,000 (£450,000)	Jim Holton (S'land) £64,000 (£900,000)
Jimmy Greenhoff (Stoke) £100,000 (£1.5m)	Gerry Daly (Derby) £170,000 (£2.6m)
Ashley Grimes (Bohemians) £40,000 (£600,000)	
TOTAL IN £195,000 (£2.925m)	**TOTAL OUT £264,000 (£3.95m)**

1977–78

Joe Jordan (Leeds) £350,000 (£4.5m)	Gordon Hill (Derby) £275,000 (£3.6m)
Gordon McQueen (Leeds) £450,000 (£5.8m)	
TOTAL IN £800,000 (£10.3m)	**TOTAL OUT £275,000 (£3.6m)**

1978–79

Tom Connell (Coleraine) £20,000 (£200,000)	D. Bradley (Doncaster) £5,000 (£50,000)
Tom Sloan (Ballymena) £32,500 (£325,000)	Jonathan Clark (Derby) £50,000 (£500,000)
Mickey Thomas (Wrexham) £300,000 (£3m)	
TOTAL IN £352,500 (£3.52m)	**TOTAL OUT £55,000 (£550,000)**

1979–80

Ray Wilkins (Chelsea) £700,000 (£5.95m)	M Rogers (QPR) £5,000 (£40,000)
Niki Jovanovic (Red Star) £350,000 (£2.975m)	Stuart Pearson (West Ham) £200,000 (£1.7m)
	David McCreery (QPR) £170,000 (£1.45m)
	Brian Greenhoff (Leeds) £350,000 (£3m)
TOTAL IN £1.05m (£8.925m)	**TOTAL OUT £725,000 (£6.19m)**

Docherty versus Sexton

Docherty: spent 1995 equivalent of £27,825,000; sold £16,278,000: NET SPEND – £11,547,000

Sexton: spent £31,705,000 (incl. 1980–81); sold £14,050,000: NET SPEND – £17,655,000

So poor Dave managed to spend half as much again as the Doc without a trophy to show for it . . . .

Reds On Duty: International Honours

Reds Capped Whilst Playing For United, December 1972–June 1980

PLAYER	COUNTRY	DEBUT	RED CAPS 72–80	TOTAL CAPS
COPPELL	England	v Italy, 1978	23	42
GREENHOFF	England	v Wales, 1976	17	18
HILL	England	v Italy, 1976	6	6
PEARSON	England	v Wales, 1976	15	15
WILKINS	England	v Italy, 1976	11	84
ANDERSON	N.Ireland	v Cyprus, 1973	6	22
BEST	N.Ireland	v Wales, 1964	2	37
JACKSON	N.Ireland	v Israel, 1969	10	35
McCREERY	N.Ireland	v Scotland, 1976	23	67
McGRATH	N.Ireland	v Scotland, 1974	15	21
McILROY	N.Ireland	v Spain, 1972	45	88
NICHOLL	N.Ireland	v Israel, 1976	32	73
SLOAN	N.Ireland	v Scotland, 1979	3	3
BUCHAN	Scotland	v Portugal, 1972	32	34
FORSYTH	Scotland	v Yugoslavia, 1972	6	10
GRAHAM	Scotland	v Portugal, 1972	5	12
HOLTON	Scotland	v Wales, 1973	15	15
HOUSTON	Scotland	v Denmark, 1976	1	1
JORDAN	Scotland	v England, 1973	16	52
McQUEEN	Scotland	v Belgium, 1974	12	30
MACARI	Scotland	v Wales, 1972	18	24
MORGAN	Scotland	v N.Ireland, 1968	14	21
DAVIES W.	Wales	v England, 1964	3	34
THOMAS	Wales	v W.Germany, 1977	9	51
DALY	Eire	v Poland, 1973	9	48
GRIMES	Eire	v Turkey, 1978	8	15
MARTIN	Eire	v Austria, 1972	14	51
MORAN	Eire	v Switzerland, 1980	2	70
ROCHE	Eire	v Austria, 1972	7	7
JOVANOVIC	Yugo.	v Luxembourg, 1980	2	?

The following Reds weren't capped whilst at Old Trafford during Dec '72 to June '80 but had already been capped, whether before Dec '72 or when somewhere other than OT:
CHARLTON, KIDD, SADLER, STEPNEY, STOREY-MOORE (England); LAW, McCALLIOG (Scotland); DAVIES R. (Wales); DUNNE (Eire).

'Red Army Years' players who were later capped elsewhere:
MacDOUGALL (when at Norwich; Scotland), RIMMER (when at Arsenal; England), CONNELL (when at Coleraine; N.Ireland).

Players already on United's books in the 1970s who went on to be capped in the 1980s:
BAILEY, DUXBURY (England); ALBISTON (Scotland); DAVIES A., BLACKMORE*, HUGHES* (Wales); WHITESIDE* (N.Ireland).
* = associate schoolboy during 1970s.

Attendances Home and Away 1972–80

Season	Lge Home Av	(Div 1 Av)	Away Av	Best Home	Worst Home	Best Away
1972–73	48,623	(30,299)	41,171	61,500 v City	36,073 v S'ton	56,194 at Arsenal
1973–74	42,721	(28,292)	35,337	60,025 v Leeds	28,589 v Cov C	51,501 at Arsenal
1974–75	48,388	(27,301)	25,556	60,585 v S'land	40,671 v Forest	45,976 at S'land
1975–76	54,750	(28,331)	37,037	61,689 v Everton	44,269 v Wolves	50,094 at Villa
1976–77	53,710	(29,540)	35,357	60,723 v Spurs	42,685 v S'land	50,123 at L'pool
1977–78	51,938	(28,692)	30,424	59,547 v Ipswich	41,625 v Villa	50,856 at City
1978–79	46,687	(27,499)	30,498	56,139 v B'ham	33,678 v Norwich	46,608 at L'pool
1979–80	51,562	(26,327)	34,101	57,471 v Leeds	43,329 v Bristol C	51,389 at Spurs

- League Cup gates note: the lowest home League gates for 1972–77 were all worsened by early round League Cup ties at OT so that's something the 1990s has in common. Overall lowest home gates for these years were: 1972–73 – 21,436 v Oxford; 1973–74 – 23,906 v Boro; 1974–75 – 21,616 v Charlton; 1975–76 – 25,286 v Brentford; 1976–77 – 32,586 v Tranmere.

- The figures for best gates on our League travels were bettered in Cup competitions between 1976 and 1979 as follows: 1975–76 – 55,000 and 100,000 for FA Cup semi and Final; 1976–77 – 66,632 at Juventus in UEFA Cup, 55,000 and 100,000 for FA Cup semi and Final; 1977–78 – 60,000 at Porto in European Cup Winners' Cup, 82,000 at Charity Shield; 1978–79 – 51,800, 52,524 and 53,069 at Spurs in FA Cup 6th rd and at semi/replay plus 100,000 at Final.

- United had the best average home gate in England for every one of these seasons even when in Division Two; having temporarily lost top spot between 1970 and 1972, we reasserted our supremacy over Liverpool in 1972–73 despite their championship and our being at the foot of the table for most of the season.

- United's dominance was reflected most spectacularly in 1975–76 and 1979–80 when our average gate was *double* that of the Division as a whole; the 1975–76 average was second only in United's entire history to that achieved during the 1966–67 title season.

Invading Division Two: The Red Army 1974–75

'Ask any older United fans to name their favourite season and a good proportion will name our season spent in Division Two,' *writes Andy Pollard.* 'The away matches were most special of all: it's worth noting the enormity of the travelling divisions.' Below is Andy's list of the gates we attracted away, together with his considered estimate of the numbers of Reds in attendance.

	GATE	NO. REDS
SUNDERLAND	45,976*	6,000
ASTON VILLA	40,353	12–15,000
BOLTON	38,152*	25,000
SHEFF WED	35,067*	20,000
WEST BROM	28,666*	10–15,000
BRISTOL CITY	28,104**	8–10,000
FULHAM	26,513*	10,000
OLDHAM	26,384*	15–20,000
PORTSMOUTH	25,608*	10,000+?
BLACKPOOL	25,370*	17,000
NORWICH	25,056	8,000
HULL CITY	23,287*	12–15,000
CARDIFF	22,344*	10–15,000
NOTTM FOREST	21,893**	10,000
SOUTHAMPTON	21,866*	7,000
BRISTOL ROVERS	19,337**	5,000
ORIENT	17,772*	8-10,000
NOTTS. CO.	17,320**	10,000
MILLWALL	16,988*	unknown
OXFORD UTD	15,815*	5,000
YORK CITY	15,567*	7,000

* = home club's best gate of season
** = second-best gate

The Nottingham and Bristol clubs only got better gates for their respective local derbies. Bearing in mind that these days, getting 4,000 tickets out of a 35,000 gate is regarded as a buzzin' allocation, you can appreciate how overpowering ten thousand-plus at a 25,000 gate was; no wonder that Lou Macari, all these years later, still marvels at the memory . . .